Anne Neville

England's Forgotten Queens

edited by ALISON WEIR

Series Editor

Alison Weir has published ten books: *Britain's Royal Families*, *The Six Wives of Henry VIII*, *The Princes in the Tower*, *Children of England*, *Elizabeth the Queen*, *Eleanor of Aquitaine*, *Henry VIII: King & Court*, *Mary Queen of Scots & the Murder of Lord Darnley* and *Lancaster & York: The War of the Roses* and *Isabella, She-Wolf of France, Queen of England*. She is at present researching for a book on Katherine Swynford and John of Gaunt. Alison Weir's chief areas of specialism are the Tudor and medieval monarchies. She has researched every English queen from Matilda of Flanders, wife of William the Conqueror, to Elizabeth I, and is committed to promoting the studies of these important women, many of whom have been unjustly sidelined by historians.

Published

Arlene Okerlund, *Elizabeth Wydeville: The Slandered Queen*
Michael Hicks, *Anne Neville: Queen to Richard III*

Commissioned

Patricia Dark, *Matilda: England's Warrior Queen*

Anne Neville

Queen to Richard III

MICHAEL HICKS

TEMPUS

In memory of my parents G.E.H. and W.M.H.

This edition first published 2007

Tempus Publishing Limited
The Mill, Brimscombe Port,
Stroud, Gloucestershire, GL5 2QG
www.tempus-publishing.com

© Michael Hicks, 2006, 2007

British Library Cataloguing in Publication Data.
A catalogue record for this book is available from the British Library.

ISBN-10 0 7524 4129 9
ISBN-13 978 0 7524 4129 0

Typesetting and origination by Tempus Publishing Limited
Printed in Great Britain

Contents

Foreword

Michael Hicks' excellent reputation as a leading expert on late medieval England has long been established. Now he returns to the fifteenth century, with a fascinating and authoritative study of Anne Neville, daughter of Warwick the Kingmaker and queen consort of Richard III, the first full-length biography of this much-neglected woman, which has been years in preparation and will undoubtedly be the standard life for a long time to come.

Unlike other queens of the period, Anne's existence is poorly documented, but from the few fragments of information that have come down to us, Professor Hicks has crafted an intriguing, lively and often poignant story, rich in detail and based on wide-ranging research and an unparalleled and extensive knowledge of the period. This is no romantic tale – unlike the only previous account of Anne Neville, which was written by Agnes Strickland in the 1850s in her *Lives of the Queens of England* – but a realistic and convincing portrayal that offers new insights into the controversies that overshadowed Anne's existence, and accords her her proper place in the world in which she lived. For Anne Neville was a very important personage in her own time, and her life was closely entwined with the history of England itself.

Most compelling of all is Professor Hicks' depiction of Anne's marriage to the controversial and enigmatic Richard, Duke of Gloucester, later Richard III, a union fraught with difficulties, and which was to end in tragedy. Discarding all the popular theories that have gained currency in recent years, he presents a masterful and tantalising assessment of the relations between the two, and reveals startling new evidence that touches the very essence of their marriage.

When writing a medieval biography, it is often difficult to gain an impression of what one's subject was actually like, yet despite Professor Hicks' entirely justified protestations that there is much that we can never know about Anne Neville, this absorbing biography has nevertheless left me with a strong impression of a real flesh-and-blood woman, and I have no doubt that it will appeal not only to scholars of the period, but also to the legions of people who are interested in Richard III and his times. I am privileged to be associated with such a book.

Alison Weir

Preface

Anne Neville is the most obscure of England's post-conquest queens and, many would argue, deservedly so. I did not select her as one of the four out of twelve late medieval queens for a biography in my *Who's Who in Late Medieval England* in 1991. Even amongst Joanna Laynesmith's prize-winning *Last Medieval Queens*, much less was said of her than about Margaret of Anjou, Elizabeth Wydeville or Elizabeth of York. My previous books on Anne's father, *Warwick the Kingmaker*, her husband, *Richard III*, her brothers-in-law, *False Fleeting Perjur'd Clarence* and *Edward IV*, and her nephew, *Edward V*, who interacted with Anne at many points, demonstrated conclusively the absence of any unexploited caches of records and the sparseness of information available today. So did my brief life of her for the *Oxford Dictionary of National Biography*. As Richard III is much the most popular of late medieval English kings, however, there is much more demand for a biography of Anne than the other queens. When Jonathan Reeve, once again, proposed a book on Anne Neville, I said, with regret, that it was impossible. 'That' (I paraphrase) 'is what you said last time over Edward V' was his response. And so I agreed to write this book. Preparing a synopsis revealed some possibilities in the topic. Writing it has revealed much more. Revisiting such topics as the contract for Anne's first marriage, Richard's proposal to marry his niece and the Warwick inheritance dispute from another angle has enabled more to be extracted from the sources, more implications to be recognised and explored, and our understanding of the era, the principal characters, and their interactions to be enriched. That is one advantage of biography and, for me, the main point of the genre. Although not necessarily capturing the essence of these topics, this biography does bring together everything that is known about Anne, casts light both on her successive predicaments and on her times, and does significantly advance historical understanding of some of the key individuals, issues, and events. Thank you very much, Jonathan, once again.

Anne received a girl's education, grew up into a lady, married twice, was widowed, became a princess, duchess and queen, and spent her whole life in the grip of the Wars of the Roses, so this book draws repeatedly on historians of each of these separate fields. Her study is a by-product of those of her father Warwick the Kingmaker, brother-in-law Clarence, and husband Richard III. The life of Richard III (and hence his consort) is not merely an area of controversy but a co-operative enterprise, in which extra bits of information and perceptions are being constantly added by many interested parties. Hence the prominence of references to *The Ricardian*, journal of the Richard III Society, which has been constantly consulted, even though relatively few such items have demanded a place in the bibliographical essay. Like all other operators in this field, I gratefully acknowledge my debt first to Alan Sutton and more recently to the Society and the Richard III and Yorkist Trust, which have made so many sources available in modern editions. The contributions of Peter Hammond, Anne Sutton, and Livia Visser-Fuchs cannot easily be overstated. Just in the nick of time, Peter Hammond and Geoffrey Wheeler kindly drew my attention to Peter D. Clarke's important article on 'English Royal Marriages and the Papal Penitentiary in the Fifteenth Century' in *English Historical Review* cxx (2005). This article proves both that Anne Neville *did* have a dispensation to marry Richard III and, unwittingly, that this dispensation was inadequate – and thus that their marriage (as I had already deduced) was never valid. I gratefully acknowledge the guidance and stimulus of the late Charles Ross, who first introduced me to the Wars of the Roses, and the influence among so many others of Ralph Griffiths, Rosemary Horrox and Tony Pollard. Researching and writing books inevitably takes place out of term and out of what ought to be family time: I gratefully acknowledge the forbearance of my wife and my now adult children.

All quotations have been rendered into modern English and all places of publication are London unless otherwise stated.

University of Winchester, September 2005

CHAPTER ONE

Why Study Anne Neville?

SHAKESPEARE'S LADY ANNE

Was ever woman in this humour wooed?
Was ever woman in this humour won?[1]

The woman was Anne Neville, the wooer Richard Duke of Gloucester, and the occasion the funeral in 1471 of Anne's father-in-law King Henry VI, whom Richard had slain. The immediate sequels were Anne's second marriage to Richard, later to become Richard III. Hence in due course Anne was to accede as Richard's queen. Through Richard's speech and throughout this whole celebrated scene, Shakespeare made his Lady Anne into one of the best known figures in history, albeit – like the Princes in the Tower – seldom remembered by name. Sir Laurence Olivier and Claire Bloom brought them to millions through play and film and are still doing so today.

Richard's speech encapsulates the paradox at the centre of Anne's life that Shakespeare exploited to the full. It immediately follows after the opening soliloquy, in which Duke Richard reveals what a malicious and dissembling villain he was and that the throne of England was his object. Richard boasts

despicably that he had already slain both of the key Lancastrians,
King Henry VI (1422–61, Anne's father-in-law) and his son
Prince Edward of Lancaster (d.1471, Anne's husband), and
also Richard, Earl of Warwick, the Kingmaker (d.1471, Anne's
father). Richard states his intention to eliminate his own
elder brother George, Duke of Clarence (d.1478). He looks
forward hopefully to the natural death of his own eldest
brother, King Edward IV (1461–83). Since Anne Neville was
the daughter of Warwick, the wife (now widow) of Edward
of Lancaster, and the daughter-in-law of Henry VI, Richard
admitted that she had every reason to hate him, quite apart
from the twisted body that in a politically incorrect age disadvantaged him in courtship. Shakespeare did not bring into
his play any of the material issues that we know about today,
issues which counted for more at the time, and may well
have explained Richard's actions. Instead he dealt solely – and
perhaps anachronistically – in terms of the romantic love that
we take for granted today, a presumption that makes it hard
for us (and harder for his intended audience) to imagine a
more improbable match-making. Moreover, it was a courtship conducted over the corpse of Henry VI, the strongest
possible reminder of Richard's crimes, whose funeral cortège,
led by Lady Anne, Duke Richard had intercepted and arbi-
trarily interrupted.

Lady Anne preceded the corpse, lamenting eloquently the
deaths of her loved ones and bursting out into curses against
he – Richard – who was responsible.

> O, cursed be the hand that made these holes!
> Cursed the heart that had the heart to do it!
> Cursed the blood that let this blood from hence!

Let the curses fall from the father onto his son and onto
his wife! Let any son born to the murderer be premature,

physically crippled and affright his mother, and be a source of unhappiness to him! May the murderer's wife suffer more sorrow than did Lady Anne herself at the death of Edward of Lancaster! If ever uttered, such curses, of course, should have fallen on Lady Anne herself. They did not, for Lady Anne was no prophet – Richard's son was not to be crippled and Richard's wife did not outlive him – but certainly Shakespeare's Lady Anne at this point perceived Richard to be every bit as villainous as he actually proved to be. Her mood, obviously, was unpromising for any suitor, least of all her husband's murderer. There follows one of Shakespeare's most brilliant and witty exchanges of repartee between the duke and the widow. Lady Anne's reaction to Richard's murder of King Henry was a mixture of shock, loathing and contempt, in which she upbraided him for his 'heinous deeds', 'homicide', 'butcheries', and 'foul deformity', stated that he knew 'no law of God' and was thus inferior to the irrational beasts, and denounced him as 'a hedgehog', 'fiend', a 'fouler toad' and 'even foul devil'. In a keen exchange of wits, Richard deflected her insults or excused them, landed a succession of skilful compliments and put his case, to which, eventually, the lady succumbed. (Shakespeare portrays Lady Anne throughout as a mature woman: doubtless he was quite unaware that she was only a susceptible fourteen).

Lady Anne was the trophy of what was a truly virtuoso display, as Richard admitted to himself.

Was ever woman in such a humour wooed?
Was ever woman in such a humour won?
I'll have her; but I will not keep her long.

Shakespeare of course knew what was to follow twelve years later: a time span made to appear much shorter by his play.

What? I, that kill'd her husband and her father,
To take her in her heart's extremest hate,
With curses in her mouth, tears in her eyes,
The bleeding witness of her hatred by,
Having God, her conscience, and these bars against me,
And I no friends to back my suit at all,
But the plain devil and dissembling looks?
And yet to win her, – all the world to nothing!
Ha!

It is the medieval equivalent of the modern goal-scorer's punch to the sky. It was 'not so much for love, as for another secret close intent', undisclosed, that Shakespeare's Richard married Shakespeare's Lady Anne.

For Lady Anne had sex appeal. Richard lauds 'your beauty' and 'sweet bosom' and eagerly anticipates joint occupancy of her bedchamber and her bed: Lady Anne was no virgin. Addressing her as his 'sweet saint', 'heavenly face', and 'divine perfection of a woman', Richard certainly presents her in the most attractive light, which her passion, intelligence and wit, and articulacy strongly reinforces. Yet she was too easily persuaded – for the harsh facts were, after all, facts. She was out-argued and lost out to the stronger personality and reveals, surely, a frailty both of purpose and of morality: provided, of course, that the events and their contexts were as Shakespeare portrayed them. [2]

So, too, Lady Anne accepted Richard's accession. As devoted a subject to the young Edward V as his own mother and grand-mother, she (now Duchess of Gloucester) is on her way to visit the young boy in the Tower when her way is barred by order of the king – a king who proved to be not Edward V, but her husband Richard III. Evidently Anne had not been consulted. She was not complicit at all in Richard's crime, the illegal usurpation of the crown. Nor indeed did she carry much weight in her husband's illicit regime. She was not able even as the king's wife to secure access to the princes. Receiving a summons to be crowned, she exclaimed:

Despiteful tidings. O unpleasing news!

She was remorseful and regretful that she had ever married him. Though disapproving of the usurpation, she feebly succumbed despite her sharp misgivings.

Anointed let me be with deadly venom
And die ere men can say 'God save the queen'.[3]

That was indeed prophetic! For Queen Anne quickly fell mortally sick, which Richard eagerly anticipated, so that he could marry his niece Elizabeth of York, sister of the by-now murdered Princes in the Tower.

I must be married to my brother's daughter,
Or else my kingdom stands on brittle glass; -
Murder her brothers and then marry her!
Uncertain way of gain! But I am in
So far in blood that sin will pluck on sin;
Tear falling pity dwells not in this way.

In a repeat exchange of crisp repartee, Richard persuaded the initially hostile Elizabeth, queen to Edward IV and mother to the princes and Princess Elizabeth, to put to her his case.[4] To Shakespeare's thinking, therefore, Anne died irrelevant, a passive instrument who had served her purpose and had passed her sell-by date, just as much Richard's victim as were his brother of Clarence, his nephews the princes, or his cousin of Buckingham. The victory over Richard in 1485 at Bosworth of Henry VII was Anne's posthumous victory too.

The wooing scene is wholly Shakespeare's invention. There is nothing about the courtship in the *History of Richard III* of Sir Thomas More or the *English History* of Polydore Vergil, which are Shakespeare's ultimate sources of information. The playwright seized on the remarkable paradox that Richard III, whom *Hall's Chronicle* presented as Edward of Lancaster's murderer,[5] was to marry his widow. Richard certainly fought in the army that slew Warwick and today appears quite probably to have participated in the deaths of Henry VI, Edward of Lancaster, and indeed Clarence. Yet there was nothing discreditable or blameworthy about such actions. Always he was a secondary player, a follower rather than an initiator, authorised and justified by the command of King Edward IV, who alone was answerable before God for such actions. If Richard killed Warwick and Edward of Lancaster in battle or afterwards, his conduct was acceptable at the time and indeed legitimate in terms of the laws of war and military honour. All four were traitors against his king, therefore deserving of death, to which both Henry VI and Clarence had been sentenced by parliament.[6] Henry VI was actually buried at Chertsey Abbey in Surrey, not at Westminster Abbey where Shakespeare locates his funeral, perhaps summarily and certainly without the publicity and pomp normal for the burials of kings. Nor did the battles and funeral in 1471, and the wooing and marriage around 1472, coincide with the deaths of Clarence in 1478 and King Edward IV in 1483, historically seven and a dozen years later. Shakespeare had, for dramatic reasons, compressed these events. Such telescoping rendered the sequence of events dramatically manageable and heightened the intensity of the drama. Also, incidentally and unintentionally, it juxtaposed the beginning and ending of Anne's second marriage, and thus highlighted the paradox at the heart of her life.

Like any other writer of his age, Shakespeare was convinced of the wrongfulness of Richard III's seizure of the crown and of his destruction of the princes. King Richard was a usurper, a tyrant, and a murderer. How then could Anne possibly have believed his claims and gone along with them? Since she did, she had to be presented as a passive victim, albeit adding to the prophecies of destruction that lie ahead. Here imagination, not evidence, reigns. The descent of the play to destruction proceeds too rapidly helter-skelter to allow Anne's death, Richard's incestuous plans for his niece, or even the murder of the princes, for all of which he possessed good sources, to be presented on stage. The build-up to the crown presented other villainies in such detail that explicit treatment of those that followed was not required. Shakespeare may also have been understandably reluctant to make too much of a mercifully unfulfilled matrimonial project for the ancestress of the ruling royal house, Elizabeth of York, and the arch-villain himself.

Though incorrect in detail and sometimes indeed depicting what can never have happened, Shakespeare certainly did capture the family character of the Wars of the Roses. Then, as now, most murders occur within the family: besides fratricide, most homicides, regicides, and infanticides were perpetrated by relations of the victim. In such a context, Shakespeare was right to perceive the necessity for co-existence, co-operation and even intermarriage amongst former foes, between those wronged and their wrongdoers, all of which Anne Neville's career so poignantly and repeatedly illustrates.

Shakespeare forged Richard III into one of the theatre's greatest villains and into one of the worst of history's kings. Essentially that was what he had extracted from his sources. Sir Thomas More was not at all unusual in perceiving Richard as unnatural, his unnatural life and violent death foreshadowed by an unnatural birth, his inner vice betokened by his twisted body. Most of these elements appeared twenty years before in the *History* of John Rows, who had known Richard at first hand. For More, Shakespeare and their age, physical disability was not mere misfortune to the sufferer, but an indication of the distorted character that lay within. Richard was a usurper, a tyrant, a murderer of innocents comparable to the biblical King Herod, and a monster. Anne, therefore, was the wife of this usurper, tyrant, murderer and monster, shared her bed with this cripple and her private life with this villain, tyrant and monster. What this meant in practice even Shakespeare could not conceive. He depicted a Lady Anne who had entered into her marriage with Richard with her eyes open, but was seduced by his charm and way with words, and who came bitterly to regret their liaison. Thus he presents Anne Neville as just another of Richard's victims. This was the 'tradition [that] declares she abhorred' Richard's crimes that was still current in the 1840s.[7]

Actually, Shakespeare knew only the half of it. He offers us no access to the rest of Anne's life, much of which is as impenetrable to us as it was to him. Anne Neville (1456–85) was the consort of one of the most short-lived of English medieval kings. She had reigned for only twenty-one months: less than any English queen since the Norman Conquest. Her only son, whilst still a child, predeceased her. Her kingly husband was to lose his throne. Defeated and disgraced, notorious in his own lifetime as a usurper, tyrant, and slayer of the princes,[8] for half a millennium Richard has been numbered amongst the most wicked of medieval kings, into whose character and motivation no further exploration or perception was required. If Queen Anne was his victim or his instrument, we cannot perceive it in the evidence we have. If she was his partner or accomplice, it can only be by inference, for actually she is quite obscure. We know as little about her as any of our medieval queens and much less than most of them. If Perkin Warbeck and Edward V are dubious candidates for biography, why should historians bother with a consort who appears to have done nothing independently or of note and is frankly unknown?

Yet Anne was engaged in great events – the Wars of the Roses of 1455–85 – and lived out her whole life amongst them. Both a victim and a victor, she was an important participant, who had her own decisions to make and whose status gave her behaviour a special significance. That we can seldom divine her conduct does not reduce its significance. Her interactions with such key actors as her father and husbands really mattered. Even a 'pawn in politics' deserves attention. 'Tacit acceptance' of Richard's crimes was a decision. Even passivity, acquiescence, or deference to the men in her life is revealing. For Anne should not be perceived just as an individual. She also represents a type of person and progressed through a series of roles or stereotypes during the twenty-eight short years of her life. There are models to which she conformed and from which she diverged, and these offer us access both to Anne herself and to her time. Moreover, her life illustrates not just well-worn topics such as the critical importance of lineage, inheritance, marriage and gender stereotypes within her era, but also others, less often examined, which underpinned, conditioned and perhaps determined public opinion and hence on occasion had an impact on political events.

As far as we know, Anne did not have her portrait painted. Certainly none survives, unlike those of her husband, Edward IV's queen Elizabeth Wydeville, and all subsequent queens. There are several stylised images of Anne Neville, in the *Beauchamp Pageant*, *Rows Rolls*, and *Salisbury Roll* as a queen, or in a lost stained glass window at Skipton-in-Craven (Yorks.),[9] but these are not realistic or representative of reality and probably tell us little if anything of her actual physical appearance. Was she tall, short, fat or thin? All we do know is that she was like her niece Elizabeth of York in build and complexion and that they probably fitted the same clothes:[10] that Queen Anne, at twenty-eight, after at least one pregnancy, was of similar height, build, and measurements as a girl of eighteen.

Later in life, after several pregnancies, Elizabeth of York appears somewhat stolid in her portrait, which depicts her aged thirty-seven – the date of her death – or less. Elizabeth is portrayed at Canterbury Cathedral in glass with flowing golden tresses. That was a contemporary ideal that was applied to both ladies and to Elizabeth's own mother in illuminations, but which may nevertheless be telling us the truth. It is best therefore to imagine Anne Neville as an English rose – a slim blonde, so Laynesmith suggests,[11] – and probably unremarkable.

Anne has no monument. Her tomb at Westminster Abbey is marked only by a modern brass and archaeology would be required to detect it.[12] We do not know how King Richard intended to mark her resting place; nor indeed can we know whether Westminster was actually destined to remain her resting place, rather than – for instance – York Minster, where, it has been speculated, Richard hoped to be interred himself. After her death – or, at least, by five months after her death, when her husband was destroyed – there was nobody who cared enough about her memory to commission even a modest tomb. They may have been afraid of associating themselves too closely with the disgraced usurper. Henry VII himself, who did provide honourable interment after an interval for King Richard, failed to do the same for Queen Anne. Because Richard III left no heir to continue his memory, no cause to be continued, and attracted no historian in a position to speak out for him, so Anne, too, has been forgotten. Glimpses of her are provided by the Crowland Continuator and by the cantarist John Rows, but neither can be said to have known her in person – as opposed to her rank and pedigree – and what they have recorded for us can be counted in a few sentences.[13] Yet there was much more than this to Anne and more, fortunately, can be recaptured and reconstituted.

We can never know Anne Neville the individual as well as, for instance, Margery Kempe or Margaret Paston, whose autobiography and correspondence survive, or even Alice Bryene or Margaret Hungerford, whose household accounts or pious dispositions expose much about their everyday life or inner thoughts. Yet historians cannot confine themselves to the best documented individuals in the past. That would be elitist and sexist, would rule all but a tiny handful of unrepresentative individuals out of historical study, and would render history impoverished and limited indeed. Anne is capable of being studied. Moreover she is worth studying. And finally, because of who she was and especially because of who her husband was, many historians and many ordinary people today want to know about her – to know whatever there is to be known. That is the justification for this book.

WOMAN, LADY AND QUEEN

Anne, of course, was a woman. Historians used to suppose that there could be no history of women, especially medieval women, and certainly none that was worth the recounting. Initially, perhaps, this was because historians (especially male historians) had no wish to write about members of the other sex. They subscribed to the presumption that history was about politics, in which women have traditionally played little part. Women's failure to participate in what really mattered in the past meant that women themselves were unhistorical and unworthy of the historian's attention. It is certainly true that there is relatively little evidence relating to women in the conventional historical sources that deal with high politics. Women were, of course, everywhere in the past, as numerous if not more numerous than the men, sharing their upbring-ings, their adult lives, social and economic activities, their households and their beds, conceiving, bearing and bringing up each future generation. Women's presence *en masse* cannot be denied. And new generations of historians, not necessarily themselves women, have decided that these other aspects of the past and women themselves are as worthy of research as the most eminent of politicians. Moreover, they have demonstrated triumphantly that if one wishes to know about women, then the appropriate sources and techniques to do so can be found. There are now relative riches published in this field.[14] Anne Neville played many roles in her short life and can be perceived in all these contexts.

Of course women do pose further problems to the historian that relate to their inferior status and restricted opportunities. In a patriarchal society which was becoming more patriarchal, according to Goldberg and as enjoined by St Paul, women were inferior and rightly subordinate to men.[15] No matter how active and strong in character, first as spinsters and then as wives, they were obscured in the sources by their menfolk, who made the formal decisions for them, held their property, and represented them in politics. It was only as widows that women could create their own records and emerge into the light. We do know about many late medieval widows, aristocratic or burgher. Yet widows are hardly representative. Some widows admittedly were young, but most were not, and their study by definition cannot reveal them as spinsters, wives, nor during their reproductive years. Besides, it is only certain aspects of their lives, in particular their piety, that are usually illuminated. Even the best known widows are obscure. They suffer the disadvantages of all the subjects of medieval biography, that we lack the revealing sources of later eras, and that we cannot really grapple with their personalities. Yet women can be categorised as recognisable types, whose characteristics can be deduced rather than observed. Anne, as we shall see, passes through several such types.

Of all these types, queens were pre-eminent. Each queen was particularly prominent, in history as in life. It is not surprising that, as the most eminent of females in their own age and the leaders of female society, all English queens achieve the salute of a life in the new *Oxford Dictionary of National Biography*, some admittedly fuller and more elaborate than others. None is shorter or more vestigial than that by the present author of Anne Neville.[16] Of course, her husband Richard III had one of the shortest reigns of any post-conquest English king, a mere twenty-six months, and she predeceased him. Anne therefore had little time to make an impression. None of her own records survive. Almost no independent actions can be identified. That does not make Anne into a personal nonentity nor indeed render her insignificant, but it does make her quite exceptionally inaccessible, which is all the more regrettable given the fame, notoriety, and modern fascination with her husband Richard III. How much we would like to know the inner secrets of his family life! What did his wife think? We cannot know.

Before she became queen, Anne Neville was a noble lady, a spinster, princess of Wales, a widow, and duchess of Gloucester. She illustrates a whole series of the 'life-cycle stages' that are now perceived as 'modifiers' of 'medieval women's gendered identity'.[17] In each case, regrettably, there are no special sources. Anne was amongst the most obscure instances of her type. If Anne had not become a queen – and queen, moreover, to Richard III – nobody would have selected her for study. Yet each of these categories is a type that historians have studied and illuminated. Much is known about young medieval women, medieval widows, medieval ladies and medieval queens, and whole books have been written recently on each.[18] In the last five years there has been a relative epidemic of studies of the last medieval queens.[19] These provide templates against which Anne can be measured and contexts into which she can be set. Anne symbolises a series of stereotypes. She was successively a stage on her family tree, her father's daughter, the consort of two husbands, and the queen of a reigning king. She was also a bride, widow, a bride again, a mother, moreover a bereaved mother, and almost, anachronistically, a divorcee. But Anne does much more than pose for these established tableaux. Merely to reveal that she conforms to norms is hardly worth the undertaking. But actually Anne Neville did not conform to type. What little we know about her reveals her life to be remarkable, not merely for its eminence, and well worth investigating. Close analysis casts more light on Anne herself and also – and perhaps more intriguingly – on the extraordinary men who shared her life. Poor Anne. She died so young and suffered such a sequence of tragedies in her short life. Much more than an object of the activities of others and a victim, it is nevertheless as a victim that Shakespeare has commemorated her. Most historians have followed.

Shakespeare's view of Richard III no longer prevails. Most people today suppose Richard to be not as bad as Shakespeare presented him. Many think him the victim of Tudor propaganda. That is the achievement of many individuals – perhaps most influentially Josephine Tey and Paul Murray Kendall – and of the Richard III Society, which allows no opportunity to pass to correct critical comments in books, paper, television and other media. If Richard was a good man and a good king, then perhaps he was also a good husband and Queen Anne was happy with her lot. Perhaps theirs was a love match, their marriage companionate, and we should imagine them like any happily married couple of today. At times, certainly, it has seemed essential to the new Ricardian myth to cast a romantic aura over their relationship. If so, the loss of Anne's son and her own childlessness – Anne's failure to fulfil this essential function – looks more tragic yet.

LOVE AND MARRIAGE

Anne Neville did matter. She was a queen. She did bear Richard his only legitimate son, the tragically short-lived

Prince Edward of Middleham. She brought him the resources in her Neville inheritance that enabled Richard to dominate the North and the means to usurp the throne. She shared his coronation and other regal ceremonies of his reign. And she survived too long, apparently to be spurned by a husband to whom she was a political burden, an obstacle to the reconstruction of his power, and supposedly, indeed, his victim. She packed into her short life incident enough for many adventurous careers, but always, apparently, as a passive instrument of a succession of others. This book seeks to research her career properly, to bring out its implications, and to explore in depth the remarkable shifts and turns of her fraught and ultimately unrewarding career.

The life of Anne Neville illustrates much that makes medieval England different from today. Clearly Anne is an example of a medieval lady, whose life illustrates both the normal experiences of medieval ladies and contemporary attitudes towards them. Her life illustrates repeatedly the making of the medieval marriage. However we might wish it were not so, Anne may never have married for love, but was rather the object – and the financial beneficiary – of two materially prudent marriages. In her life the key role played by inheritance – its sanctity, both theoretical and practical – has to be constantly reiterated.

Anne Neville was born to be a wife and mother. So far as we know, the only respectable alternative – life in a nunnery – was never considered. From early childhood, her parents were seeking an appropriate spouse – to arrange a marriage, certainly for her benefit, but with many ulterior motives in mind. The arranged marriage was the norm. People of her station did not marry merely to please themselves and those who did, like Edward IV and Margery Paston, offended contemporary standards and were strongly condemned. The love match, which we take for granted, was deplored. Anne's first marriage was the handiwork of her parents. When it was terminated by

Prince Edward of Lancaster's death, a further marriage was the only palatable option: another, less acceptable, may have been broached. Although apparently the work of the two parties, Anne's union to Duke Richard was unexceptionable and unobjectionable – what her parents would have approved and may indeed once have sought – and was furthermore approved by the king. If the partiality of Anne for Richard went beyond the businesslike – even to Shakespeare's stormy wooing – it fell within the parameters of eligibility and mutual advantage.

Yet Anne and Richard were not as free in their choice of partner as we presume today, because there was a much longer list of people, scores or perhaps hundreds strong, that each was forbidden to marry. This was because they were related within the prohibited degrees. More significantly, perhaps, this book is a commentary on the prohibited degrees. The rules on eligibility that applied – a framework both legal and moral – recognised as kin much more distant relatives than we do today and forbade marriage amongst relations whom we would scarcely acknowledge today. Canon law was here rooted in the laws of Moses set down in the Old Testament in the book of *Leviticus* chapter 18: 'None of you shall approach to any that is near of kin to him, to uncover their nakedness'. Kinship was either consanguineous, where blood relatives shared a common ancestor, or affinal, the result of marriage or at least sexual intercourse, that had made the two participants one flesh and their in-laws into relatives. Consanguinity (blood relationships) and affinity (relationships created by marriage) were expressed as degrees; there were also spiritual ties created by acting as godparents at baptism. Unions between partners within four degrees of kinship whether consanguineous or affinal were incestuous and were therefore banned. *Leviticus* had actually forbidden only a few close relationships, which were regarded as examples for others equally close, but the Church had extended the ban, originally to the seventh degree, which prohibited marriage amongst those sharing a great-great-great-great-great grandparent living two centuries or more ago, of whom most descendants may have been quite unaware. From 1215 the prohibition applied only to relationships in the fourth degree: to those descended from a common great-grandparent or whose blood relations had sexual intercourse with their prospective in-laws in the last four generations. Any man was barred from marrying the third cousin of any woman with whom he had 'carnal dealings'. These rules constituted a moral code that was strictly enforced by the Church, sometimes by debarring couples from marriage, if necessary by abrogating marriages after the event and bastardising any resultant children. The code was internalised as the moral expectations of the general public. We certainly must not suppose, writes Helmholz, that 'the rules about consanguinity were trifles'. For most people they were absolute barriers and there was no way out. For royalty and aristocracy, however, the situation was different. They were closed elites who frequently intermarried with their kin. For such notables a bull from the Pope dispensing any prohibitions that arose not from divine law as set out in *Leviticus* but from human law, the extensions made by the Church, was not only possible but commonplace. The busy clerks of the papal penitentiary routinely dispensed away literally thousands of these impediments. Penitentiaries and notables may indeed have viewed the impediments less as moral precepts than as the dispensable technicalities that we tend to suppose nowadays. Princes and nobles often did not wait for a dispensation, but married in the expectation of one; even if set asunder by the Church, they might well be allowed to marry again. Not always, however.[20]

On the other hand, compared with today, the age of consent mattered much less. There were ages of majority and ages of discretion, both younger than we permit today and surprisingly not identical for the two sexes. The age of consent, supposedly that of puberty, was twelve for women and fourteen for men, the age of majority was fourteen for women and twenty-one for men. Such restrictions were not as absolute as they are today: whilst marriages younger than seven were disapproved and had to be confirmed at the age of consent, yet marriages at a young age – as with Anne Neville's father Warwick – did happen.

Where fifteenth-century people denounced as incestuous the marriages of cousins and in-laws that we permit without any qualms, sexual relations were perfectly acceptable between those of different ages: relations that today we might label paedophilia and prosecute as child-abuse. The match between Anne and the future Richard III, apparently contracted when she was fifteen, would today label Richard as a sex offender, guilty of sexual relations with a minor or, in American parlance, of statutory rape, yet it excited no such condemnation or even disapproval in their own age. There are no rules on such issues applicable everywhere even today. Child-marriage at puberty, later ages of discretion, bigamy and gay marriage are to be found in other countries, religions and cultures, permitted in some parts of the world and prohibited in others. Doubtless their practitioners, like us, consider their standards to be the best. From our third-millennium, British, western, post-Christian and liberal standpoint we must be careful not to assert dogmatically that our own laws and conventions, which have changed enormously in the last forty years and are still evolving at breakneck pace, are right, absolute for all time, and applicable to the past as well as the present. Of course standards and values do vary with era, country, class and culture and are very largely why the past is so different from the present. Nor, indeed, should we be surprised if such unfamiliar standards framed patterns of conduct unfamiliar to us today. Why shouldn't many children short of puberty with parental consent and support have been gearing themselves for courtship and arranged marriage? Some girls, quite legitimately and legally, experienced pregnancy and childbirth and embarked on motherhood before they were fourteen. Henry VII was one such end product. It was not the problem we perceive today. Even if we believe, as surely we do, that we manage such things better today, our predecessors lacked this perspective. We cannot understand their actions unless we can suspend our disbelief and appreciate the standards that they lived by and applied. Nor can we impose our values on the past.

Anne Neville illustrates repeatedly the operation of these rules in practice. Yet the rules were far from absolute. Most bars, though not quite all, could be dispensed by the Church and set aside. It may even be that members of the elite, who almost always required dispensations for some impediments when it came to marrying their social equals, came to regard such matters as mere technicalities to be rectified for the appropriate fee, even retrospectively. Two princesses in this book appear to have taken this view. Perhaps aristocratic morality was somewhat deficient even by the current contemporary standards. Such issues did matter. Such matters constantly recurred throughout Anne's life and were absolutely crucial at its end.

CHAPTER TWO

Who Was Anne Neville?

PRE–NATAL INFLUENCES

Anne Neville (1456–85) was the younger of the two daughters – and hence one of the two co-heiresses – of Richard Neville, Earl of Warwick and Salisbury ('Warwick the Kingmaker') and his consort Anne Beauchamp. Anne Neville was thus born into the highest nobility, the top rank of English society, and was assured from birth of a great future. The course that her life was to take owed much more to her lineage and family wealth, the circumstances of her family and her birth, the careers and renown of her ancestors and parents, than it did to her own efforts. Such factors determined who she was and ensured that she mattered. Rarely indeed can Anne be demonstrated to have done anything at all, yet her role was often crucial and her significance not in doubt. Before detailing her own life, therefore, it is necessary to establish her context.

Who Anne Neville was, what she was to become, and what factors shaped her development were pre-determined, at least to some extent, by her pedigree. Pre-natal influences, most notably lineage and inheritance, are the essential keys to understanding Anne's context. What follows is therefore a commentary on Anne Neville's pedigree.[1]

Anne's father, as we have seen, was Richard Neville junior, who made himself a household name as Warwick the Kingmaker in his own time and in all generations down to today. Richard was the son of another Richard Neville senior (d.1460) and Alice Montagu (d.1463). Richard Neville senior was the eldest of the children of Ralph Neville, Earl of Westmorland (d.1425) by his second wife Joan Beaufort. Earl Ralph was the most outstanding head of the great house of Neville – the culmination of many generations of Neville barons of Raby (Durham), Middleham and Sheriff Hutton (Yorks.) who had distinguished themselves repeatedly against the Scots ever since the Norman Conquest. Joan Beaufort, his second wife and his first countess, was the daughter of John of Gaunt, Duke of Lancaster (d.1399) and third son of Edward III (1327–77), by his mistress and eventual third duchess Katherine Swynford. This royal marriage explains in part Ralph's promotion as earl in 1397. He had the requisite qualifying income anyway and he had earned promotion by good service to the crown. However his elevation coincided with that of Joan's brother John Beaufort as earl of Somerset. The Countess Joan was thus half-sister of the Lancastrian King Henry IV (1399–1413), aunt of Henry V (1413–22), great-aunt of Henry VI (1422–61), whole sister of Cardinal Beaufort (d.1447) and Thomas Beaufort, Duke of Exeter (1425), both Lord Chancellors, and the aunt and great-aunt of the four Beaufort dukes of Somerset. Such a marriage made the Nevilles themselves royal. Earl Ralph, Henry IV's brother-in-law, was frequently described in royal records, according to contemporary usage, as the king's brother. His proximity to the king brought him high favour, a string of grants of office and of property that was settled in tail on the earl and his eldest son by his royal wife, Richard Neville, not the eldest son by his first marriage who was heir to the earldom of Westmorland. Doubtless persuaded by the Countess Joan, Earl Ralph also transferred many of his ancestral Neville estates to her children – to Richard senior and his heirs male – away from the main Westmorland line. Following Earl Ralph's death, the Westmorland Nevilles objected violently, but were obliged to accept reality in 1443. They retained the Durham properties, but it was Richard Neville senior who secured the Middleham estates in Richmondshire and Sheriff Hutton, Penrith and other properties in Cumbria, and the royal wardenship of the West March that made him the military commander west of the Pennines against the Scots. It was this patrimony to which Anne's father Richard Neville junior was born in 1428.[2] It was also this power-base that Anne Neville was to transfer to her second husband Richard, Duke of Gloucester in the 1470s. Gloucester used it to make himself dominant in the North and to usurp the throne in 1483.

Another fruit of the kinship of the Nevilles to the house of Lancaster was the most remarkable series of child marriages in medieval England. Earl Ralph fathered no less than twenty-two children, nine of them by his second wife Joan.[3] The Nevilles were able to exploit the favour of the Lancastrians to secure grants of the marriages of the most desirable heirs and heiresses to marry their children, which Henry IV and V willingly conceded, especially when they were the offspring of former traitors whom they wanted safely married into loyal families. Neville spouses had become attractive to noblemen seeking husbands for their daughters. Hence Richard Neville senior was married to Alice Montagu, sole daughter and heiress of Thomas Montagu (d.1428), Earl of Salisbury, by Eleanor, one of the five heiresses of the Holland earls of Kent. Richard and Alice were Anne Neville's grandparents. Quite apart from the title, which gave Richard Neville the earldom that his great estates demanded, and extensive lands mainly in south-central England, his countess could trace herself through both lines back to Edward I. If not quite of the front rank – only the Stafford, York and Warwick inheritances were – Richard

Neville's combined estates placed him firmly in the second rank among the top half-dozen dynasties of the 1430s and 1440s. He was certainly the equal of his rival and brother-in-law Henry Percy, 2nd earl of Northumberland.[4]

Anne Neville's grandparents the Earl and Countess of Salisbury started searching in the nobility for partners for their own dozen children well before they reached their teens and indeed before the younger ones were yet born. Richard Neville junior, the future kingmaker, was their eldest son, heir to the earldom of Salisbury and to all their Holland, Montagu and Neville possessions. He was a considerable matrimonial catch. Given how many marriages the Nevilles had already contracted amongst the nobility, there were in reality few partners of sufficient standing who were not already too closely related to them within the prohibited degrees of affinity and thus genuinely eligible. One of the most promising of these was undoubtedly Anne Beauchamp, the youngest daughter of Richard Beauchamp, Earl of Warwick (d.1439) by his second wife Isabel Despenser (d.1439). Born in 1426, Anne Beauchamp was not an heiress, for she had an elder brother Henry (d.1446), the future duke of Warwick, but only his single life stood between her entitlement to a share, with her four half-sisters, of the Beauchamp and Despenser heritage. In any case, even the greatest families could not confine themselves to heirs and heiresses unless they were prepared to intermarry with those of lesser rank, mere gentry rather than nobility.

No objection could be found to Anne's pedigree. The earls of Warwick traced themselves to the legendary Guy of Warwick. Earl Richard Beauchamp was the sixth Beauchamp earl, a soldier and indeed hero of chivalric renown, the 'father of courtesy', the tutor to King Henry VI himself and about to become king's lieutenant in France.[5] The Countess Isabel had been daughter and sole heiress of Thomas Despenser (d.1400), briefly Earl of Gloucester, who traced his descent from Edward

I, and Constance of York (d.1416), another granddaughter of Edward III. Her daughter Anne Beauchamp was indeed the 'noble lady of the blood royal' that John Rows alleged.[6] The combined Beauchamp and Despenser estates, principally in the West Midlands around Warwick, Hanley Castle (Worcs.) and Tewkesbury (Gloucs.) and in south Wales (but including Barnard Castle in County Durham), placed them decisively in the front rank, one level above the Nevilles. Evidently it was Salisbury who really wanted a matrimonial alliance, most probably to unite his daughter Cecily Neville with Warwick's son Henry, heir to the only magnate family to which the Nevilles were not yet closely connected. Earl Richard Beauchamp, we may deduce, was not so enthusiastic to dispose of the hand of his heir in this way. Henry was, after all, the greatest heir of any contemporary noble house, who ought really to have been advancing himself by marriage to a royal princess or to a well-endowed heiress, neither of which Cecily Neville was. Salisbury, however, made him an offer even Earl Richard Beauchamp could hardly refuse. Not only did he offer him a dowry with Cecily of 4,700 marks (£3,233 13s 4d), one of the largest marriage portions recorded in medieval England and very welcome given the great earl's financial embarrassments, but Salisbury also threw in as makeweight the hand of his son Richard for Anne Beauchamp, which would make her a countess. This was decidedly better than the mere baronies that were all that Warwick had secured for his three elder daughters by his first wife. The double marriage, Henry Beauchamp to Cecily Neville and Richard Neville to Anne Beauchamp, was celebrated at Abergavenny in Wales on or about 4 May 1436.[7]

In the short run, as we shall see, these splendid matches produced the intended results. Following the deaths of the earl and countess of Warwick, their son Henry succeeded as earl and Cecily Neville as countess. Henry was elevated in quick succession to be premier earl and then duke, but died in 1446. His infant daughter followed in 1449 and Cecily, now Duchess of Warwick, in 1450. What was unexpected was that in 1449 Anne Beauchamp scooped the pool. Richard Neville junior became earl of Warwick and acquired the whole of the vast Beauchamp and Despenser inheritance, to the chagrin, violent protest and ineffective resistance of his sisters-in-law. It was as earl of Warwick that he made his reputation – he was not Salisbury the Kingmaker, but Warwick the Kingmaker – and his parental inheritances did not fall in for another decade. This was why Anne Neville was born at Warwick, why her child-hood homes were on the Beauchamp and Despenser estates, and why John Rows of Warwick was her family chronicler.[8]

Queen Anne Neville, as we have seen, was a product of this union. Her parents were destined to careers as great landown-ers in Yorkshire and the North-West and also in the central South. During the 1450s they periodically visited London for parliaments and great council, and regularly interacted with all the other great houses whom they numbered as their kin and with the royal family. Every generation that passed, of course, moved the Nevilles further from the throne, repeat-edly creating more intimate royal families, so that by the 1450s the Nevilles were among the more remote of the 200 or so individuals who regarded themselves as royal.[9] They ceased to benefit from extraordinary royal favour during the 1440s: the Kingmaker's younger brothers, Anne Neville's uncles, and his younger sisters, her aunts, had to wait until they were adults to marry, and even then matched themselves to mere barons and the heiresses of wealthy gentry. Even if no longer ranked with the royal by those who were undoubtedly royal, never-theless Richard Neville and Anne Beauchamp – and hence their daughter Anne Neville herself – could pride themselves on descent from Edward III and earlier monarchs through five distinct lines. Her pedigree is a case study in endogamy, the tendency of the nobility to marry within a limited circle of existing kin. Royal descent linked her inevitably with other royal lines: Valois, Wittelsbach, Bruce and Luxemberg, rulers of the Empire, France, the Spanish kingdoms and Scotland, back to Charlemagne and into the mythical mists of time. Genealogical rolls traced them back to Woden, Adam and Noah. The Warwick historian John Rows was right therefore to address Anne Neville as 'the most noble lady and princess born of the royal blood of divers realms lineally descending from princes, kings, emperors, and many glorious saints'.[10] Perhaps he was thinking of St Louis (Louis IX of France) and St Margaret of Scotland? Understandably Anne and her family took pride in its lineage, burnishing their buildings, glass, plate and vestments with the coats of arms and badges that they had inherited. Most probably it was Anne Neville who was to commission the *Pageant of Richard Beauchamp Earl of Warwick* – a celebration of her distinguished grandfather – and an updated edition of the *Salisbury Roll*: John Rows' *Roll of the Earls of Warwick* was a worthy gift.[11]

Yet inheritance was not merely a matter of accumulation – of castles, lordships, wealth, honours, titles and progeny. There was a genetic inheritance too. No doubt, as always, there were family likenesses. Anne's genetic inheritance may perhaps have been a negative one. It makes sense to argue that inheritances accrued because families ran out, that heiresses then occurred only when their families failed to produce or successfully to bring up sons, and that families that repeatedly married their sons to heiresses rendered themselves more liable to inherit infertility, sterility or susceptibility to disease, and hence to produce no heirs themselves. Such an argument must be mere speculation uninformed by the medical lore or genetic know-how that we can bring to the subject today, but some of the circumstances are suggestive. Alarmingly fertile though the Nevilles had been, several of the branches were to terminate only in daughters. Salisbury's brother William Lord Fauconberg left three daughters. Salisbury's three married sons produced numerous daughters, but not a single son that they raised to maturity.[12] Whereas Anne Beauchamp, as we shall see, bore only two daughters, these daughters had only five children between them, three of whom died young. Anne Neville herself produced only a single son who died before the age of ten. Gynaecological misfortune, perhaps a genetic inheritance, shaped Anne Neville's whole life and came ultimately (and tragically) to overshadow it.

The marriage of Anne's parents, in the meantime, took years to become a reality. Richard, after all, was only seven years old, his bride Anne Beauchamp being already ten. Whilst they grew up, Warwick's three brothers reached maturity – the youngest, George, becoming a bishop – and his sisters were married off to the earl of Arundel, Lord Stanley and Lord FitzHugh. Anne's four sisters had peers for husbands. Moreover, the older generation survived – in the 1450s Salisbury had four brothers and five brothers-in-law in the House of Lords.[13] Almost everyone who was anyone was related to the Nevilles. Anne Neville had a host of uncles, aunts, even great-uncles and great-aunts. The Wars of the Roses, when they happened, were genuinely a family affair. Kinship, which often entails disputed inheritances, can divide as well as unite. Different branches of this vast family network developed contradictory interests and antagonisms. It was to slay two brothers-in-law that the Neville earls were to fight at St Albans in 1455;[14] other kin followed at the battles of Northampton in 1460 and Towton in 1461.

It was crucial that Anne Neville was born not to rank and wealth, but to ancient lineage, ancient contacts and ancient loyalties. The Beauchamps, Despensers, Montagus and Nevilles had held their titles and their estates by right for so long that they had come to be seen as natural, permanent and enduring. Such long-established families were stable, capable of surmounting temporary minorities and forfeitures, and were extremely difficult to uproot. 'New men' raised from the dust by royal grants found that it took time to make more of their estates than the chance and temporary agglomeration of properties. They needed strength of character, attractive personalities and material inducements to secure the service they desired and which ancient families could take for granted, to construct the connections that were required in politics, and to ensure that these held firm at the first shock. That took decades, even generations. Long-standing inheritances, which had endured over time, conferred all these advantages on each successive tenant for life. Nobody doubted their right to exist and their natural associates – the tenants on their estates, retainers and officers – expected them not only to remain, but their heirs to continue after them. Such dependants had an interest in the inheritance, in the family and in its traditions. All the components of the Warwick inheritance were ancient, by medieval standards, and possessed this character. They had traditions remembered by lords and servants alike, whose memory was cherished and perpetuated by such custodians as the monks of Tewkesbury Abbey, canons of Coverham Abbey and the Warwick chantry priest John Rows, and as imparted to successive lords and their offspring, certainly to Anne Neville. The interest of the lords was to foster and ideally develop these traditions, which indeed Duke Richard and Anne Neville did. Anne Neville inevitably was imbued with these traditions, if not always at first hand.

Anne Neville was born at Warwick, the principal seat of the earls of Warwick, where there remains today one of the most imposing seigniorial castles to survive and which was still inhabited by its lord until very recently. Apart from its castle, the modest Midlands town was dominated by the religious foundations of successive earls, who had also enhanced it with privileges, walls, parks and other improvements. The earls of Warwick proudly traced themselves back beyond the Norman Beaumonts to the legendary past. The first earl, it was believed, had been a giant, Guy of Warwick, a hero of medieval romances, whose cave at Guyscliff to the north of Warwick still survived. The Beauchamps' respect for the legend was displayed by nomenclature – there was one Earl Guy of Warwick (d.1315) and a grandson was scheduled to be a second – and there was a huge Guy's Tower at Warwick Castle. Guy's supposed arms were quartered with their own and were to be quartered indeed with those of Anne, her sister, their husbands and Anne's sons. It was in the Warwick tradition that Anne Neville's maternal grandfather Earl Richard Beauchamp was credited with an ambitious, extremely expensive and perhaps technologically impractical plan to transform Warwick economically by making the River Avon navigable from Tewkesbury up to Warwick. In 1423, when he had feared that the inheritance would terminate with his daughters and he yearned for heirs male to continue his line, the Beauchamp name and title, Earl Richard Beauchamp had remarried to the much younger Isabel Despenser. He had also rebuilt Guyscliff Chapel, with its giant statue of Guy hewn from the rock, and had endowed a two-priest chantry to serve it. The chapel was only finished in 1454. Anne Neville's father, the kingmaker, supposedly planned to augment it with an almshouse of noble poverty for retired retainers like that which he had despoiled at St Cross, Winchester.[15] So attests John Rows, the graduate who was cantarist there for almost sixty years until his death in 1491. Rows made himself into the historian both of Warwick and its earls so successfully that he superseded whatever it was that had previously reminded the family of their heritage and which, regrettably, has been lost. Earl Richard Beauchamp bound his son Henry, if promoted, to retain the Warwick title, which indeed he did when created in 1446 duke of Warwick. Moreover, through another line, the Thonys, the Beauchamps were heirs of the legendary Swan Knight, another hero of medieval romance, whose golden cup was kept at Warwick Castle and shown to visitors. From the fourteenth century, the Beauchamps made the ancient college of St Mary Warwick into their mausoleum. It was there that Earl Thomas I (d.1369), Earl Thomas II (d.1401) and Earl Richard (d.1439) were buried. They rebuilt the choir. In his will Earl Richard Beauchamp commissioned for himself the Beauchamp Chapel, one of the finest – if not the finest – chantry chapels of medieval England, which was under construction throughout Anne Neville's childhood and was consecrated only in 1472. From 1459, when Earl Richard Beauchamp's monument was completed,[16] Anne could identify her parents by their coats of arms amongst the weepers ranged alongside the effigy of her grandfather. Doubtless she did.

En route from Warwick to Cardiff lay Tewkesbury Abbey, the mausoleum of Anne's De Clare and Despenser forebears, where her grandmother Isabel Despenser lay buried and where Anne's own sister still rests. The Benedictine monks of this greatest religious house still in lay patronage regarded themselves as repositories of their founders' ancestral renown. The eastern apse had been refashioned by her Despenser ancestors, who were all depicted in its early-fourteenth-century glass, and a semi-circle of chantries commemorated the founders from the legendary origins down to Anne's own grandmother the Countess Isabel (d.1439). Most of them, including Anne's father, are depicted in miniature in the *Founder's Chronicle*.[17] Presumably the same role was performed by the Augustinian canons of Bisham Priory, the mausoleum of the Montagus, in the earlier versions of the Salisbury Roll.[18] A younger lineage, undoubtedly, the Montagus nevertheless had their hero – William Montagu, the 1st Earl of Salisbury (d.1344) – and a century of distinction, to which Anne's maternal grandmother the Countess Alice was the last heir.

Although he was not to inherit until 1460, the kingmaker was acutely conscious of his own lineage, the Nevilles, who, as we have seen, traced themselves back to the Norman Conquest and indeed beyond. Their family genealogy, originating at the abbey of St Mary at York and continued at Coverham, as revised for Earl Ralph and updated c.1443, celebrated their roots in Richmondshire, where Middleham lay, and their military renown.[19] Some versions stressed the direct line and others all the siblings, male, female and prematurely deceased, in each generation. Surviving in multiple copies and perhaps hung up on the wall, the genealogy indicated to members of the family, such as Anne Neville, exactly where they fitted and everything to which they were heirs. The Nevilles were everywhere in the North. As Anne Neville was to find, Neville's Cross marked a notable victory over the Scots in 1346, in Durham Cathedral there was both a Neville chantry and a Neville screen, and at York her father and uncle were to found St William's College. Not only was she to feel at home in the North, but northerners regarded Anne Neville – in turn the Lady Anne, the Duchess Anne and Queen Anne – as very much their own.[20]

BIRTH 1456

A daughter like Anne Neville benefited from her complex pedigree and luxuriant traditions, but she was decidedly not their intended culmination. A daughter who was an heiress, still more a daughter who was a co-heiress, threatened to bring everything to the end – the family name, its titles, its honours, its traditions, its patronage and its connections. The future would be shaped by a husband who knew of none of these, perhaps cared little for them, and had his own counterparts to each to protect.

Joy at Anne Neville's birth (and her mother's survival) was thus accompanied by apprehension for the future. For Anne

Neville herself, of course, her birth was her beginning. What that meant – how she was greeted and how her significance evolved – is also deserving of attention.

Formally married in 1436, Richard Neville junior and Anne Beauchamp needed time to grow up. Even allowing for that, however, their marriage was slow to bear its intended fruits: inheritance, children and heirs. Richard Neville senior (henceforth Salisbury) lived to be sixty: still vigorous and effective, his life ended violently. His countess Alice Montagu, our heroine's grandmother, survived another two years. Anne Neville's maternal grandparents died sooner, both in 1439. Her only maternal uncle Duke Henry died in 1446, his spouse Duchess Cecily in 1451, and their only baby daughter in 1449, all before Anne Neville was born. The duke's infant left five aunts to divide her Beauchamp and Despenser inheritances. Had her father Duke Henry not come of age, they would have done, but because the duke had achieved his majority his only whole sister Anne Beauchamp took precedence over his four half-sisters: there was a common-law rule that favoured the whole blood over the half blood. As we have seen, the unforeseen beneficiaries were Duke Henry's youngest sister and his daughter's youngest aunt Anne Beauchamp and her husband Richard Neville, who became earl and countess of Warwick and secured the whole of both inheritances rather than merely the quarter and half shares that were all that could have been predicted. Anne Beauchamp's half-sisters and nephew objected and resisted, ultimately without avail.[21] For the heir of Richard and Alice, always heir presumptive to the Neville and Montagu lands and the earldom of Salisbury, an even greater future beckoned. Moreover, it began at once. In 1449, at the age of twenty, the younger Richard Neville became earl of Warwick. But for the Wars of the Roses and Salisbury's violent death in 1460, Richard Neville junior might have remained an heir in waiting, overshadowed by his father, for much longer than the thirteen years till his mother died. Instead he was able to become a great man at once, able to make a major impression on his age and indeed overshadow his own father Salisbury, without waiting to enter his parents' shoes. It was not a hopeful heir, but the greatest of earls who begat Anne Neville.

As yet, however, there was no heir: no offspring of either sex. By 1449 the new earl and countess had been married for thirteen years. The absence of heirs is surprising. Without pretending the union of Richard and Anne to have been a love match – how could it have been, given their youth and differences in ages? – the Nevilles at least must have intended children to result. Child grooms and brides did not live together or indeed consummate their marriages until they were considered old enough. Even by contemporary standards, 1436 – when Richard was aged seven and Anne ten – was too soon. Margaret Beaufort was twelve, and bore the future Henry VII when only fourteen. Girls came of age at fourteen, which Anne reached in 1440 when Richard, at eleven, was still too young. After the death of both her parents in 1439, if not earlier, Anne was surely living with her in-laws. We have no evidence when Richard and Anne first slept together, first lived together, or first had their own establishment, but it was surely by 1446, when Duke Henry died, Anne being at the relatively advanced age of twenty and Richard aged seventeen, still more so by 1449 when they became earl and countess of Warwick, she being twenty-three years old by then and he aged twenty. And yet it was only on 5 September 1451 that their daughter Isabel was born[22] – their eldest child so far as we can be aware. Presumably she was conceived at Christmas 1450 or New Year 1451. Given the committed interest in such events both of John Rows and the Tewkesbury Abbey chronicler, historians respectively of the Beauchamps and the Despensers, we should surely expect to know of any earlier daughter to be born and certainly of any son on whom the future of both houses depended, if not necessarily of miscarriages and still-births. Richard and Anne must have been trying to beget children. Twenty-five was an advanced age for Anne to bear her first child. Perhaps the Countess Anne came to puberty very late. Perhaps she had miscarriages of which we are ignorant. That certainly is indicated by the papal dispensation she secured in 1453. Because 'she is weakened by former illnesses and the birth of children', she was allowed when pregnant to eat eggs and meat in Lent.[23] Did she also have difficulty in conceiving? The second daughter and future queen Anne Neville was born when Anne was thirty, which was an early age for a lady to cease child-bearing. Women who experience puberty late today have early menopauses. We can presume, once again, that Warwick himself was anxious to breed a son and was engaging in the requisite intercourse with his countess. Nothing more materialised. If infertility could have been his fault, his bastard daughter Margaret is evidence of a sex drive that the Countess Anne alone did not satisfy, for he was married throughout his fertile life. Anne Neville's genealogical inheritance included a gene bank that, it appears, may well have included the gynaecological problems which, perhaps, explain or contributed to her own disappointing record of procreation.

Young though they were, Richard and Anne were programmed by class and family expectations to reproduce, all the more so once her inheritances had devolved on them. Heirs were needed to perpetuate their line. Additionally heirs were of signal value as they combated the rival claims of their rival cousins. We may be sure therefore that Anne Beauchamp's first pregnancy was welcome, how eagerly her first confinement was anticipated, and how disappointing was the birth – when it came – of a daughter. There can be little doubt that Isabel Neville was given the name of her maternal grandmother, the countess's mother Isabel Despenser. Even daughters had their dynastic and political uses, however, and Isabel's birth was moreover an earnest of better things to come. Yet four years passed before the next childbirth, when events repeated themselves. It was in recognition that the countess's pregnancies were few – and that the hoped-for son might materialise – that a special christening was prepared. Undoubtedly Anne Neville was wanted – but how much more disappointing must have been her sex. Anne was given her mother's name. And so, in the absence of evidence, sexual intercourse persisted and the waiting continued. How soon it was that the Warwicks realised that there would be no more pregnancies or childbirths we cannot tell. Certainly by 1464, when the countess was forty, Warwick appears to have made his will and invested his hopes in heirs that did not include a son. The countess herself, of course, will have known when her periods ceased. Not to have a son that they both wanted so much was surely one of the sharpest disappointments of their married lives and perhaps their personal tragedy.

Earl Richard and Countess Anne thus produced only two daughters, Isabel and Anne Neville. Probably conceived at Warwick Castle, their principal seat and the countess' home, it was there that Isabel was born on 5 September 1451.[24] Most probably Warwick himself was present in the castle, although the labour was an all-female preserve. Nothing is recorded about her christening. Anne Neville also was born at Warwick on 11 June 1456 and 'in our lady church there with great solemnity was she christened'[25] at St Mary's, Warwick College, the Beauchamp mausoleum where Earl Richard Beauchamp and his father were interred. Since Warwick missed the poorly attended great council that met at Westminster from 7 June, almost certainly he was at Warwick for the birth and for the christening, although the son that he so desired failed to materialise. Regrettably the Warwick cantarist John Rows, who reported the occasion, has not transmitted to us details even of who Anne's godparents were. Presumably it was for the intended son that the ceremonial (and noble godparents) were prepared: the most public statement possible to the Warwick connection that the Neville line was to endure.

UPBRINGING

The young married couple who unexpectedly became earl and countess of Warwick in 1449 fought off rivals for the Beauchamp, Despenser and Abergavenny elements of Anne's inheritance. The earldom of Salisbury fell in following the deaths of Warwick's father in 1460 and his mother in 1463. Substantial additions to his estates were added from the forfeited property of Lancastrian families such as the Percys, Cliffords and Rooses. Warwick now was the richest nobleman in England by a large margin – richer even, almost certainly, than Richard, Duke of York and than any other subject since John of Gaunt (d.1399). He had moreover accrued a host of offices – captain of Calais, chief forester of the North and chief steward of the northern estates of the duchy of Lancaster, great chamberlain of England, keeper of the seas, warden of the West March, constable and steward of a host of castles and lordships, even briefly king's lieutenant of the North and steward of England. He conquered the North for Edward IV, not once but repeatedly, was the king's principal ambassador, presided over the queen's churching and, to foreigners at least, he appeared greater than King Edward himself. He dominated his brothers, whose personal success, John as earl of Northumberland and warden of the East March, and George as archbishop of York and chancellor of England, enhanced his own.[26]

Warwick's success happened very quickly, but not all at once. The first years of his first daughter, Isabel, were surely spent with her mother the Countess Anne principally at Warwick. That was where Anne was born. But her father's career took off first as keeper of the seas and then as captain of Calais, the principal military commands of the English crown in the aftermath of military defeat. Never had Calais and its captain been more important. Remarkably Warwick chose to take up residence in Calais. That was in May 1457.[27] Earlier captains, such as Earl Richard Beauchamp and Humphrey, Duke of Gloucester, had been absentees who acted through deputies. It was a formal decision by Warwick, not a chance visit that was somehow extended. Even more remarkably, Warwick took his countess with him. Perhaps he did not wish to be parted indefinitely from his lifelong partner and soul mate; more cynically, he could not pass by several years of opportunity to father a son. Probably, therefore, both his daughters were at Calais too. It could hardly have been intended to separate them from their mother for the space of years. Probably Anne Neville moved to Calais before her first birthday. Probably she, her mother and her sister Isabel resided at Calais for three years.

Restless and apparently tireless, Warwick himself was frequently away, often on activities that carried a high degree of risk. Obviously his countess and daughters did not join him for his naval depredations against foreign shipping nor for negotiations with foreign neighbours in Calais' hinterlands. The chroniclers do not record either whether his family joined him for his visits every so often to England for great councils, notably the three-month peace conference that culminated in the Loveday of St Paul's in the winter of 1458–9, and which allowed him at least to make lightning visits to Warwick and other properties. These were political fraught occasions not without their own dangers: the first blows of the Wars of the Roses had been struck and there was an assassination attempt on Warwick in Westminster Hall in November 1458. Most probably, therefore, his countess and daughters remained at Calais.

Certainly the Countess Anne was again at Calais, perhaps with her daughters, when Warwick arrived there on

2 November 1459 in flight from the debacle at Ludford. He was accompanied by his father – his daughters' paternal grandfather Richard, Earl of Salisbury – and by Edward, Earl of March, son of Richard, Duke of York and the future King Edward IV. All the Yorkist peers were attainted as traitors at the Parliament of Devils. When Warwick consulted York in Ireland, many chronicles report what was evidently a celebrated feat, and he returned to Calais with his mother (and Anne's grandmother), the now aged Countess Alice.[28] Left behind during the successful invasion of the Yorkist earls in 1460, the two countesses (and presumably also Isabel and Anne) received the victorious Warwick in triumph at Calais on 7 August and were transported back via Sandwich to England, catching up with King Henry VI at Greenwich on 19th and proceeding with him to London.[29] At that point Anne had just embarked on her fifth year.

Young though she was, Anne's earliest years in Calais ought to have been a formative experience. She was not in England in her early childhood. Physically she did not live in England, although she must have been told often enough, nostalgically, that it was her real and permanent home. The great household that she inhabited was little different from what it was in England, but her apparently static existence in Calais Castle was very different from the peripatetic nature of noble life in England. The beleaguered frontier town of Calais, a garrison town and an English colony in a foreign hinterland, was quite unlike anywhere else in England, except possibly the northern marcher fortresses of Carlisle and Berwick-upon-Tweed, and was certainly dissimilar from the provincial seats where her parents resided when in England. She may not have known Warwick, Hanley Castle (Worcs.), Tewkesbury, Cardiff or her mother's other residences in Wales and the West Midlands as well as her sister Isabel, particularly as the earl's northern heritage seems to have taken precedence after 1460; perhaps Rows knew her less well also. For six months in 1459–60 she lived in close proximity to her grandparents. Moreover at Calais Anne was exposed to francophone culture. If English was the principal language of her parents, their entourage, and indeed the people of Calais, French and Flemish were frequently spoken by native Frenchmen and Burgundians in her parents' household and everywhere outside, doubtless sometimes to Anne, whom, one might surmise, quickly learnt to understand and also to speak French herself – a language that was both useful and a polite accomplishment. Surely she encountered Flemish too. If Anne grew up bilingual, it could have smoothed relations with her first mother-in-law Margaret of Anjou. Unfortunately, like so much else about Anne, there is nothing to confirm what was the impact in later life of her sojourn in Calais.

Little more than a toddler and at a distance in Calais, Anne was insulated against the first of the Wars of the Roses of 1459–61, though her father's absences – and some sense of the risks, the reliefs, and the victories – surely permeated down even to his youngest daughter. After the Greenwich reception in August, the earl and countess and presumably both daughters too went next to Warwick, before the earl met up with Richard, Duke of York at Shrewsbury, and preceded him to London,[30] where the duke bid for the crown. The decisive battles ensued. Where the countess and daughters were in the meantime we cannot know. Warwick survived. He also won. The right side, the Yorkists, prevailed decisively at the battle of Towton on 29 March 1461. The Yorkist King Edward IV, whom his cousin Anne knew from his nine-month sojourn at Calais, supplanted the Lancastrian King Henry VI.

Perhaps Anne Neville at four and certainly her sister Isabel at nine were old enough to understand the high dramas of 1460–1, when the Yorkists secured control of the government, their grandfather was slain at Wakefield, their father was routed at St Albans and the Lancastrian army menaced London where, most probably, they were at the time. Given the prominence of their parents, they were probably observers both of the formalities of King Edward's accession on 4 March and his coronation in 1461. Their father set off northwards for the decisive battle of Towton and returned as victor. If never visible in our sources, Isabel and Anne cannot have been ignorant either of the stakes and risks nor other than grateful at consequences that surely answered their prayers.

Warwick was certainly head of his household and a model of the male authority to which daughters like Anne were taught to defer. To an extent even greater than as head of his great household in his provincial seats, the Earl of Warwick was in charge in Calais, where he actually ruled and where, when in rebellion, he actually was the final authority. He operated martial law and exercised power of life and death, notoriously despatching Osbert Mountford, King Henry's naval commander, when he fell into his hands.[31] Warwick's power was the reality of Anne's earliest years. Return to England did not radically change that situation. As early as Anne Neville became conscious of such things, her father was a great man. When she was four he was second only to the king or – so some said – greater than the king himself. Laden with honours and responsibilities, 'he had all England at his leading and was dreaded and feared [doubted] through many lands', and was 'a famous knight and excellent greatly spoken of through the most part of all Christendom', whose 'knightly acts had been so excellent that his noble and famous name could never be put out of laudable memory'. That was the public face of what was to her 'the most famous and dread and beloved lord'.[32] How close that relationship was, how domestic was the comital household, how well Anne knew her father and what he meant to her in practice we cannot tell.

Of Anne's mother we know a little more. The earl and countess resided principally at Warwick up to 1456, when Anne was born, and then in Calais until 1460. Thereafter during the 1460s Warwick was constantly away on military or diplomatic business, most commonly in the North, at Westminster, and on continental embassies, on which his family can rarely have accompanied him. Clearly the earl and countess were less often together. Quite frequently recorded at Middleham and at Carlisle, the earl was rarely at Warwick after 1461 and does not occur again in Wales. Did the countess also base herself in the North? For the whole of 1464–5, the only year for which accounts survive, the Countess Anne was not at Middleham. Or did she reside more usually on her own estates in the West Midlands whence she came? She must certainly have possessed a household capable of operating apart from the earl and of moving about. After the earl's exile in 1470, his countess lived in turn abroad, at Beaulieu and in the North, and returned to Warwick, if ever, only after John Rows had finished writing. Although this Warwick cantarist knew his countess well, and knew all about her subsequent sufferings and her reactions to them, yet he encountered her principally in 1449–57 rather than later. What he saw her daughters witnessed also. As a clergyman, Rows reports with approval that the countess 'was ever a full devout lady in God's service' – that she attended religious services assiduously and fervently: he had more that was positive and distinctive to say about her elder siblings and would have liked, we may presume, to have something more concrete to praise about her piety. Rows also perceived in her 'a noble lady of the blood royal' and 'by true inheritance countess of Warwick', neither of which Anne can have overlooked. Anne's mother was also an excellent example of feminine conduct for her daughters, even through masculine eyes. 'She was also gladly ever companionable and liberal', Rows wrote, 'and in her own person, seemly and beauteous, and to all that drew to her ladyship, as the deed shewed, full good and gracious'. Translated into modern English, Rows tells us that the countess was pleasing to the eye and acted with decorum. She was affable, courteous to all comers, and generous. She addressed all members of her household whatever their rank 'according to her and their degrees'. A strict sense of hierarchy and etiquette and condescension to inferiors, which contemporaries thought proper and we call snobbery, is implied. Although apparently only twice in childbirth herself, Rows reports that the countess was 'glad to be at and with women that travailed of child, full comfortable and plenteous of all things that should be helping to them'.[33] Presumably these mothers-to-be were the gentlewomen of her household and the wives of her retainers and officers. It sounds as though they were her friends as well as her employees. Pregnancy, childbirth and babies were entirely familiar. Here surely Rows provides some insight into the feminine ambience within which Anne Neville was raised up to her early teens. Thereafter, as we shall see, she leapt into married life.

Whilst obviously coming together much more frequently than we can know, for procreation, on important feasts and perhaps on many other occasions, it was normal for lords and ladies to have separate and self-sufficient households, and for them often to be apart. Warwick's busy life often kept him and his family separate. In the absence of direct evidence, the households of the earl and countess were surely like many others that we do know about. Most members worked in the service departments that handled the food, drink, transport, laundry and washing up: the lower household that sustained the upper household, where the lord and lady lived and entertained. Warwick's household came to be exceptionally large and the scale of his open-handed hospitality quite outstanding.[34] When the Neville daughters were there, they found roasted meats prominent on the menu. Bar the laundress, the earl's household was entirely male, but in the smaller replica that was the countess's establishment there were females, both

gentlewomen (damsels) and domestic servants. Based on other
parallels, there were probably both married women, the wives
of his officers, and spinsters, although actually only one widow
– the earl's flighty cousin Dame Margaret Lucy[35] – is known
by name. It was a female world that aristocratic girls like the
Neville sisters inhabited. Men there were in plenty, both in the
service departments, in office upstairs, in business transactions
with their mother, and in polite society, but such maidens were
always chaperoned and insulated against potential male preda-
tors except under the most strictly controlled circumstances.

Whilst little, the earl's daughters lived with their mother.
Mothers took general responsibility for the upbringing of their
children.[36] The image of St Anne teaching her daughter the
Blessed Virgin Mary to read become popular in the fourteenth century. At this stage in history ladies did not suckle
their babies or undertake themselves the physical care of their
offspring. That was the work of a wet-nurse, from whom girls
progressed to a governess – in a great household a gentlewoman – and boys to a master. The Warwicks, of course, had
no sons, but at least two other boys, their ward Francis Lord
Lovell and also the royal prince Richard, Duke of Gloucester,
were brought up in their household;[36] female wards and other
girls may also have been. Whatever their sex, all the children
learnt at least to read and write in English, perhaps in Latin also,
to say the Lord's Prayer (*Paternoster*) and Hail Mary (*Ave*), and
were taught about religious observance: there were religious
services everyday, usually several times a day. They also learnt
who they were: their family, its genealogy, its traditions, legends
and renown. It was here, surely, that Anne Neville learnt about
Guy of Warwick and her remarkable grandfather Earl Richard
Beauchamp, about her Despenser, Montagu and Neville forebears. They must all have learnt to ride. Thereafter the routes
for boys and girls separated. Boys were taught to a higher
academic standard and also about the martial arts appropriate

to future warriors. The upbringing of girls was designed to fit them for their role in life as gentlewomen, mothers, managers of households and members of polite society. They needed to attract good husbands and to make the most of their married lives. For the latter role, they needed to learn housewifery. Sewing and the working of textiles feature prominently in all the books of instruction. They learnt how to handle servants. Girls also needed to learn courtesy, proper deportment, the etiquette, procedures and good manners expected of polite society. The Neville girls must have been taught to eat as daintily as Chaucer's *Prioress.*

The content of education, as ever, was not everything. The Knight of the Tower wrote his book so that his daughters 'ought to govern them self and to keep them from evil'. Academics and caring fathers alike sought to set girls on the right course, to inculcate proper values, and to cure them of the besetting female sins, of which a considerable list was compiled. Girls should avoid gossip, take care in what they said, not answer back, eschew idleness, extravagance and over-attention to their physical appearance, such as the painting of faces and plucking of eyebrows, and hence both vanity and pride. 'Every good woman' should 'behave herself simply & honestly in her clothing and in the quantity of it'. Humility, obedience to men and silence were enjoined. That such advice had to be devised implies, of course, that many girls were not like this. If we cannot be sure that Anne Neville conformed, nevertheless great effort and staffing was surely deployed to ensure that Warwick's daughters were brought up properly. Above all, girls must be chaste, virgins before marriage and monogamous afterwards. Girls were of course secluded from male society and chaperoned at all times, but that alone was not enough. Knowing that their future lay in marriage, even young girls were surely alert to male suitors and sexually aware, at least in theory, and liable to temptation. From their own first-hand experiences, both the Knight of the Tower and Peter Idley warned against predatory and ineligible males, who flattered inexperienced girls, promised marriage to seduce them, and threatened their reputations. Girls should curtail such inappropriate conversations and preserve their reputations – for honour was crucial among females – and hence their attraction to serious suitors. Constancy and courage were urged as antidotes to the temptations they were bound to encounter. As models they were offered the virgin martyrs, like themselves always beautiful, nubile and desirable, who had successfully resisted all blandishments, worldly advantage and threats to preserve their chastity. We may safely presume that Anne was kept unsullied for her marriage at fourteen.

The virgin martyrs were maidens, what we call adolescents, suspended between childhood and adulthood. 'Sufficiently physically developed to engage in procreation, and sufficiently intellectually and morally developed to understand the nature of the bond' of marriage, maidens had reached the perfect age of the 'youthful, sexually mature yet virginal young woman'. The late medieval ideal was that female 'beauty was associated with the slenderness of youth and virginity'.[37] By the mid-1460s, Isabel and Anne Neville too were maidens shaped by their upbringings and were still being shaped to an ideal devised by men to make them attractive to male suitors and good wives and mothers thereafter. Anne was blonde and conventionally described as 'beauteous' by John Rows.[38] Heiresses did not have to be beautiful, with even the insane finding husbands, but as they attracted royal dukes perhaps the Neville sisters were.

Damsels like Isabel and Anne were commonly placed in other gentle households, where perhaps they were more easily disciplined in their adolescent years. We have no evidence of this for the Neville sisters. There was no queen's household in which to place them until 1464, when Isabel was twelve and Anne eight. Perhaps Warwick did not want to place them with Edward's Wydeville queen, about whom he had decided qualms, and whose kinsfolk competed vigorously for such places. We should imagine Isabel, Anne and other girls living in an upper household dominated by mature and married gentlewomen with their mother and accompanying her wherever she moved, albeit less frequently than their restless father. With both parents they are recorded making offerings with the king at St Mary's Warwick, probably in January 1464.[39] Most likely they were also with their parents at York in September 1465 in company with young Duke Richard, their two uncles by marriage Lords FitzHugh and Hastings and hence probably their aunts, Warwick's sisters Alice and Katherine. That, regrettably, is all.

Probably Warwick's two little girls moved increasingly into society during the 1460s. From historical records, of course, it was only on occasions – and very special occasions – that they did emerge from obscurity and into our vision. Always they were in their best clothes and on their best behaviour. It was only their presence that was reported. Although unrecorded by the heralds, almost certainly both were present with almost all their kindred at Bisham Priory on 14 February 1463, where their grandfather Richard, Earl of Salisbury and their uncle Thomas Neville, both slain at Wakefield in 1460, were ceremonially reburied, and their recently deceased grandmother the Countess Alice was first interred. The king's own father and brother, both also killed at Wakefield, were not to receive their similar reburial until 1476. The heir of the throne, the king's brother George, Duke of Clarence, was among Warwick's distinguished array of guests at Bisham. So splendid was the occasion that the heraldic record became the model for the funeral of an earl. There is no record of the wedding of their youngest aunt Margaret c.1462 to John, Earl of Oxford. Just as remarkable as Bisham in September 1465 at Cawood Palace near York were the celebrations of the enthronement of their uncle George Neville as archbishop of York. Two thousand guests were feasted on the most lavish scale at thirteen tables in the great hall, in the chief, second and great chambers, the lower hall and in the gallery. Almost all their relations were there. Their father Warwick himself was engaged as steward, his countess was seated with other adults in the second chamber, and 'two of the Lord of Warwick's daughters' were placed in the great chamber: testimony, perhaps, that their society manners at twelve (Isabel) and nine (Anne) could be trusted. Also at their table was another child, the earl's ward, the thirteen-year-old Prince Richard, Duke of Gloucester, 'the king's brother', and three adult ladies to keep order. The ladies were Duke Richard's grown-up sister Elizabeth, Duchess of Suffolk, a cousin of the Neville girls, their distant in-law the countess of Westmorland, and their aunt by marriage (and Warwick's sister-in-law) Isabel, Countess of Northumberland. It was both a family get-together and the nursery table.[40] The heraldic records of the other major ceremonies of the 1460s, which the countess and her daughters may well have attended, such as the marriage of Queen Elizabeth (1464), her coronation (1465) and churching (1466), over which Warwick presided, and the Smithfield tournament of the Bastard of Burgundy with Lord Scales in 1467, prioritised male participants and made no mention of either Isabel or Anne. Presumably they were absent from the marriage of the Princess Margaret in Burgundy in 1468 since the earl himself was elsewhere.

Neither Isabel Neville at seventeen nor Anne Neville at fourteen were particularly young by contemporary standards when they were married. They were the products of the sort of upbringing that has been described. How successfully they internalised its messages we cannot tell. Anne's moral code, as we shall see, may have been imperfect. It was at fourteen that she left her parents' hearth. She may never have returned to Warwick again until she was queen. Hence John Rows knew her less well than her mother or her sister and therefore has little that is personal to tell us. If he could, he would have recorded distinctive details, especially of her piety, but was instead reduced to the most general of platitudes. Her manner was decorous and amiable, he records, her conduct commendable and virtuous, and she was 'full gracious'. The *Great Chronicle* also records her reputation as gracious.[41] At least, therefore, she had been brought up to her rank.

MARRIAGE

The destiny to which all aristocratic ladies were born was marriage and motherhood. That was the fate of both Isabel and Anne. Maidenhood, childhood, and even infancy, was not too early to ask. The earl and countess of Warwick had been children aged seven and eleven when they were married. Warwick's own father Salisbury had been part of the most remarkable child marriages in medieval England. If the Countess Anne's parents had been adults when they married, in each case for the second time, both had been under-age on the first occasion, her mother indeed not yet fourteen. Child marriage was a family tradition. Logically the earl and countess ought to have been thinking along these lines. Yet there seems to have been no intention to marry Isabel, the eldest, until the mid 1460s, when she was at least thirteen. At least there is no such record.

The delay is easy to explain. The Nevilles had contracted brilliant dynastic matches in the first forty years of the fifteenth century with extraordinary ease, principally because of their close kinship to the Lancastrian royal house, but as the generations passed their relationship had ceased to be special. Warwick's brother John was not married until 1458 and his youngest sister Margaret did not wed John, Earl of Oxford until about 1462. Providing for his siblings took priority in Warwick's time over his daughters. Secondly, as head of his family, Warwick took a direct interest in advancing all his kindred: nephews, such as George Neville, son of his brother John, Earl of Northumberland; his niece Alice, daughter of his sister Alice Lady FitzHugh; and Margaret Lucy, daughter of his great-aunt Anne, Duchess of Exeter, who tried to conceal her sexual and matrimonial adventures from her disapproving cousin. Warwick expected – and was expected – to choose spouses for his daughter. Father did know best. He was very choosy, quite unwilling to match his heirs to any but the noblest in the land. The progeny of mere barons and knights – even the earl of Oxford and Lord Lovell – were insufficiently grand. And, to be fair, with the Wars of the Roses and the repression of the northern Lancastrians, Warwick had plenty on his plate.

The status of Isabel and Anne was an important third factor. The girls had no concerns about their material future. They were too young for that. Moreover, as daughters of an earl, actually the greatest and best connected of earls, they had obvious attractions on the marriage market. Warwick could easily have found well-breeched husbands for them, the heads of prosperous gentry families and even of the lesser nobility, who were well able to maintain them in genteel comfort, had he so wished. Had he possessed a son to take precedence, or even extra daughters, that perhaps is what he would have arranged. However, Isabel and Anne were heiresses – amongst the greatest heiresses of their era. Precisely when it first occurred to their parents – and then became painfully apparent – that there was to be no son to carry on the huge accumulation of family estates, titles and honours, we cannot tell. Reality seems to have been recognised, however, by 1464, when Isabel was thirteen and Anne was only eight. That they were heiresses made them much more attractive on the marriage market and probably also made their parents far more selective in their choice of bridegrooms.

The vast estate that the earl and countess had collected could remain united only for their lives. Sadly they could not transmit it intact to the next generation. For that, a son was needed. Their son. There was no divorce as such in the fifteenth century and with two daughters Warwick could hardly plead non-consummation. Even if the Countess Anne had died and the earl had remarried, any son by a second bride could have succeeded only to his Neville and Salisbury lands. The countess did not expire until 1492, when Warwick, had he survived, would have been sixty-four years old: not too ancient to procreate, but old by fifteenth-century standards. The Countess Anne had twenty years to remarry, but her menopause had surely come and reproduction of a son of her own was no longer a possibility. Even a single daughter, had either Isabel or Anne died, could not have kept everything together, because the estates were not all held by the same title. Inherited through different lines, they were subject to different entails. Whereas the Beauchamp, Despenser, Holland and Montagu lands were heritable by children of the earl and countess of whatever sex, the Neville lands were entailed in the male line (tail male). If Warwick had no son, the right of inheritance would devolve first on his brother John (d.1471) and his male descendants, and thereafter on the male lines of Salisbury's brothers George Lord Latimer (d.1469) and Edward Lord Abergavenny (d.1476) in succession. Warwick's two daughters, Isabel and Anne, could divide the rest. By 1464, it therefore appears, the earl and countess were reconciled to the division into three of their great accumulation of property. The Neville lands in tail male, comprising a couple of manors in Essex and the three great northern lordships of Middleham, Sheriff Hutton (Yorks.) and Penrith (Cumbria), were destined to pass to Warwick's brother John and his son George Neville. All the rest, from Barnard Castle in County Durham, the Welsh marcher lordships, the Warwick and Despenser lands in the

West Midlands, to properties in twenty other counties, would be divided between Isabel and Anne as co-heiresses.[42] Even in three unequal parts, the divided estate was sufficient to make George, Isabel and Anne amongst the greatest heirs (and matrimonial catches) of their time.

By 1464, if not earlier, it appears that Warwick had resigned himself to never fathering a son. It was in this year, perhaps not for the first time, that he was resettling his estates and most probably writing his will. Thirty-five was not unusually young to be planning for eternity. Actually it was only the year before that he had secured a royal licence to settle £1,000-worth of lands in trust for the payment of his debts and the performance of his will.[43] Early in 1465 he had lands settled on him, not in tail male as on previous occasions, but on his heirs, executors and assigns, clear evidence not only that he was thinking of his soul, but also that he was resigned to lacking a son and was providing for the eventuality that it was daughters whom he wished to inherit.[44] Moreover, in 1466 he compromised with his Beauchamp sisters-in-law.[45] Whilst he was alive, he could continue to frustrate their claims on his estates, but how would his daughters cope should he die? A handful of manors to each sister-in-law and an entail that promised them the succession should his countess die childless were prices worth paying to ensure that his daughters' tenure of the Beauchamp estates and the earldom of Warwick would not be challenged when he himself was gone. His sisters-in-law did not however give up their claims on their father's trust: Elizabeth Lady Latimer (d.1480), the youngest sister-in-law, regarded the trust and the Beauchamp Chapel as their family assets.[46] Presumably Warwick felt no need to compensate the powerless St Cross Hospital, Winchester, which he had already wronged, and could not persuade the Nevilles of Abergavenny to abandon their claim to a half-share of the Despenser inheritance. Warwick had recognised reproductive reality. He was investing in his heirs and ensuring their future security.

If Warwick could not himself become a king or indeed a duke as he more feasibly aspired, his heirs could be ducal or royal and could satisfy those ambitions that he yet had to fulfil. That he possessed such exalted ambitions is shown by his decision to marry Francis Lord Lovell, the heir to a decidedly wealthy barony, not to one of his daughters but to his niece, when he was granted the boy's wardship and marriage in 1465.[47] Anne Neville was the younger, of course. When we think of these two young ladies, Isabel − the eldest − must always have taken precedence and been more important. She would have had the pick of their inheritance. Inevitably it was Isabel who embarked first on the marriage market. Nor should we overlook George Neville. Although only a baby, born on 22 February 1465,[48] he and his father were the heirs presumptive and future heads of Warwick's house of Neville. Warwick was as concerned for the future of the main line, the male line, as for his own daughters.

Actually it was as early as 1464 that the Burgundian chronicler Waurin located Warwick's plan to marry his two daughters to their cousins and royal dukes, the king's brothers George, Duke of Clarence and Richard, Duke of Gloucester.[49] At that point Anne was at most eight years old. Undoubtedly Warwick did plan to wed Isabel to Clarence, whom she did indeed marry in 1469, but any proposal to wed Richard to Anne during the 1460s is unsubstantiated and appears unlikely. Certainly 1464 is too early. What seems more likely is that Warwick intended the young Henry Stafford, Duke of Buckingham for one of them, since the earl's 'secret displeasure' was recorded by the chronicler pseudo-Worcester at the duke's marriage to Katherine Wydeville, sister of Edward IV's new queen, in February 1466.[50] It is telling that no such anger is attributed to the marriages of the less well-endowed heirs of the newly created earls of Essex, Kent and Pembroke, down to whom Warwick was apparently unwilling to stoop for either Isabel or Anne. Certainly Warwick did support the proposal for the marriage of his brother John's baby son George Neville to Anne, the heiress of the Duke of Exeter. It was a match that should have made young George into a duke and certainly made him royal, for the mother of the infant bride was Edward IV's eldest sister and the father, though exiled, was also of Lancastrian royal descent. We know of Warwick's attitude because of his anger – 'his great secret displeasure' – when Anne of Exeter was poached instead for 4,000 marks (£2,666 13s 4d) by Edward's new Wydeville queen for her own son Thomas Grey in October 1466.[51] Queen Elizabeth had readier access – pillow talk – to royal favour, and the nobility were anxious to exploit (or guard against) this new avenue of patronage. The young king attached inflated worth to his new in-laws and provided for each of them on an unprecedented scale. Warwick moreover was disadvantaged by his family's previous success: in each case, Buckingham, Clarence, Exeter and Gloucester were already related to his heirs within the prohibited degrees and a papal dispensation was required, so weddings could not be concluded quickly.

Individually and collectively all these matches would have provided for Warwick's heirs, advanced them in rank and wealth, strengthened his own position at court and extended his hold yet more firmly in diverse localities. We have seen that the Buckingham and Exeter marriages were frustrated. So, too, was the union of Isabel and Clarence, which King Edward, for reasons unknown, vetoed. Pseudo-Worcester locates this around October 1467.[52] Probably Edward wanted to make use in his diplomacy of Clarence's hand and did indeed proffer it.[53] Hence Warwick suddenly found his influence eclipsed in one of his areas of principal concern – the future of his dynasty and his daughters. It has been identified as an important

contributory factor in his quarrel with the king and its subsequent escalation into renewed civil war. What Warwick had
in mind next for his daughters when the dukes were taken is
unclear, because actually he refused to take no for an answer
and married Isabel to Clarence nevertheless.

Certainly the teenaged Isabel Neville was old enough to
appreciate that a suitable bridegroom had been found for
her and denied to her by the king. Whether the eight- or
nine-year-old Anne knew of any of the very preliminary
manoeuvres on her behalf appears unlikely. There was no need
for haste. That Warwick could secure none of these matches
and was opposed at every juncture by the king and queen was a
factor – perhaps merely contributory, but significant nevertheless – in the deterioration of their relations that ended in the
renewal of civil war in 1469 with the earl and king on opposite
sides. If the Countess Anne, Isabel and almost certainly Anne
Neville engaged themselves with the matrimonial issues, neither daughter can have been consulted on the bigger political
issues and the countess's input, if any, was not decisive.

CHAPTER THREE

Her Father's Daughter 1469–71

ISABEL'S MARRIAGE AND STILLBIRTH

The second phase of the Wars of the Roses, from 1469 to 1471, commenced with the marriage of Anne Neville's sister Isabel. It was a conflict in which Anne was a major player.

George, Duke of Clarence (1449–78), the middle of the three York brothers, was younger than King Edward IV and older than Richard, Duke of Gloucester, the future Richard III. At his marriage on 12 July 1469 he was still only nineteen. Since Duke George had been in control of his own affairs since his majority was advanced in 1466,[1] he may have appeared older, though it was not very mature of him the previous year to point out in public that Lord Mayor Oulegrave had fallen asleep whilst presiding over a treason trial at the London Guildhall![2] That was not strictly what Rows meant when he described the duke as 'right witty',[3] but rather that he was intelligent. Crowland also praises his abilities.[4] Such testimonies, however, need not mean that Clarence had any common sense. Duke George was a prince and a royal duke, possessed of enormous wealth and presiding over a most impressive household, for which Warwick had helped compile model ordinances only the year before.[5] He was thus most eligible of all the available bachelors to reproduce the grandeur to which Isabel Neville had been brought up. Moreover, George was 'seemly of person and well-visaged',[6] which may have been just as important to his cousin Isabel Neville, now aged eighteen. What mattered to Clarence is suggested by a note entered into his household book that Isabel was 'one of the daughters and heirs of the said Richard Earl of Warwick',[7] the other being Anne Neville. This reminded him and us that George's marriage to Isabel promised a share in due course of Warwick's great estates and titles. The earl had promised Isabel to the duke at least a couple of years before they were married. The two teenagers were of age and were entitled legally to bind themselves to one another if they so wished. Not only the bride's parents approved, but also, it appears, the groom's mother Cecily.[8]

That Edward IV objected to the match and vetoed it could not be decisive – there was no Royal Marriage Act in 1469, although to flout a king regnant was definitely ill-advised. In this instance, however, the king had more say. George and Isabel were first cousins once removed, related in the second degree, and were also related in other degrees: Isabel's great-grandmother was George's great-aunt and both were descendants of Edward III. Moreover, George's mother Cecily, Duchess of York had been godmother to Isabel – a spiritual relationship. Although not explicitly forbidden in the book of *Leviticus*, intermarriage between such close relations was prohibited without a dispensation, to be solicited from the Pope, and which under most circumstances those of noble birth could normally expect. Often enough such couples married on the expectation of a dispensation later, but this carried a risk that the union might be nullified, which clearly Warwick was not prepared to take: indeed, he was even more unwilling after he encountered obstacles. King

Edward's wishes counted for more at Rome than did those of Warwick and Clarence. He used his contacts to obstruct any such application. Warwick's agent, Master Lacy, could obtain no audience with Pope Paul II.[9] But Edward's opposition proved indecisive, because Warwick refused to give up and used James Goldwell, the king's own representative at the Curia, to negotiate on his behalf.[10] The necessary dispensation was dated 14 March 1469.[11] Although King Edward could no longer prevent their marriage in England, Warwick secured a licence from Cardinal Bourchier, another cousin, for George and Isabel to be married at Calais, where he was still captain, by his brother Archbishop Neville.[12]

The wedding took place on Tuesday 12 July 1469 at Calais. This was the first visit there of Warwick's daughters, so far as we know, for eight years. No clandestine affair like the king's, the marriage festivities were a splendid five-day celebration comparable in splendour to Archbishop Neville's own enthronement. It was a society wedding that left the validity of the marriage in no doubt. The bride's parents, the earl and countess of Warwick, were present and perhaps also the groom's mother, Cecily, Duchess of York, who is recorded with them at their embarkation from Sandwich. Despite its peripheral location, there attended 'five other knights of the garter, and many other lords and ladies, and worshipful knights, well accompanied with wise and discreet esquires, in right great number, to the laud praising of God and to the honour and worship of the world'.[13] We do not know who all the guests were, but their presence, especially at such an out-of-the-way venue, indicates that the king's opposition was regarded as unreasonable and that his malevolence could be risked. Anne Neville, though not separately mentioned, was undoubtedly present. Apart from what it meant to the conjugal couple, it was the moment for Anne when the two girls at home became one, when Isabel moved out, and Anne's own marriage moved up her parents' agenda. She was now part of the inner royal family: the Yorkist family tree had now become her own. Anne Neville was now sister-in-law (or, in contemporary terms, sister) of the Duke of Clarence, of King Edward and his queen, of Clarence's sisters the duchesses of Burgundy, Exeter, and Suffolk, and of their husbands the three dukes. Kinship was a powerful force in fifteenth-century England, yet it – and especially kinship by marriage – could divide as well as unite.

Important though the marriage was in itself, it also sealed an alliance of great political moment, of which, most probably, Warwick's two daughters were in ignorance. The Duchess Isabel and probably also the Countess Anne and Anne Neville herself remained in Calais,[14] whilst the earl, duke and archbishop launched their political takeover of the realm of England. A rebellion that Warwick had fomented in Yorkshire was accompanied by his own invasion from Calais, which resulted in victory over the king's allies at Edgecote in Oxfordshire, the elimination of the king's principal favourites and the seizure of the person of King Edward himself. Edward IV was imprisoned first at Warwick Castle and then at Middleham Castle, whilst his government was conducted at Westminster at Warwick's direction by the archbishop. Initially this was designed to restore to Warwick the control of affairs that he had formerly enjoyed, not to depose the monarch. That, however, may also have been intended. Charges of sorcery against the queen's mother were most probably meant to invalidate the king's marriage and hence the legitimacy of his offspring. The slur of bastardy against Edward that also circulated[15] could also have invalidated the king's own legitimacy and right to rule. If Edward's children were discounted, Clarence was once again his heir. If the king himself was a bastard, it was Clarence who was heir to their father Richard, Duke of York and to the Yorkist line. Taken together, therefore, these aspersions were grounds for Edward to be replaced at the next parliament by his brother

Clarence, which would have made Anne's sister Isabel into a queen. None of these allegations can be attributed directly to Warwick, but they emanated from his circle and surely had his consent. The parliament that he ordered to be summoned (but which never met) might have given all this effect or, at the least, legalised Warwick's control over the government. At some point after Warwick's invasion, the Countess Anne and Anne Neville crossed to England and proceeded, most probably, via London to Warwick.[16]

But it all went badly wrong. Warwick had to release King Edward, who resumed control of affairs and held a great council at which he replaced his deceased favourites with new ones. This involved also the betrothal of George Neville, son of Warwick's brother John, to the king's eldest daughter and heiress presumptive Elizabeth of York. Both bride and groom were three years old. George was created Duke of Bedford and John into Marquis Montagu. Young George Neville was thus offered the promise of a throne as alternative to that to which Clarence and his duchess had aspired. It was food for thought for Warwick, so it was reasoned, that not his co-heiress, but his heir male could yet attain the throne. Whatever Edward may have wished, however much he may have hoped to avenge himself on the earl, duke and archbishop, as the royal household men predicted, yet the council induced him to receive them and to reconcile himself to them. The culprits submitted and resumed their allegiance. The king in turn accepted their submissions and loyalty.[17] Apart from the marriage of George and Isabel, which made Anne Neville Clarence's sister[-in-law], Warwick and Clarence had gained nothing but forgiveness for their misdeeds. They were as far from power as ever, for King Edward had found new magnates to replace the old, one of whom threatened the earl's lands and dominance in the North, and had besides removed Warwick and the archbishop from the offices in which they had inserted themselves.[18]

As earnest of the reconciliation, the duke and earl stayed in the capital for the Christmas and New Year celebrations that they shared with the king. Although not separately recorded, the Countess Anne, the Duchess Isabel, and Anne Neville herself were most probably also present. Since Isabel was advanced in pregnancy, she may have been grateful for the attendance of her mother, who was something of an expert in such circumstances. Thereafter they apparently went into the country, to Warwick's western estates as the ignorant Burgundian Waurin uninformatively expressed it,[19] probably with Clarence, who returned to London on 4 March 1470, and put up – with his brother the king – at the house of their mother the Duchess Cecily, Baynards Castle.[20] Following Edward's departure to quell a rebellion in Lincolnshire, Clarence and his father-in-law set off from London on 7 March for Warwick.[21] Probably Anne Neville and her mother were also there.

Although Edward IV had received Warwick and Clarence into his grace and allowed them to keep their property, other acts of the Westminster great council in December 1469 were designed permanently to deny them the power they had sought in the summer. It was not Warwick who succeeded the Herberts as power-brokers in Wales: that was the king's youngest brother Richard, Duke of Gloucester as front man for the Herberts. In the East March and the North the natural rivals of the Nevilles, the Percys, earls of Northumberland, were restored. Warwick's brother John, now promoted to be Marquis Montagu, was reassigned abruptly from the North-East to the West Country. His other brother Archbishop Neville ceased to be Lord Chancellor. Montagu's new title, which gave him precedence over Warwick himself, the elevation of his son George to be duke of Bedford, and the latter's betrothal to King Edward's heiress (and Warwick's goddaughter) Elizabeth of York – potentially to be queen, but unlikely ever to succeed – did not compensate for their real exclusion from real power.[22] Warwick and Clarence, we may deduce, were unhappy with these arrangements. We may presume, moreover, that they were unpersuaded of Edward's good faith. In due course, when the time was propitious, would he not wreak vengeance on those who had so humiliated him? Still set on the power that they had sought in the summer, they planned a repeat performance, this time however intending Edward's deposition and his replacement by his male heir, Clarence himself. The core was the Lincolnshire Rebellion of March 1470, nominally a popular insurrection, but actually orchestrated by Sir Robert Welles at the instigation of Warwick and Clarence. When the king marched northwards from London to suppress it, the duke and earl promised help and proceeded in force eastwards from Warwick, where they probably left their ladies. They promised to support the king, but hoped instead to ambush him, a project that was revealed by captured rebels and correspondence after Edward had scattered the insurgents at Losecote Field. He turned his attention next to Warwick and Clarence, who were not strong enough to resist him in battle, and fled instead to France.

Their flight was not altogether precipitate. Warwick's artillery train accompanied them and was left in safe-keeping at Bristol, where the earl was able to recover it the following year. [23] En route, moreover, most probably at Warwick, the fugitives were joined by their ladies, Warwick's countess and her daughters, Clarence's duchess and the still unmarried Anne Neville. Anne was 'the child' who accompanied her parents and the Clarences when they embarked from Dartmouth on 7 April,[24] may have been repelled with them at Southampton where Warwick's newest ship the *Trinity* was lost, and then sailed with them to Calais where, much to their surprise, they were excluded by Warwick's deputy John Lord Wenlock. That was on Monday 16 April.[25] At anchor and confined to the ships, exposed to unfamiliar motions and decidedly alarmed, Anne's sister Isabel,

Duchess of Clarence went into labour. As the duke and duchess had celebrated and had presumably first consummated their marriage on 12 July 1469 and forty weeks fell on Tuesday 17 April 1470, the baby could have been almost exactly full-term. More probably it was premature – a few days, a few weeks, or a few months – and was stillborn: the result surely of the stress to which the mother had been exposed. George and Isabel lost their son and heir.[26] The earl and countess were deprived of their first grandson and Anne herself of her nephew. Isabel's mother, well accustomed to childbirth, and most probably Anne, were in attendance. This familiar tragedy certainly brought a private reality to Warwick's miscalculations.

THE MAKING OF A PRINCESS

The stillbirth of his eldest grandchild did not deter Warwick from political activity. A campaign of piracy, with his ladies in train, enraged the Burgundians, and was followed by a safe landfall in the Seine estuary in Normandy about 1 May. Much though he wished to help, King Louis XI of France was bound by treaty not to assist Burgundy's enemies, so he was obliged to make his support for Warwick surreptitious. So he explained by letter of 12 May. The exiles' ladies were different, however, non-combatants deserving of chivalry, so Louis proffered hospitality to the countess of Warwick, duchess of Clarence, and by implication their entourage, who certainly included Anne Neville[27] It is unlikely that they took his offer up, since Warwick chose to keep them near him. We know that on 8 July the three ladies were with Warwick at Valognes in the Cotentin peninsular conveniently near to Barfleur, where Warwick's expeditionary force to reconquer England was being prepared.[28]

Now defeated traitors, Warwick and Clarence feared execution if they returned home. Moreover, they had both forfeited all their possessions. If not yet destitute, they and their ladies faced a future of relative privation in exile much like that endured for the past few years by the Lancastrian Queen Margaret of Anjou and her adherents at Bar and elsewhere. Anne's privileged life and comfortable future as daughter of an earl, great heiress and titled lady, consort and mother, was abruptly terminated and gave way to something far less certain and unattractive. The three Beaufort brothers, also exiled, had been unable to marry and Frideswide Hungerford, though still resident in England, had abandoned any plans of marriage for a nunnery. Anne's future therefore was bleak. Her fate depended entirely on whatever her father could conjure from the current catastrophe. There was no mileage in reconciliation with the Yorkists. Since Edward IV was in an unforgiving mood, there was no immediate prospect that the exiles could negotiate their way back. If insufficiently powerful to defeat Edward with all the advantages of surprise, the exiles could hardly expect to launch a successful invasion by themselves. They needed help. Warwick wasted no time over scruples: he realised almost at once (by 12 May)[29] that he must ally with the Lancastrians, who could offer him not only extra manpower, but the moral authority of King Henry VI, which proved still to have great popular appeal. Clarence and Isabel's hopes of a crown were necessary casualties and had to be abandoned. From Warwick's angle, the losses of one daughter were balanced by the gains of the second, for the marriage of his younger daughter Anne Neville to Edward of Lancaster, son of King Henry and Queen Margaret, was the seal to any deal. Although first mentioned on 2 June,[30] the topic had probably been broached by 12 May, and was duly agreed.

'My enemy's enemy is my friend' was a maxim that had occurred as early as 1467 to Queen Margaret's brother John, Duke of Calabria, and subsequently in 1470 to Queen Margaret's chancellor Sir John Fortescue as they heard of the widening breach between the Nevilles and Edward IV.[31] In 1468 Warwick had seen more future within England in persuading Edward or restraining him than in transferring his allegiance to the Lancastrians, which had no appeal for Clarence at all. Then they had other fish to fry. Margaret of Anjou was therefore open to a deal with Warwick in 1470 – indeed, eager and enthusiastic for one – although the marriage alliance was something she had to think about. Prince Edward's hand in marriage, potentially that of a future king, was too important to be lightly conceded. The alliance was agreed by 29 June, but 'on no account whatever', the Milanese ambassador reported, 'will she agree to send her son with Warwick, as she mistrusts him'.[32] What if Warwick betrayed him to the Yorkists? Was not the capture of Prince Edward – the whole future of the house of Lancaster – a benefit so great that Edward IV could even be persuaded to pardon Warwick and Clarence in return? Mistrust ran both ways of course. If Henry did resume his reign, how could Warwick (his former enemy and traitor) be assured of his own safety and the restoration of his estates? Prince Edward had been Margaret's principal diplomatic card: as early as 1461 she had agreed a marriage for him with Princess Mary of Scotland that had not taken effect.[33] If Margaret were now to marry Edward off to Anne, this was a card which henceforth she could no longer play. A grandchild, of course, would strengthen her hand. The same argument, albeit weaker, applied to Anne, Warwick's unmarried heiress. Her marriage (and inheritance) was too valuable to concede lightly. Such potential alternatives had to be balanced against current realities. In the juncture where they found themselves in 1470, the solution for both queen and earl was the espousal of Prince Edward to Anne Neville. The union of Warwick's daughter to the Lancastrian heir and future king assured the earl of his future and moreover fulfilled his highest ambitions – a crown for his daughter, albeit the youngest rather than the elder. The match moreover bound the earl to the Lancastrians. Once the prince was his son-in-law, Warwick was obliged to favour his cause and could no longer treat him as a bargaining counter. Nor, indeed, could he refuse to concede formal authority to his new son-in-law should the invasion be successful, however much he might hope to bend the new regime to his will.

Alliance between the old adversaries by itself was not enough. Both Warwick and Margaret recognised the participation of King Louis to be essential. Against his personal preferences, Louis XI was obliged to engage in mediation, to receive both parties publicly at court, and to endure the increasingly critical and justified diplomatic notes of Charles, Duke of Burgundy, whose subjects Warwick had robbed. The earl overrode the qualms of the king, ignored his urgings to depart prematurely and forced him to take on the financing, supply and equipment of the expeditionary force to invade England on a scale, quality of preparation, cost and timescale much beyond what Louis had wished. Louis' agents backed Warwick rather than their master. Urged to depart on 23 June, his unwanted guests sailed only on 9 September.[34] Meanwhile, Warwick had been preparing his retainers in England – diversionary uprisings were launched in Yorkshire and Kent – and the Lancastrians also communicated with their adherents. The result was a complete success. Now, on behalf of Henry VI, the progress of Warwick and the Lancastrians from the West Country to Coventry received unprecedented popular support, whilst the incumbent King Edward IV was isolated, bereft of support, only narrowly evaded capture, and fled abroad. Henry VI reigned once more, amazingly. 'You might also have come across innumerable folk', wrote the Crowland chronicler, 'to whom the restoration of the pious King Henry was a miracle and the transformation the work of the right hand of the All Highest'.[35]

Anne Neville's marriage was essential to this remarkable *bouleversement*. Mutual advantage alone sufficed to achieve the rapid and complete agreement of Warwick and Margaret in principle, although the details as always took time and the right appearances also had to be preserved. Since Warwick had been the greatest foe of the Lancastrians, Queen Margaret had to appease her devoted, resentful and understandably vengeful followers by maintaining her moral ascendancy. Instead of applauding the discomfiture of their persecutor, they had to be convinced of the desirability and wisdom of alliance with him. Warwick must be perceived as a subject, not treated as an equal. He had to be presented as contrite for past faults, properly submissive, soliciting the queen's forgiveness in formal ceremonial and on bended knee, whilst she graciously condescended to receive him back into her allegiance. As for the marriage alliance,

> The queen would not in any wise consent there unto for any offer or any manner of request that the King of France might make her. [For] some time she said that she saw neither honour nor profit for her nor for son the prince. Another [argument] she alleged that, if she would, she should find a more profitable party and of a more advantage with the King of England. And indeed she showed unto the King of France a letter which she said was sent here out of England the last week by which was offered to her son my lady the princess [Elizabeth of York], and so the queen persevered fifteen days ere she would any thing attend to the said treaty of marriage.[36]

This, of course, was ridiculous. There is no other evidence that Edward IV was ever prepared to marry Princess Elizabeth to Prince Edward, an offer that might have brought the struggle of York and Lancaster to a peaceful conclusion, ostensibly promised the succession to the English crown to Margaret's son Edward of Lancaster, but would have certainly alienated the blameless John Neville. There is a superficial resemblance here to the Treaty of Troyes of 1420, which made Henry V the son-in-law and heir of Charles VI in preference to Charles' own son. Similarly, Lady Margaret Beaufort somewhat later negotiated to repatriate her son Henry Tudor, the future Henry VII: Henry – like Edward of Lancaster – was not himself attainted and such obstacles could anyway be negotiated away. What was supposedly proposed here was the match of a three-year-old girl to a youth of seventeen that theoretically could have brought the latter to the English throne, but probably would not, since Edward IV intended to breed sons and the future Edward V was indeed born only three months later. Was Queen Margaret really so gullible as to overlook this intended eventuality? The match would moreover break the betrothal of Princess Elizabeth to Montagu's son George Neville and untie the bonds by which Edward had just bound them. Was Edward IV really prepared to take that risk? There is nothing else to suggest that Margaret would have contented herself with anything else than the crown, for example with Anne Neville's share of the Warwick inheritance, and much evidence that this was not so. If Margaret ever took this line, it was another bargaining counter to raise the stakes in negotiation with Warwick: it cannot have been based on an authentic or honest letter from Edward IV. Besides, there were not fifteen days available for them to negotiate.

That such poses were struck, that there was some such pantomime, emerges both through the strictly contemporary ambassador's reports and the manifesto *The Manner and Guiding of the Earl of Warwick at Angers*. This was the manifesto that Warwick had had written for his supporters in England and that presumably he despatched to them: the only surviving version was apparently copied from one amongst the papers of a London alderman. From Warwick's angle, this manifesto showed that he did not admit any fault on his part or that of his followers in ousting the Lancastrian regime. 'He had a righteous cause to labour their undoing and destruction', he declared, 'and that therein he had not done, but what a nobleman outraged and despaired ought to have done'. Furthermore, Warwick presented the agreement as of his own making. *The Manner* depicted him as persuading the queen to do his will whilst conceding to her only in essentials. It induced his committed followers in England to back him in this latest desperate enterprise. Warwick had conjured victory out of defeat, had secured the alliance of the Lancastrians at no material cost to his followers, and had moreover won the Lancastrian heir for his daughter. This was a triumph indeed. It must not appear too easy however, too unprincipled, too self-evidently the desperate grasping at the last available straw of two discredited exiles concerned only with their own advancement. Hence *The Manner* states that negotiations about the marriage took fifteen days,[37] yet Edward and Anne were betrothed on 25 July, only three days after the beginning of the formal proceedings at Angers on 22nd, and indeed the ambassador reports all the essentials to be settled by 20 July, before the conference had even commenced.[38]

The crown of England was the objective for both parties. The Lancastrians wanted to re-assert their title to the kingdom, to restore King Henry VI and Queen Margaret to their thrones, to make Edward of Lancaster once again heir apparent, prince of Wales, duke of Cornwall, and earl of Chester, and in due course king of England. His consort, already a titular princess, was destined to become first Edward's princess and then his queen. That role was marked out for Anne Neville. Edward and Anne's progeny would be royal – princes, princesses, further generations of Lancastrian kings, and grandchildren of the earl of Warwick himself. That was the plan. It sufficed. We possess no evidence that the earl thought about any further ramifications from the marriage, yet surely he did, such as young Edward's claims to the rest of the Angevin inheritance of Margaret's father King René. Although apparently secure, the rapid deaths of René himself, his brother Charles, Count of Maine, his son Duke John and his grandson Nicholas of Taranto were rapidly to make Margaret into the residuary heir. Such a chain of mortality uncompensated by issue was unexpected in 1470, but it was not unusual for the time and cannot have escaped Warwick's calculations, nor indeed those of King René, who took part in these negotiations. Even if the worst befell and Henry VI could not be restored to his throne, on which Warwick staked everything including his life, yet his daughter Anne as consort of Prince Edward and their issue might nevertheless have succeeded on Margaret's death to the duchies of Anjou and Bar, the marquisate of Provence, the county of Maine and claims to the kingdoms of Jerusalem and Sicily. Was there any airy speculation on the union of this greater Angevin inheritance with the crown of England by King Louis, Margaret or Warwick? What implication might this have had on longer-term Anglo-French relations? It cannot have been desired by the prince, who did not intend the extinction of his kindred, nor by Anne herself. Nor indeed can Anne's heritage – accessible only if the Lancastrian line was restored and scarcely princely – have been of much interest to Prince Edward or Queen Margaret.

For the roles of the bride and groom were surely completely passive. Anne herself was only fourteen years of age. Not too young for an English lady to be married, she was older than either of her parents when they were wed. Indeed, she was already past the female age of majority. Yet she was only a child in terms of making choices and decisions. Aristocratic daughters like Anne were used to being bestowed in marriage by their fathers. Marriage contracts did assure them of their futures – security and wealth for life come what may – but

the motive for such matches was commonly advantages perceived by their menfolk. Daughters could decline the proffered
match, at least in theory. To refuse an eligible spouse, however,
was eccentric and apparently rare. The objections that occur
to us today – that Anne did not know the bridegroom, may
not have liked the bridegroom, nor loved him – would have
been thought unreasonable at this time. There is no evidence
that any of these objections occurred to Anne. If she had met
Edward before the summer of 1459, their last possible encounter, when she was three and he was six, it was too long ago for
either to remember anything significant. Presumably they did
meet momentarily in July 1470 before they were betrothed,
but we cannot know whether there was instant attraction,
mutual liking, or mere compatibility. Anne's father negotiated
as though the decision was his alone, as aristocratic marriages
normally were. His daughter was bestowed on Prince Edward.
Anne must certainly have been aware that she was expected to
marry well and at her father's command. Very obviously, it was
her duty in the disastrous circumstances of 1470 to accept this
particular match, which was to be the salvation of her whole
family. Now aged fourteen, Anne was fully able to consent.
She did. There is nothing in any of the surviving correspondence to suggest that her consent – or that of Prince Edward
– could not be taken for granted. So, too, in the absence of her
kingly spouse, Queen Margaret decided on her son's behalf. He
could not doubt her commitment to his interests, which had
shaped all her actions for the past ten years. Margaret may have
needed to persuade the prince that the sacrifice of his hand in
matrimony to a mere commoner was worthwhile and indeed
a necessary price to pay. The very little we perceive of Edward
of Lancaster, however threadbare the reality of his life in exile,
is of a boy who had been brought up to think of himself as a
prince and who was keen to have his opponents' heads off[39]
– a sharp contrast to his father Henry VI. Yet, at seventeen, he

was old enough to make the calculations and to contribute to any debate in his own right. Too much hung on the marriage, for Anne at least, the fortunes of her whole family – father, mother, sister and brother[-in-law] Clarence – for her to pull back even if she had wished.

What Anne should have gained from her marriage was the status and wealth of a princess and the spouse of the heiress of the throne. Her husband should have recovered his principality in west Wales, his county palatine of Chester, and his duchy of Cornwall, with its swathe of estates from Cornwall in the far west to the modern Kennington Oval. Anne should have had her own establishment, her own obsequious attendants, extensive apartments and numerous household. She should have lived in a series of royal palaces and castles, attired herself in the most luxurious fabrics and jewels, and played a central role in court ceremonial of all kinds. We cannot tell whether Anne looked forward to this, all of which she had already experienced in a smaller way and for which she was trained, nor even whether married life suited her, because it did not happen. Neither she nor her husband secured any of the material wealth or shared in the rule of her father-in-law Henry VI: only the marital rights, the status and respect materialised. Neither was to reach England until it was too late.

On 25 July 1470 Anne and Edward were formally betrothed in the cathedral of St Mary at Angers, perhaps by proxy.[40] Richard, Earl of Warwick and Queen Margaret swore oaths of assurance to one another on fragments of the true cross. Betrothal, the free exchange of vows of a man and a woman – two consenting adults in modern parlance – was as binding a tie and as unbreakable in the fifteenth century as the formal marriage ceremony in church. This was so in theory at least, for there were actually many instances involving royalty where diplomatic engagements were broken as international alignments changed: Edward IV's daughter Elizabeth is the

classic victim. Hence Warwick was not content with mere
betrothal. He insisted at once on the next step, the formal
marriage ceremony, and actually made it a precondition of the
departure of his invading force. Accordingly, on 31 July, Queen
Margaret, the earl and countess, and the engaged couple set off
for Normandy, where they were to marry.[41] Probably Warwick
had also prescribed the immediate consummation of the union
to ensure that it could not be invalidated.

Yet the marriage was delayed. By 7 August, it was Warwick
who could wait no longer and had returned to the fleet. 'He
did not wish to lose time in waiting for his daughter's marriage', the ambassador reported, which would, he understood,
be celebrated before King Louis back at Amboise.[42] There was
a hitch. Genealogical investigation had revealed that Edward
and Anne were related by blood in the fourth degree. Distant
though their relationship was, it nevertheless fell within the
prohibited degrees. No valid marriage could be contracted
without a dispensation. A dispensation would take time and
time could not be spared. The restoration of Henry VI could
not be postponed. Warwick had to trust in Margaret's good
faith after all. He realised of course that she needed to be as
assured of his fidelity as she of his. Hence the passage inserted
as explanation at this point in *The Manner* that Anne was to
remain in Margaret's hands and 'that the said marriage shall
not be perfected [consummated] until the Earl of Warwick
had been with an army over the sea to England' and had
conquered the kingdom.[43] There was no point in commit-
ting Prince Edward to the marriage until the intended fruit
was guaranteed! *The Manner* thus explained Anne's continued
single state, blamed the delay on Margaret, and, crucially, concealed the existence of an impediment to the marriage itself.
Warwick's followers were reassured that the crucial match
would happen. Meanwhile, Anne 'shall be put and remain in
the hands and keeping of Queen Margaret'.[44]

The bride and groom had been found to share a common great-great-grandfather in John of Gaunt, Duke of Lancaster and son of Edward III, father both to Edward's great-grandfather Henry IV (d.1413) and Anne's great-grand-mother Joan Beaufort (d.1441). Their consanguinity was slight enough for a dispensation normally to be a formality, but so much hung upon this match that in the interests of both parties it was necessary to be quite sure. Hence King Louis despatched Matthew Fontenailles to the ambassadors of the Pope at Lyons to seek a dispensation. Fontenailles' journey took place not later than 24 July, when payment of his expenses was ordered, possibly even after his return. King Louis himself was quite willing for Edward and Anne to marry ahead of any dispensation, even though to do so was itself sinful and required absolution and a payment to the apostolic datary. Actually, three dispensations were granted to cover all eventualities: first, for them to marry (if they hadn't yet done so), second, if they had married, whether aware of the impediment or not, for them to remain married and to be absolved, and third, for any resultant offspring to be legitimate. As approval was given on 17 August at Rome, the whole process was very quick, but it was nevertheless too slow for the timetable of the intended invasion. Warwick had probably embarked for England before the dispensations reached the king. Hence alternative options also had to be pursued. For such a remote connection, it was hoped that a dispensation could be secured from closer to hand. King Louis therefore wrote to the bishop of Beauvais 'to know of him if he had power to dispense for the marriage of the Prince of Wales and the daughter of the Earl of Warwick'. Apparently the answer was no. Again, on 2 August, King Louis wrote also to the archbishop of Rheims and the Bishop of Laon, evidently receiving the same negative response.[45] To Louis XI and his court, the dispensation was a technicality, for Anne was accepted – and paid for – as 'wife of the said prince' in August, September and October 1470.

By October, the dispensations had surely arrived from Rome. That the search for a dispensation continued afterwards indicates that, unfortunately, all were deficient. All three dispensed Edward and Anne for the fourth degree of consanguinity, which appears to be correct. The two that presumed the couple had already married were obviously redundant. The problem evidently arose with the other one. This authorised the marriage of two nobles, Edward of England, layman of the diocese of London, and Anna de Warwyk, damsel of Salisbury diocese (*domicella Sarisberiensis diocesis*).[46] It is in these descriptions that the problem most likely lay. Whereas Edward of Lancaster was indeed born at Westminster in the diocese of London, though not resident there for the past decade, Anne Neville had never lived in the diocese of Salisbury: that her father was, incidentally, earl of Salisbury was immaterial. Louis' dispensation failed on this technical point. Another dispensation was required. Further investigation revealed that the patriarch of Jerusalem, who in his capacity as bishop of Bayeux lacked the power to dispense the original impediment, could remove the remaining obstacle. On 28 November, at last, his representative, the grand vicar of Bayeux, granted the necessary dispensation. On Thursday 13 December 1470, Anne Neville and Edward of Lancaster were at last married at Amboise.[47] If it was a quieter occasion than had been intended – neither the bride's father Warwick nor her brother-in-law Clarence nor the bridegroom's father Henry VI could attend as they were all absent in England – yet Anne was surely reassured that the invasion had succeeded and that she really was marrying the Prince of Wales. Queen Margaret was present in person. So too were Anne's mother the countess of Warwick and her sister Isabel, Duchess of Clarence.[48] Next, presumably, Edward and Anne went to bed and consummated their union: sexual intercourse was the seal that rendered the union unbreakable. No longer merely a great heiress and future countess, Anne was now Princess Anne and was destined in due course to become Anne, queen both of England and France.

For the fourteen-year-old princess, no doubt, this was one of the defining moments of her life, no less important for the fact that it has passed into history almost wholly unrecorded. Nothing came of it. No pregnancy ensued. It should not have mattered: there should have been plenty of time. Had Anne become pregnant and borne the house of Lancaster a further heir, one wonders what might have befallen. Perhaps she would have remained in France. Regrettably, this eventuality did not materialise.

WIDOWING A PRINCESS

From November 1470 the arrival of the royal party in England was often predicted, yet they did not come. On 15 December Queen Margaret, the new princess of Wales, the duchess of Clarence and countess of Warwick set off for Paris, where a splendid reception was laid on at King Louis' command.[49] Even after solemnisation and consummation, they strangely languished in France, perhaps whilst the French embassy to England concluded its treaties with the new regime. Warwick was assured of the free hand that he promised in *The Manner* without the more consensual and conciliar regulations under the aegis of Prince Edward proposed in the model constitution of Sir John Fortescue.[50] It was not in fact until 24 March that the queen, princess, countess and duchess returned to Harfleur.[51] They had then to endure seventeen days of contrary winds.

Waiting to get married had delayed the departure to England not only of Anne and her mother, who did not matter much politically, and of Edward of Lancaster, who did, but also crucially of his mother Queen Margaret of Anjou. The absence of Margaret and Edward may have been fatal for the success of Henry VI's second reign, commonly known as the Readeption. Warwick, Clarence and his supporters worked well with Somerset and the other Lancastrians in the invasion and in restoring Henry VI to the throne. They could unite against a common enemy. It was afterwards that co-operation was more difficult. There is nothing to suggest that Henry VI was much more than a figurehead. He was allowed to take some actions in areas that interested him, such as clerical appointments,[52] but on issues that mattered, he was not. Even the Lancastrians, prior to their return, had no intention of allowing that. A memorandum composed by Chief Justice Fortescue, Queen Margaret's chancellor, envisaged a government largely run by a royal council and presided over by Prince Edward as the king's lieutenant or protector.[53] Although now seventeen and hence regarded as of age, Edward would surely have been guided in his actions by, as Margaret must have hoped, his mother or, as Warwick probably hoped, by his father-in-law. But neither Margaret nor Edward was accessible. Indeed, Prince Edward does not crop up on the patent roll until 27 March 1471,[54] almost the very end of the Readeption. He was never formally granted the titles, estates and offices that went with his position: he may, of course, have been regarded as having resumed them after a decade's interruption. In the absence of Margaret and Edward, the lead in government was taken by Warwick, who was the king's lieutenant: if Clarence, his other son-in-law, was joint lieutenant as several sources suggest, he was very much the junior partner.[55] Some Lancastrians, such as the duke of Exeter and earl of Oxford, valued Warwick's qualities and followed his lead.

But what was intended to be temporary, a matter of a few weeks, continued for six months – six months of crucial decisions and policy-making. First one session of parliament, then a second, and a full round of negotiations for a set of treaties with France passed under Warwick's aegis. John Tiptoft, Earl of Worcester, apart, there was not the blood-letting against the Yorkists that Lancastrian vengeance demanded and, so far as we know, no new forfeitures. The Lancastrian leadership, whether returned magnates like the royal dukes of Exeter and Somerset or lesser men, recovered their forfeited properties and received some patronage, but they did not secure the rewards or the decisive say in affairs that their loyal sufferings deserved, or so they thought. No doubt they considered that too much had been conceded at Angers to Warwick, their erstwhile foe. It even appears that Clarence was made Henry VI's heir in reversion after the prince if he died childless rather than the junior Lancastrian lines. Clarence resisted surrendering lands to the Lancastrians which they, in contrast, thought the absolute minimum that they should recover.[56] An alliance between former victims and victors inevitably meant that there was too little to share out.

Had Margaret and Edward arrived, it could have been very different. Whether Fortescue's plan of government could have materialised is unlikely, since his academic theorising, however cloaked in concrete detail, was ill-suited for critical circumstances that demanded decisions and leadership. However much Fortescue may have deplored the dominance of magnates over functionaries, the Readeption was certainly a time when it was the powerful who counted. The leadership of Margaret and Edward gave that legitimacy to the actions of the regime that it lacked to some Lancastrian eyes. Margaret and Warwick might have smoothed over differences between the unwilling allies: though neither feature amongst history's great conciliators. Warwick surely did not welcome any reduction in power or any of the transfers of Lancastrian forfeitures from himself to their original owners that could be expected to ensue, although he, at least, could understand the necessity.

Certainly the authority of the queen and prince was more acceptable to former Lancastrians than was Warwick's. One would like to think that a note of caution might have tempered the commitment to an aggressive alliance with Louis XI against Duke Charles of Burgundy, which disastrously caused the duke to resource Edward IV's return, to which originally he was adamantly opposed. That, however, is unlikely, for Margaret's obligation to Louis was particularly strong. By the time Edward and Anne arrived in England, sadly, all these opportunities were past.

Isabel, Duchess of Clarence did cross over ahead of the main party to join her husband the duke.[57] She was therefore in England for the heart-searching that the duke underwent, although perhaps neither in his company nor in his confidence. Probably she failed to influence a man, who proved particularly susceptible to the blandishments of other kinswomen. Clarence was urged to resume his allegiance to his own house of York rather than that of Lancaster by his mother Cecily, Duchess of York, his uncles the earl of Essex and Cardinal Bourchier, his sisters the duchesses of Exeter, Suffolk and 'most specially, my Lady of Burgundy', and Bishop Stillington,[58] who surely played his part when the duke was recruiting from his episcopal palace at Wells. That was en route to join Warwick against Edward IV, who had landed in Yorkshire and marched southwards to Warwickshire. Clarence succumbed. Actually the duke carried his troops into his brother's camp. Clarence was not much concerned about breaking faith with the Lancastrians, it appears, but he did not wish to part company with his father-in-law Warwick – one or the other must lose the forthcoming battle – and persuaded King Edward to offer forgiveness to the earl. Warwick refused, in honour certainly, since nobody would ever accept his word again if he was to turn his coat once more, but also, one would like to suppose, in faith to his daughter Anne, now the Lancastrian princess of Wales, and his countess, also still with the Lancastrians in France. Their fates did not apparently weigh heavily on Clarence's mind. At Barnet on Easter Sunday it was Anne's father who was slain, her sister's husband Clarence – her brother[-in-law] – who survived. Anne, too, was no party to these changes, but merely found, on arrival in England, that the alignments she had expected were no more.

Warwick had despatched his Lord Treasurer Sir John Langstrother, Prior of St John, with the veteran John, Lord Wenlock to fetch the queen, countess of Warwick, prince and princess. They had embarked from Harfleur on 24 March. Unfortunately, however, nature intervened: contrary winds prevented their voyage until 13 April, Easter Saturday. Anne's mother the countess of Warwick landed at Portsmouth; the queen and the others, including Princess Anne, at Weymouth.[59] This was the day before Easter and the battle of Barnet, at which Warwick and his brother Montagu were defeated and slain. London and Henry VI were already in Yorkist hands. To aggravate the situation, Clarence was now on the other side. With her husband dead and her elder daughter a Yorkist once more, the Countess Anne was not inclined to repose her trust in Warwick's new Lancastrian allies. Instead she deserted them and (in the process) her younger daughter Anne Neville. Nearer to the capital and proceeding westwards, it was she at Southampton who first heard of her husband's demise and chose not to proceed to Weymouth, but instead to take sanctuary at Beaulieu Abbey, a Cistercian abbey of royal foundation in the New Forest,[60] whence she could not be removed by her enemies. Actually Edward IV would probably have consigned her to a nunnery anyway had she come into his hands. He required the abbot to keep her safe.[61] The countess may have feared that, now that Warwick was dead, his foes would wreak revenge on her. Perhaps she also feared that she was personally so deeply implicated in her late husband's plots that she might

suffer attainder just as her mother-in-law Alice, Countess of
Salisbury had done in 1459. In consequence her younger
daughter Anne, still aged only fourteen, now fatherless, was
also deprived of her mother's company, support and advice for
the next two years – two crucial years in her life.

'The Queen Margaret and her son' and obviously also
Princess Anne, although always unmentioned, landed at
Weymouth in Dorset and proceeded thence to Cerne Abbey,
which they made their base. There they were joined by the
rest of their entourage and by a reception party from London
made up of the Beaufort brothers, Edmund, Duke of Somerset
and John, Marquis of Dorset, and also John Courtenay, the earl
of Devon. There on 15 April, only one day after the battle,
they heard of the disaster at Barnet. Not surprisingly, Margaret
'was therefore right heavy and sorry'.[62] The reaction of her
daughter-in-law Anne to the loss of her father is again unrecorded but easily imagined. How distressed she was depends
on the nature of their relationship, which we cannot divine,
but certainly shock, sorrow, alarm and anxiety for the future
must have been ingredients. Unlike her mother, Anne had
no choice what to do. Her future was irrevocably tied to her
new-found husband, to her mother-in-law Queen Margaret,
and to the Lancastrians, as they embarked on their final cast of
the dice, carrying Anne with them. If Anne had heard what the
Yorkist *Arrival* reports was said within the Lancastrian camp,
that the Beauforts at least thought their cause not weakened
by her father's death but rather strengthened,[63] she was surely
yet more distressed. Now that Warwick's Neville allies were
defeated, was the unfortunate girl herself branded an encum-
brance by her Lancastrian in-laws? It was fortunate that her
marriage was legally watertight.

In 1470 Warwick had swept through the West Country
to Coventry, where his army was reported as 60,000 strong.
Whilst doubtless an exaggeration – could any English army

of these dimensions supply itself in the field? – it is obvious that the invaders had benefited from popular enthusiasm for Henry VI and that Edward IV in contrast had been left bereft. The support was more than Warwick had enjoyed earlier in the year and doubtless more also than the Lancastrians could have raised without his aid. Now the Lancastrians sought to repeat the exercise. They lacked Warwick's leadership and probably also his adherents. Never strong in the far west, the Neville connection may have been defused, just possibly transferred to Warwick's son-in-law Clarence, but surely not to the earl's other daughter the Princess Anne. Evidently some hoped that potential Lancastrians put off by Warwick, formerly their greatest foe, would now enrol. We cannot tell whether they did. What we can be sure of, nevertheless, is that they did not reproduce the outflow of popular enthusiasm of the previous year or consequently that vast army. They did exploit the talismanic names of Beaufort and Courtenay, 'old inheritors of that country', still strong after ten years of exile, but not powerful enough. The noblemen, the queen and the prince strove to mobilise their supporters in Cornwall, Devon, Somerset and Wiltshire.[64] The army they raised was substantial, but not huge. In March, Clarence, on his march northwards via Wells to the Midlands, had raised 4,000 men in support of Henry VI from their particular pool.[65]

From Cerne Abbas the Lancastrians proceeded to Exeter, thence (presumably via Wells) northwards to Bath, which they reached on 29 April.[66] After recruiting for a fortnight – the whole duration of some of the campaigns of the Wars of the Roses – the Lancastrian forces were still too few to take on King Edward with confidence. Their preference was to join up with the Lancastrians of Wales, who were being recruited by Henry VI's half-brother Jasper Tudor, Earl of Pembroke, and of Cheshire and Lancaster, which done, so they hoped, they could defeat the Yorkists.

Edward IV had other ideas. Instead of waiting to be attacked, he took the initiative, proceeded to Cirencester, and sought out the Lancastrians in battle. Although initially evaded, he was able to prevent them from combining their levies, forced them to stand and fight, and decisively defeated them at Tewkesbury (4 May 1471).

The Yorkist *Arrival* records the elaborate manoeuvres, feint and counterfeint, and then the desperate chase northwards from Bristol through the Vale of Berkeley to Gloucester and on to Tewkesbury. If the forced march of thirty-six miles on the last day saw the ladies on horseback,[67] it was surely exhausting, frightening and dispiriting for a princess who was still short of her fifteenth birthday. Doubtless the ladies preceded their weary army, which reached Tewkesbury only about 4p.m., and were accommodated within the abbey or the manor house. These were familiar surroundings for Anne, who had visited the town and abbey frequently. Her grandmother Isabel was buried there, together with her Despenser and De Clare ancestors. Her mother was foundress of the abbey. Perhaps she and her husband stayed in her family's residence; perhaps at the abbey itself. Since Prince Edward took his leave of his mother early on the morrow, Queen Margaret and Princess Anne were probably lodging together.[68] That Saturday morning the Lancastrian army was drawn up with its back to the abbey and the town, into which it was scattered by the victorious Yorkists. The town, the abbey, and doubtless the foundress' residence were sacked. Although unrecorded, we may presume – as soldiers habitually behave in such circumstances – that violence, wanton destruction, sacrilege and rape were visited on the non-combatant civilians, priests, women and children. Those Lancastrians who took refuge within the abbey were lured out, on royal promises of immunity, and some of them were then executed: a story that the Yorkist *Arrival* took pains to conceal. Others were slain in the abbey cemetery. Both the abbey and churchyard were polluted and had to be reconsecrated later by the bishop of Worcester. Most of the Lancastrian commanders who survived the battle were executed afterwards – Somerset, Dorset, Devon, Wenlock and St John among them. This was on Monday.

Also slain was Anne's husband of six months. Prince Edward of Lancaster was fighting his first battle. His presence was important for Lancastrian morale, although the direction of the battle appears to have rested in the older but inexperienced hands of the duke of Somerset, disastrously. The prince 'was taken, fleeing to the town ward, and slain, in the field', reports the *Arrival*. A Tewkesbury Abbey chronicle and other early sources take the same line. 'And there was slain on the field, Prince Edward', states *Warkworth's Chronicle*, 'which cried for succour to his brother-in-law the Duke of Clarence'. A much later source, *Hall's Chronicle*, states instead that he was taken alive, hauled before King Edward to whom he was impertinent: the king struck him and those about him, the king's brothers Clarence and Gloucester and Lord Hastings, then despatched him.[69] Since Gloucester was to be second partner of the prince's wife Anne Neville, Hall is the source and inspiration for Shakespeare's belief that Anne remarried to her first husband's killer and of the celebrated (albeit wholly fictional) scene of the duke's wooing of the widowed princess. Professor Myers has applied the accepted academic principle that the earliest accounts are closest to the original and hence more reliable to demonstrate the elaboration of the story down to Hall.[70] A desire by later writers to blacken the failed tyrant Richard III, formerly duke of Gloucester, also may have played a part. Hall's tale lacked any contemporary authority and was dismissed as fiction. Recently, however, historians have become aware of an illustrated French version of the *Arrival*, perhaps dating to this very year, which shows a scene very like that described by Hall. Pinioned, the prince, identified by his coat of arms, faced King Edward wearing his crown, and was struck down.[71] Whether Gloucester was one of the killers is not apparent, nor is it material, since it was his role as constable of England to preside over the summary military proceedings that duly despatched those taken in battle and other traitors. In any case it was the king's responsibility. Like Henry VI, who was killed soon afterwards, Prince Edward was too dangerous to let live. It seems therefore that Hall's account may be authentic: that we should credit this last picture of the spirited, arrogant, fearless adolescent who was Anne's first husband.

Where was Princess Anne during the battle and its aftermath, the sacking and the bloodbath? Not at Tewkesbury, we must hope, but we cannot know for sure. What happened to Anne was of no interest to the author of the *Arrival*, who did not recognise his future queen, and left her out of his history. Most probably she escaped the terror of the defeat, the sacking and the bloodbath because she was with Queen Margaret, who 'withdrew herself from the adventure of the battle' early that Saturday morning 'for the surety of her person' to some 'poor religious place' across the River Avon on the Worcester road. Probably Evesham Abbey was meant, although it does not match this belittling description. There, reports the *Arrival*, King Edward found the queen (and most probably the princess) on 7 May on his way to Worcester. Queen Margaret 'was borne in carriage before the king at his triumph in London'.[72] She was never to be at complete liberty again. This refuge of the queen and princess is consistent with the listing by the abbey chronicle of thosehere taken and presented to the king, and pardoned', who included 'Lady Margaret, Queen, [and] Lady Anne, Princess'.[73] The *there*, however, surely betokened Tewkesbury. Two other ladies who were also pardoned, the countess of Devon and Lady Katherine Vaux, were probably attendant on the queen. It is possible therefore that Margaret and Anne were brought back to Tewkesbury prior to the king's departure. If so, they witnessed the aftermath of defeat – the destruction, the bloodshed, the display of quartered bodies of their kin and friends, and so on: traumatic sights. Thereafter their paths diverged, Queen Margaret as the king's prisoner and Anne as Clarence's charge: they may never have met again. Nor indeed was Anne to meet her father-in-law Henry VI, probably last encountered in 1460, who was eliminated a few days later in the Tower.

Neither Margaret nor Anne saw Prince Edward alive after he left their company that Saturday morning. Whether they could have seen him dead or attended his funeral may depend on where the king took them into custody. Presumably no burial service or masses were possible in a church that had been deconsecrated by bloodshed.[74] Prince Edward was interred in a prime position 'in the midst of the convent choir'[75] – an appropriate position for a member of the founder's family, given that the circle of chantry chapels around the high altar was complete and that in 1477 the vault even of Anne's sister Isabel had to be located in the ambulatory. Perhaps, therefore, Edward's burial place reveals Anne's choice, but it may be that the convent selected such a prominent site on its own account. A simple brass was erected over his tomb. The cult of Edward II, which financed the remodelling of Gloucester Abbey's choir, was a nearby reminder of the potential value of political saints. There are two references to a cult for Edward of Lancaster, but it failed to take off.[76] As their founders' chronicle makes plain, the monks of Tewkesbury saw themselves as safeguarding the interests of their patrons. All the other Lancastrian leaders also received honourable burial within the church and a careful record was compiled of who was buried where. The king may also have had some input in the final resting place of his former royal rival. Although there is no indication that any monument ever marked the prince's tomb or that any special masses were ever held in his honour, yet Princess Anne could certainly have located Edward's tomb without difficulty had she returned to Tewkesbury. This was to be expected, given Tewkesbury's status as the greatest of her family's religious foundations. Actually, however, her future lay elsewhere. There is no proof of her presence at Tewkesbury again. It is just possible that in 1483, when she took a different route from King Richard III from Windsor to Warwick, that Queen Anne dropped in at Tewkesbury Abbey and searched out her first husband's tomb, but, if so, it is not recorded. It is possible, but not likely.

CHAPTER FOUR

Between Princes
1471–5

Anne was scarcely married before she was widowed. Her acquaintance with her first husband Prince Edward was brief indeed: not more than nine months in all, at most six months of matrimony. Briefly, ever so briefly, she was a princess, by name and in the estimation of that limited company that was with Queen Margaret in France and returned with her to England and amongst Lancastrians generally, but without ever the courtly and luxurious life that should have gone with it. With her husband's death at Tewkesbury, Anne found herself a widow. She was dowager-princess of Wales. She was entitled to dower from the possessions of her husband – the principality of Wales, duchy of Cornwall and earldom of Chester. She should have had a right to her jointure too, but no jointure had been settled on her. But of course there was a hitch: her husband Edward had been a Lancastrian prince and after 4 May England was Yorkist again. Anne was princess only to a Lancastrian audience. Who dared to be Lancastrian after Tewkesbury? Since 1460 Yorkists had discounted any hereditary rights to the house of Lancaster. In 1471 King Edward IV firmly rejected the house of Lancaster, the Readeption, and hence any claims that Prince Edward had possessed either to the crown or his principality. To King Edward IV and the Yorkist victors after

Tewkesbury, Edward of Lancaster had never been prince of Wales. He had never taken seisin of any of the possessions that normally belonged to the king's heir; had he done so, it would have been wrongfully. Thus Prince Edward had nothing with which to dower his princess. Moreover, he had perished an enemy and a traitor. If he was never attainted, this was because there was nothing to confiscate. Furthermore, King Edward now had his own infant prince, the future Edward V, on whom he was to confer all the properties earmarked for the heir of throne after resuming whatever had been granted to anybody else.[1] As princess, therefore, Anne was entitled to nothing. Her title of princess of Wales was obsolete, empty, useless, probably unusable, and raised undesirable associations. Although more elevated, princess of Wales was a title that she ceased to use once she became duchess of Gloucester, if not before.

At least King Edward had received her, accepted her submission, and had pardoned her. He could do no less. The Wars of the Roses were not waged against women. None were slain in battle, only three attainted as traitors by parliament. Even the most partisan ladies were merely confined (usually in monasteries) and restrained from supporting their recalcitrant menfolk.[2] Princess Anne posed Edward no threat. If the wife or widow of a traitor peer was reduced to begging, like Anne's aunt Margaret, Countess of Oxford, King Edward was induced to relieve her:[3] it was chivalric expectation. Just as Edward was expected to, and did, see his rival honourably buried, so too he had to tolerate Prince Edward's consort and, if necessary, finance her. Until 11 June 1471, moreover, Anne was only fourteen years of age.

Laynesmith has revived speculation about what might have been had Anne been already pregnant by Prince Edward.[4] That was certainly an objective of the marriage which Prince Edward surely strove for. If Anne had been with child, she could have renewed the Lancastrian line that had just been eradicated. Whilst nobody could have been certain, the fact that Henry VI perished unnaturally on 20 May, a murder that was pointless as long as he had an heir living, may be evidence that Anne was believed not to be with child. Had she been pregnant, an accident – life-threatening to her baby if not herself – might have been engineered. Such speculation, however, is more than usually groundless. There is no contemporary evidence of any such interesting condition, not even any contemporary suspicions.

Anne was above the age of majority. Although entitled in law to half the Montagu/Salisbury lands (less her mother's dower and jointure), she was not a royal ward. She was also a widow and thus *femme sole*: a single woman entitled to manage her own affairs without male intervention, unlike any spinster or wife. A fifteen-year-old widow without property, however, had no means to exercise her theoretical independence. Nor could Anne look to her mother for sympathy, guidance or protection, except perhaps by post, since the Countess Anne was in custody at Beaulieu and was also unable to assert her own rights.

Anne Beauchamp, now dowager-countess of Warwick, could expect no dower from her late husband's estate, since, to Yorkist eyes, her husband Warwick had been a traitor. She was still entitled to her jointure – the properties settled jointly on her and her husband at their marriage.[5] Moreover, her vast Beauchamp and Despenser inheritances were still legally her own. That all the lands that Warwick held in his own or her right were seized in 1471 and occupied by Clarence was a common enough error that should have been corrected when better evidence of the actual title was produced. Whatever the legal situation, however, many bereaved ladies seem to have had difficulties with their jointures, apparently sometimes because they were not properly secured at law: the king's own queen and two of his mistresses found their in-laws unwilling to

honour the deals after their husbands' death.[6] Their inheritances, however, were different: their rights of inheritance were
beyond debate – quite incontestable. These were rights that
could not be denied. Understandably the countess found it
difficult to secure livery of her estate whilst in sanctuary. She
needed to come to the king and make her case direct as, for
instance, the king's future bedfellows Dame Eleanor Butler,
Dame Elizabeth Grey and Dame Margaret Lucy had done.[7]
But the countess found that realising her rights was in practice
quite unattainable. As she was to protest to parliament, she had
not done anything wrong. She had not betrayed King Edward
as Warwick himself had done. She had taken sanctuary for her
own safety and to pray 'for the weal and health of the soul of
her said [deceased] lord and husband as right and conscience'
demanded. Within five days or thereabouts, therefore even
before the battle of Tewkesbury, she had asked the king for a
safe-conduct. Instead, 'to her great heart's grievance', he had
ordered her strict confinement, so that she was unable as she
wished to come to court to sue for livery of her inheritance,
jointure and dower. In October 1472 or even later, not less than
eighteen months after she first took sanctuary, the countess
was still not allowed to leave Beaulieu Abbey, where she was
living poorly and lacked even a clerk, she said implausibly, to
pen her plea. She

> hath written letters in that behalf to the King's Highness, with
> her own hand, and not only making such labours, suits and
> means to the King's Highness, sothely also to the Queen's
> good grace, to my right redoubted lady the King's mother
> [Cecily Duchess of York], to my lady the King's eldest daugh-
> ter [Elizabeth of York], to my ladies the King's sisters [Anne
> Duchess of Exeter and Elizabeth Duchess of Suffolk], to my
> lady of Bedford, mother to the Queen [Jacquetta Duchess of
> Bedford], and to other ladies noble of this realm.[8]

Obviously she expected other ladies to be sympathetic to her in her predicament: the Duchesses Cecily, Anne and Jacquetta had all struggled to recover their rights after their husbands' death or forfeiture. She expected the intervention of this ladies' union to be effective with the men. Given that the war was over, surely nobody thought that the widowed countess posed any further threat to national security? Yet she was confined to Beaulieu at the king's command. Why did the king command it? Why did the countess not solicit the intercession of her daughter Isabel or her son-in-law Clarence? The answer in all cases is surely the same. Surely she did seek the support of Isabel and Clarence, to no avail. Actually it was Isabel and Clarence (and perhaps later Anne and Gloucester) who opposed her rights. It was in their interests that the king kept her confined to Beaulieu after any risk to the public had passed. The royal ladies, to whom the countess wrote, may well have put first the interests of their brothers and brothers-in-law Clarence and Gloucester. In the meantime, of course, the countess could be no effective help to her daughter Anne.

We left Anne in the king's company at Tewkesbury or at Worcester in early May 1471. Whilst we cannot delve into her first marriage, we may safely presume a succession of emotions – fear during the long pursuit and decisive battle, apprehension at the result, grief at her husband's death, trauma at the bloodshed, and undoubtedly also concern for her own safety and for her own future. What was to befall her was far from clear. If safe from actual destitution or execution, her prospects now looked very bleak. Personally dowerless, she had only her expectations of inheritance to sustain her and to attract a male protector. At midsummer 1471, in view of her father's death at Barnet and her mother's flight, that heritage was purely speculative. Under such circumstances, the protection of her powerful brother [-in-law], her sister Isabel's husband Clarence, was surely very welcome. All the more so if, as seems likely, he took her in at Tewkesbury itself, immediately after the battle and her submission to the king, and conveyed her home to Warwick en route for London, whence he engaged in a further campaign in Kent against the Bastard of Fauconberg. Clarence was Anne's guardian angel. As with other wives of traitors, the king may well have consigned Anne to Clarence's custody by word of mouth or in some undocumented way, but he cannot have granted him the wardship and marriage of a widow who was of age.

COURTSHIP OF A PRINCESS

Unfortunately we have no detailed knowledge of where Anne was and what she did for the next eight crucial months. We must deal in likelihoods. Clarence's easiest course of action was to receive his widowed sister-in-law into the household of the Duchess Isabel. We may doubt how agreeable were the relations now resumed of the two reunited sisters, the elder of whom was married to the man who had betrayed the younger's father and husband, both with fatal results. Probably Anne accompanied her sister wherever she went, to London, and into society. A widowed princess was an honoured guest. Also probably it was during this period and at London, most probably at the Christmas and New Year celebrations of 1471–2, that Anne again encountered her brother[-in-law] Richard, Duke of Gloucester, resumed their acquaintance, and determined to take him as her second husband.

Anne cannot have planned all this in advance. Doubtless she was relieved initially to be rescued and was pleased to lie low. Her mother remained in sanctuary at Beaulieu. Isabel was to hand, but the interests of the two sisters were not identical. When Clarence had deserted Warwick and rejoined King Edward, the two royal brothers were reconciled. Clarence's offences were wiped out. Subsequently he had served in the king's army at Barnet, a close-run battle in which the duke's contingent, estimated by the *Arrival* as 4,000 strong, was essential for victory. As reward for his defection and services at Barnet, Clarence had immediately been granted all the Warwick inheritance which Isabel had been entitled to inherit. A court was held in their name at Erdington in modern Birmingham as early as 16 April.[9] The Neville lands in the North, to which Isabel had no claim, were excluded. Having secured everything to which she had rights of inheritance, naturally George and Isabel wanted to keep it all – it was the heritage of their unborn children – and did not want to surrender any of it to the Duchess Isabel's mother, nor indeed to divide it with her sister Anne. In her distant sanctuary at Beaulieu, the countess of Warwick was out of the picture: indeed, she was kept out of the picture, the abbot receiving 'right sharp commandment' from the king to hold her there.[10] Naturally also George and Isabel wished to prevent Anne marrying again, for any husband would surely wish to assert her rights and recover for himself her half-share. Their case cannot be put more succinctly than it was somewhat later by the Milanese ambassador: 'because his brother King Edward had promised him Warwick's country, [Clarence] did not want the former [Gloucester] to have it, by reason of the marriage with the earl [of Warwick]'s second daughter'.[11] They wanted to keep what was theirs, their entitlement, what the king had given them. Presumably it was only after Gloucester had showed an interest in Anne that they concealed her from the prying eyes of aspirant husbands. This apparently was at the duke's London house, Coldharbour, near Dowgate. Whether she was concealed as a maid in the duke's kitchen, as Crowland claimed, sounds unlikely[12] – women were not normally employed in great households and Anne cannot have possessed many relevant skills – but the concealment story is surely authentic. Crowland's kitchen story is reminiscent of the Cinderella rags to riches story. It implies that Gloucester was a knight errant who rescued her rather than, alternatively, a predatory seducer. We cannot know what the Clarences had in mind for Anne next. In similar circumstances we know of male heirs who consigned their nieces to nunneries – William, Earl of Suffolk in 1423, for instance[13] – and of brothers-in-law who tried to exclude their sisters-in-law from their inheritance.[14] If the Clarences offered Anne the alternative of taking the veil, we must presume that she declined. As an heiress, in theory, she was materially secure, but to make good her rights she needed a male protagonist and to marry.

The pressure that George and Isabel, her protectors, could exert on the fifteen-year-old Anne may have appeared almost irresistible: though we cannot know, of course, whether they coerced her at all. The best evidence of such pressure, perhaps, is that Anne was to greet Clarence's brother Richard, Duke of Gloucester as her saviour, her rescuer, and that she allowed him to whisk her away to sanctuary. In medieval parlance, this abduction was a rape – as so often committed, in medieval terms, with the full consent of the lady. By then, presumably, Anne had reconciled herself to remarrying – the destiny after all to which such aristocratic ladies were born and brought up. Independence, as a helpless and destitute *femme sole*, could not do the trick and had no attraction for her.

Whether Anne was right to see Richard in such a favourable light, however, is not so certain. Doubtless she embarked on the course that she took with her eyes open. Obviously there was an irony to such a match. Whether or not Richard had a part in her husband's death and whether this was publicly known, both of which now appear more likely in view of the rediscovered Burgundian illumination, and whether or not he had presided over the elimination of her father-in-law Henry VI, nevertheless the duke had certainly fought on the side adverse in the battles at which Anne's father, husband and uncle had been slain. This was as one of many, against a cause that was now obsolete and beyond revival. To the Yorkists and hence everybody else who mattered politically in 1471, Anne's menfolk had been traitors legitimately slain in the rightful Yorkist cause. A post-Lancastrian and post-Warwick reality had to be accepted. There was nothing to be salvaged or revived from the Lancastrian cause and no mileage in resentment or vengeance. If revenge ever featured in Anne's thoughts or emotions, she lacked the power to exact it and let it drop even when, in bed, Richard was at his most vulnerable. In the perilous limbo in which Anne found herself in 1471, such reflections were pointless, indeed counterproductive, and best forgotten. Moreover Anne had as many kindred on the winning as the losing side. Until 1470 it had been the winners whom she knew and the Yorkists with whom she interacted. The answer to Shakespeare's rhetorical question – 'Was ever woman in this humour wooed?' – was surely no, not even in this case. However ironical, the issues were never as stark or as conflictive as Shakespeare was to imagine.

Whatever Richard's physical limitations – we know him to have been short, slight, and perhaps even a hunchback – Anne had everything to gain materially from matrimony with him that she could hope to attain. She would have the ducal and royal rank her father had planned with a bridegroom that he may originally have favoured and (according to Waurin) had actually selected; respect; a princely establishment and great wealth; and the prospect of motherhood, the normal fulfilment of any late medieval lady. It was her birthright and her destiny. Given all that, her hereditary rights were of secondary importance for her, but they were crucial for Duke Richard. Without her, they were inaccessible. Neither the duke nor any other potential husband could secure Anne's inheritance except by marrying her. That was her best hope for the future and her security. Marriage, of course, was only a first step. It was perhaps attainable by mere squires, like Owen Tudor who

had notoriously coupled with Henry V's queen Katherine
of France or Richard Wydeville, who had wed Jacquetta of
Luxemberg, the widow of the Regent Bedford. There were
many for whom marriage to a princess was exaltation: already
a prince, Gloucester was not among them. To secure Anne's
inheritance in the teeth of the royal duke of Clarence required
her to marry not just any genteel squire, but somebody equally
powerful and just as influential with the king as Clarence was.
Sir John Risley was later warned by Edward IV not to buy
land with a suspect title from Gloucester, which demanded all
the power of the duke to retain it.[15] All these necessary criteria
in this case were satisfied by Richard, Duke of Gloucester and,
perhaps in the early 1470s, only by him. No other potential
suitor could be so confident of success.

Undoubtedly Richard wanted Anne for his wife. Crowland
tells us so, adding how astutely he tracked her down, found
her whereabouts, and spirited her into safekeeping.[16] He was
not deterred by any obstacles, personal or political, familial or
moral, and he confronted his brother Clarence head on. The
abduction was another crucial upheaval and another decisive
turning point in Anne's short life. We merely know, thanks to
Crowland, that Duke Richard removed Anne initially from
Clarence's custody to the celebrated sanctuary in the city of
London of the College of St Martin-le-Grand, which was
located between the Guildhall and St Paul's.[17] That was some-
time before 16 February 1472.[18] Anne may have spent half a
year or more in Clarence's care. Actually we may deduce rather
more. After receiving the submission of the Kentish rebels at
Sandwich on 26 May, Richard was sent to combat the last ves-
tiges of resistance in the North, where he tried and executed
the Bastard of Fauconberg. At Norwich about 23 August,[19] he
dated from the North grants on 30 August, 4 and 6 October,
20 November and 11 December 1471.[20] Unless therefore he
reached his understanding with Anne in the early summer, in

June and July 1471 and immediately after the death of her first husband, the whole courtship had to be fitted into the two months from late December 1471 to the Sheen council of 16 February 1472. A whirlwind wooing indeed!

It is unfortunate that this episode is so ill-documented, since it was the pivotal moment when Anne made the choices that shaped the rest of her life. If Anne was undoubtedly a victim, she was not helpless. Within the limited scope apparently left to her, she was also in charge. Widows were legally free of masculine control and free to contract their own courtships and marriages. There seems to have been nobody to whom she could turn for disinterested counsel. Gloucester, who did advise her and whose blandishments were crucial, was certainly no disinterested party. Yet it was Anne's self-conscious decision not to remain where she was, in Clarence's kitchen or wherever. She also decided self-consciously not to become a nun and against whatever future, probably not including marriage, that her brother-in-law Clarence had in store for her. It was her decision to permit her abduction to St Martin's, almost certainly with the rider that this was merely a first step towards marriage to Duke Richard. It was her decision also to marry far within the prohibited degrees. There can have been very few fifteen-year-old ladies, let alone princesses, who chose their marriage partners for themselves. Anne did. She transferred herself from one royal duke to another and duly married the second, tying her fortunes henceforth to his. All her ambitions were thereby fulfilled.

Why Anne did this is only too obvious. Her current situation and prospects were unacceptable. We have seen what she had to gain. Only Gloucester dared to outface his brother of Clarence and only he could retrieve her inheritance. She had no alternative, certainly none if she wanted the wealth, prestige and rank to which she was born and bred. Without her inheritance, even Gloucester was not available. Anne could have aspired no higher. It helped of course that Anne was acquainted with Duke Richard: they had shared experiences from his sojourn in 1465–8 in her father's household. Perhaps they knew one another quite well, despite their difference in years. In March 1472, when she was only fifteen and he was nineteen, a difference of nearly four years in age (forty-four months) was substantial. How much more significant was the gap in age in 1468, when the sixteen-year-old duke had moved out of Warwick's household and away from his twelve-year-old cousin! Any romantic interest dating back to that era appears improbable. Romance makes better sense in 1472, providing that they had the opportunity to develop their relationship, most probably before Clarence – understandably alarmed – secreted Anne away, but perhaps only following the abduction and after Anne's initial flight. How irritating that we cannot know! Evidence of any sexual attraction – or indeed sexual starvation following the abrupt termination of Anne's conjugal rights – is irretrievable. It is twenty-first-century standards that have made modern historians hope for the love-match that we take for granted today. For Anne, with her upbringing and contemporary expectations, love was not the prerequisite that we have subsequently made it. A love match appears unlikely here.

There is no need to inject sentiment as an ingredient into Richard's actions. He was a royal duke and he wanted the estates, wealth, and power within England to go with it. Not for him to be a pawn in King Edward's foreign policy! Most of the lands that he had been given in the 1460s had been returned to their original holders or resumed by the crown. That was why he ceased to operate in Lancashire and Cheshire. The chief offices in Wales received in 1469 now reverted to the 2nd Earl of Pembroke. Edward IV gave Gloucester everything that he had to bestow arising from the forfeitures of the renegade Yorkists and the Lancastrians who had been defeated in

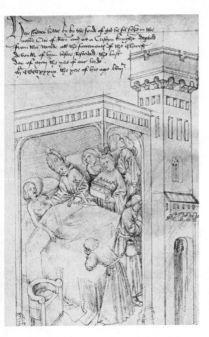

1 The deathbed of Anne Neville's heroic grandfather Richard Beauchamp, Earl of Warwick and king's lieutenant of France, at Rouen in 1439, from the *Beauchamp Pageant*.

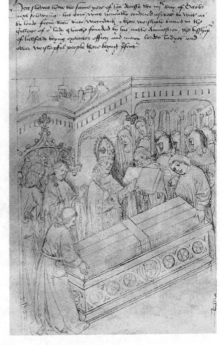

2 The *Beauchamp Pageant*'s depiction of the funeral in 1439 of Anne Neville's grandfather Richard Beauchamp, Earl of Warwick, at Warwick College, where Anne Neville was baptised in 1456. Later the earl was moved to the splendid Beauchamp Chapel, adjoining, which he had commissioned.

3 Anne's parents, Anne, Countess of Warwick and Richard Neville, Earl of Warwick (the Kingmaker) from the *Rows Roll*. The banners record how noble were their forebears (and hence Anne Neville's) on every side. Note the bear at the countess' feet and the ragged staff on the banner above.

4 Warwick Castle, where Anne was born. The huge Guy's Tower is to the rear; the incomplete Bear and Clarence towers in the foreground were the handiwork of Anne's father, Warwick the Kingmaker, and brother George, Duke of Clarence.

5 London, the largest city Anne had ever seen in 1460, showing the city's exceptional size and old St Paul's Cathedral.

Key:
1: 'Warwick Inn', London residence of Anne's father.
2: St Martin-le-Grand.
3: Old St Paul's.
4: The Great Wardrobe.
5: Baynard's Castle.

6 Calais, England's greatest fortress in France, depicted about 1483 by the *Beauchamp Pageant*. Anne Neville knew it well in early childhood, living there with her parents in 1457–60. The defeat of the Lancastrian besiegers that she witnessed had much in common with the similar events of 1436 shown here.

Edwardus dei gracia r. cn dnglie
et ffrancie est dominus hibernie

Regina Elizabetha consors
Edwardi dei gracia Regis

Left: 7 Edward IV, the first Yorkist king, at prayer, from contemporary stained glass at Canterbury Cathedral.

Right: 8 Elizabeth Wydeville, the parvenu queen to Edward IV, from contemporary stained glass at Canterbury Cathedral. Their marriage in 1464 advanced the Wydevilles at the expense of Warwick and his daughters and thus contributed to Warwick's rebellion in 1469.

Far left: 9 Statue formerly on the Welsh bridge at Shrewsbury supposedly depicting Richard, Duke of York (d.1460), father of the two Yorkist kings Edward IV (1461–83) and Richard III (1483–5), second husband of Anne Neville.

Left: 10 Micklegate Bar, the gateway to York used by Anne Neville whenever approaching the city from the south or heading southwards.

11 St William's College, York. Located immediately to the east of York Minster, this splendid college was founded to accommodate the minster's chantry priests by Anne Neville's father, the Kingmaker, and uncle Archbishop Neville.

12 Louis XI, King of France (1461–83), the 'universal spider' who brokered both the treaty of Anne Neville's father Warwick and Queen Margaret of Anjou and the marriage of Anne herself to Margaret's son, Edward of Lancaster. A likeness based on his instructions for his tomb.

Left: 13 King Henry VI, the politically ineffective but pious father-in-law who Anne never knew, depicted *c.*1500 as a saint on the screen at Ludham in Norfolk.

Above: 14 A fanciful Victorian depiction of the death of Anne's father Warwick on the battlefield of Barnet on Easter Sunday 1471.

Left: 15 Edward of Lancaster as Prince of Wales, from the *Rows Roll* in the College of Arms.

Above: 16 A modern plaque in the chancel floor at Tewkesbury Abbey commemorating the death of Prince Edward, 'the last hope of thy race'.

17 Tewkesbury Abbey, the mausoleum of Anne's Despenser ancestors, of her first husband Prince Edward of Lancaster and other victims of the battle of Tewkesbury in 1471, of her sister Isabel, Duchess of Clarence, in 1476, and of her brother-in-law George, Duke of Clarence, in 1478.

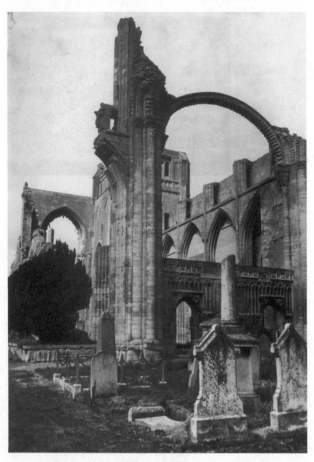

18 Crowland
Abbey,
Lincolnshire,
where
the best
chronicler of
the Yorkists
wrote in 1485.

19 Redrawing of John Rows, the aged chantry
priest of Guyscliff, Warwick, author of the *Rows
Rolls* of the earls of Warwick and partisan of the
Countess Anne, as depicted by himself.

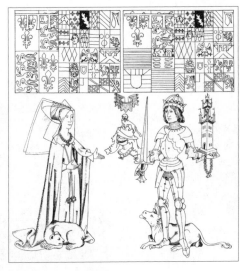

20 John Rows' portrayal of Anne's sister Isabel, Duchess of Clarence, and her husband George, Duke of Clarence, at whose feet is the black bull of Clarence and in whose hand is a tower recalling those he built at Tutbury and Warwick. Isabel has a bear at her feet. The complex heraldry of the banners was almost identical to Anne Neville's own arms before her accession.

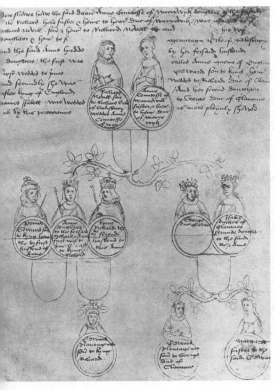

21 The family of Anne Neville from the *Beauchamp Pageant*. At the top are her parents, the Kingmaker and Countess Anne: to the left are Anne and her two husbands, Prince Edward of Lancaster and Richard III, who because of their accession are given priority over her elder sister (here styled the second sister), Isabel Neville and her husband George, Duke of Clarence. Anne and King Richard are depicted with crowns and sceptres. Depicted below are their son Edward of Middleham (left), nephew Edward, Earl of Warwick (centre) and Margaret, Countess of Salisbury.

22 Middleham Castle, Yorkshire, the best known of Anne's ancestral seats, where she and Duke Richard resided in 1472–83 and where their son Edward was born.

23 Barnard Castle towers over the Tees. Anne's ancient Beauchamp Castle was the site of the abortive college that Duke Richard founded in 1478, most probably as his intended mausoleum.

Above: 24 Surrounded by courtiers, King Edward IV receives the book proffered by the author, his brother-in-law, Earl Rivers. The earl's ward, the future King Edward V, is the child on the king's right.

Right: 25 Sir John Millais' sympathetic portrayal of the Princes in the Tower, whose legitimacy Richard III had to discredit to make himself king and Anne queen.

26 Anne and Richard III as king and queen. As the historian of the earls of Warwick, John Rows places Anne first (left) and depicts her in her coronation robes with her hair loose and her crown, orb and sceptre. King Richard in plate armour, right, is crowned and holds his orb. Note at Richard's feet his white boar and at Anne's feet a muzzled bear. Above them are shields that equate Anne's complicated arms with those of England (the three lions) and France (the fleur-de-lis).

27 Queen Anne Neville, redrawn from a lost stained glass window at Skipton church, Yorkshire. The image is ambiguous: although Anne is depicted crowned, her hair is loose. Her mantle bears her arms, yet the royal arms on her undergarment have a label of difference suggesting that Duke Richard had not yet acceded. Lord of Skipton from 1475, he gave money as king to the churchwardens in 1484, which they probably spent on this stained glass.

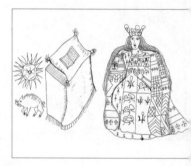

28 King Richard and Queen Anne from the Salisbury Roll. Both are crowned and carry sceptres. Anne again has her hair loose. Over the armour and kirtle depicted by Rows, they wear mantles which, in Anne's case, equate her ancestral arms (right) with those of England and France (left).

Ricaidi tertii Regis Anglie qui hanc
m....c....lxxviii

Above: 29 Anne Neville as queen of England, crowned and at prayer. From a modern memorial window at Middleham Church given by the Richard III Society in 1934. Note Anne's family coat of arms on her mantle.

Left: 30 King Richard and Anne Neville in stained glass by William Burges at Cardiff Castle. Evidently Burges made use of Richard's well-known portrait. Cardiff and Glamorgan were included in Anne's share of her parents' inheritance.

31 Elizabeth, Cecily and Anne, three daughters of Edward IV, in stained glass at Canterbury Cathedral. Allegedly Princess Elizabeth of York (left) was King Richard's choice of spouse even before Queen Anne's death. If Elizabeth and Anne were indeed alike in build and complexion, then Queen Anne looked like this.

32 John Howard, Duke of Norfolk, who was the recipient of Elizabeth of York's letter in February 1485, in which his support was supposedly sought for her marriage with King Richard. From a lost stained glass window at Tendring Hall, Suffolk.

33 The Palace of Westminster from Southwark, *c.*1550, by Anthony van den Wyngaerde. Note St Stephen's Chapel, left, Westminster Hall to the right, and Westminster Abbey (without towers) behind. Westminster was where Queen Anne was crowned, spent Christmas 1483 and 1484, and where she died and was buried.

34 Edward of Middleham, Prince of Wales. Clad in armour, bearing a crown and sceptre, and with Richard III's white boar at his feet, he is accompanied by royal crests and a shield of the royal arms with a difference: he would bear them undifferenced when he became king. Strangely, John Rows included nothing reminiscent of the prince's maternal ancestry.

Clockwise from top left:

35 Coat of arms of Anne Neville as queen.

36 Effigy, supposedly of Prince Edward of Middleham, at Sheriff Hutton. It appears from Dodsworth that before it was seriously defaced this was of a child, bearing the Warwick arms (as in Anne's coronation mantle) and the royal arms with a difference (as in the *Rows Rolls*). It sounds authentic.

37 Coat of arms of Richard III.

38 Badges of Richard III.

1471. Thus Richard accrued Warwick's Neville estates in the North – Middleham, Sheriff Hutton and Penrith – to which neither Isabel nor Anne had ever been entitled: this was at the expense of their cousin George Neville, Duke of Bedford, the son of Warwick's late brother John, Marquis Montagu. Richard was also granted all those lands in eastern England that had belonged to the earl of Oxford and a clutch of county gentry,[21] which he had little use for and most of which he later renounced. There was little to recover from the returning Lancastrians, who had been attainted once already. Many of their possessions were restored to Clarence, who had held them before, whilst the possessions of the traitor duke of Exeter reverted to his estranged Duchess Anne, eldest sister to the king and to the royal dukes. If all Richard's grants were added altogether – and assuming that Richard could overcome complications in the titles to certain estates – these grants could have brought Richard somewhat more than the qualifying income for a duke: 2,000 marks or £1,666 13s 4d. Altogether they fell well short of the revenues of the greatest magnates, such as Clarence and Buckingham. To match them – and Richard definitely wanted to match them – the duke needed to marry well within England. No potential partner offered more than the Princess Anne. From the start of his courtship, therefore, her inheritance was his key objective. Richard, moreover, was not prepared to wait for Anne's mother to die. He wanted it all now. And that meant that Richard was not interested solely in securing Anne's rights, largely prospective, but also in dispossessing Anne's mother, his intended mother-in-law the countess of Warwick.

Such an interpretation has appeared too cynical for some supporters of Richard III, who would much prefer a love match. It was 'a delicate and honourable consideration for her feelings' that prompted Richard to remove Anne from sanctuary, wrote Miss Wigram long ago, rather than his desire for her inheritance.[22] Unfortunately, this is one point about which we can be certain. John Paston II reported that Clarence conceded her person, but not her livelihood:[23] Richard, however, declined. He insisted on the inheritance also. If this appears heartless and calculating to modern eyes, bestowing women in marriage with property was commonplace in late medieval arranged marriages. Their endowment frequently determined the choice. 'Love matches sometimes occurred', wrote Jennifer Ward, 'but were frowned on by noble society'.[24]

It is surprising how quickly Anne progressed from her first husband to her second. If Anne's first marriage was definitely not a love match – she cannot have known the bridegroom before her betrothal – yet Edward of Lancaster was her husband and, however briefly, he had shared her bed. Her mourning was brief indeed. Within eight months at most, Anne had adjusted to her loss – to all her losses, her father included – and had pledged herself to another. Whilst it is not difficult to think of other young widows who moved on to further consorts with such precipitate haste, it was not what was expected – not seemly conduct – even by fifteenth-century standards. Is not a cynical and calculating materialism on Anne's part implied here? Was she one of those girls who succumbed to the material or sexual temptations that the conduct books warned against? Or was Anne merely an unstable and/or emotional and/or impressionable fifteen-year-old on whom Duke Richard had imposed his stamp? We cannot be sure.

One must moreover deplore the immorality of the match. A custodial sentence and registration as a sexual offender would result today for any man like Duke Richard guilty of sexual intercourse with a fifteen-year-old girl, but fifteenth-century standards permitted such relations and indeed regarded them as normal and legitimate. In another way, however, this match did offend contemporary values. Whilst always aware that Anne and Richard were related within the prohibited degrees, historians have downplayed the significance. The medieval Catholic Church forbade marriages between kinsfolk who were much more distantly related than those that exercise us today. Often we are scarcely conscious of our first cousins, let alone aware who are our second cousins and more remote relatives, and, in this age of divorce, we are generally unfazed by the coupling of in-laws and even step-siblings unconnected by any blood ties. Such unions are not infrequent in soap operas, feature films, and real life. Incest, for us, involves parents and children, siblings, uncles and nieces. Hence we regard Clarence's need for a dispensation to marry his first cousin once removed as a curious technicality. Even less objectionable, to us, was Anne's first match, when neither party was closer than four generations from their common ancestor John of Gaunt (d.1399). A dispensation had to be obtained for that too. We have seen that Warwick would allow neither of his daughters to marry until impediments had been removed. The spiritual kinship created by Clarence's mother as Isabel's godmother appears scarcely conceivable to us. Dispensation, from our angle, was simply a necessary mechanism to remove technical obstacles to what ought to have been perfectly acceptable. That, however, was not how fifteenth-century people regarded the issue. For them, marriage within the prohibited degrees was incestuous and therefore rightly prohibited. It was because they were related in the third and fourth degrees that the wedding of Edward IV's second son in 1478 was barred at the door of the chapel royal at Westminster, an impediment that was removed very publicly when the dean produced the requisite papal bull.[25] Breaches were sinful even if accidental. To contract such matches deliberately and in full consciousness of the offence was a heinous sin and potentially damnable. Such unions ran the risk of being compulsorily dissolved and any consequent children bastardised. Bastards were excluded from inheritance. *The Calendar of Papal Letters* contains many instances of partners who discovered the defect after their marriages and were so troubled by conscience that they revealed their offence to the papacy and secured papal authority to remain married and for their offspring to remain legitimate. Often, admittedly, impediments were set aside and illicit matches were confirmed retrospectively, but dispensations were sometimes refused, even for princes.[26] Warwick had had great difficulty in securing the necessary dispensation for Clarence and Isabel. Dispensations could not be presumed.

Gloucester and Anne were already related in the same degrees as their siblings Clarence and Isabel, to which a further distant tie was created by Anne's first wedding to a distant cousin of them both, and they were yet more closely connected by the marriage of Richard's brother to Anne's sister. The impediments multiplied. Anne and Richard were brother-in-law and sister-in-law, related in the first degree of affinity. In fifteenth-century parlance, Richard was Anne's brother and Anne was Richard's sister. This was not just a matter of words: to their contemporaries, that was their relationship. Any sexual encounter between them, in or out of wedlock, was incestuous, sinful, prohibited, deeply shocking and probably incapable of being dispensed. Neither Richard nor Anne can have been ignorant of this. Each should have rebuffed anything beyond fraternal friendship. To persist nevertheless, to pledge to each other and to resolve on marriage, required both parties to reject contemporary standards of morality – to flout what others thought – and to override the law in pursuit of their own wishes. Whether Anne was motivated by sexual attraction, ambition or merely by a desire to escape from an impossible situation, she was, by contemporary standards, quite wrong. She ran the risk, moreover, that her marriage would be dissolved after the event, that she would be left in limbo – unmarried, property-less, unmarriageable – and her children illegitimate. However difficult her situation may have appeared, it cannot,

on current evidence, have been sufficiently impossible to jus-
tify such a step. As for Richard, desperation cannot be pleaded
in extenuation. That they appear to have escaped the penalties
for a dozen years does not alter the case.

Past historians have had good reason to deduce that Anne
and Richard had no papal dispensation to validate their marriage. Long ago, C.A.J. Armstrong twice searched the Vatican
archives in search of one, unsuccessfully. In his day, the registers
of the papal penitentiary were not accessible. Now that they
are, it has been discovered that a dispensation was actually
applied for on behalf of Richard, of Lincoln diocese wherein
he had been born (at Fotheringhay), and Anne Neville, woman
(*mulier*) of the diocese of York. This was to dispense impediments in the third and fourth degrees of affinity. His petition
was approved by the papal penitentiary on 22 April 1472. A
declaratory letter was also issued,[27] which doubtless stilled the
objections of Cardinal Bourchier, the officiating clergyman, or
any other cleric present at their subsequent wedding. Richard
and Anne were related in the same degrees as their siblings
Clarence and Isabel in 1469: that is, in the second degree (as
first cousins) and twice in the fourth degree of consanguinity.
As Richard, like Anne's first husband Edward of Lancaster,
was a great-grandson of John of Gaunt, there was yet another
fourth degree of consanguinity to be dispensed. Finally, of
course, Richard and Anne were brother-in-law and sister-in-
law, related in the first degree of affinity. What they needed was
a dispensation that covered impediments in the first degree of
affinity, another in the second and three in the fourth degrees
of consanguinity. This one, which dispensed only in the third
and fourth degrees of affinity, not consanguinity, was therefore insufficient to validate their marriage. If the clerks of the
penitentiary routinely dispensed impediments in the third and
fourth degree, the second degree of consanguinity (as Clarence
had found) was more serious, and affinity in the first degree

was yet more so. Such a dispensation was more difficult to obtain. It would certainly take more lobbying, more time, and might indeed prove unattainable. Rejection was predictable.

The 1472 dispensation was therefore inadequate, as Richard must have perceived. At no point can he have been unaware of the consanguinity that linked Anne to him, that they were first cousins once removed and siblings-in-law. Another, more wide-ranging dispensation was needed before Anne and Richard could contract a valid union, but they did not wait for that. That they decided to marry in defiance of canon law is astonishing. To marry before securing a valid dispensation – and, indeed, in full knowledge of it – was a further sin to be absolved. Both partners had to be eligible to marry one another and to make a valid marriage, even though by 16 February 1472 (at the latest) they had evidently pledged themselves to one another, all that in normal circumstances was required to make an unbreakable contract in this period. Even Clarence was obliged to accept that the marriage would happen – John Paston's phrasing, however, indicates that it had not happened yet.

> The King entreats my Lord of Clarence for my Lord of Gloucester, and (as it is said) he answers that he may well have my lady his sister-in-law, but they shall divide no livelihood, as he says.[28]

Even though Clarence thought of both parties as his siblings, the morality, so it appears, was at this stage not his concern. Whilst the dukes themselves debated in council, they represented Isabel and Anne and not necessarily purely formally. At this stage Clarence fought to keep all the property, but found himself opposed by the king. Posing improbably as arbiter and 'loving brother', so Crowland ironically reports,[29] Edward imposed a settlement that was much to Clarence's disadvantage. At this royal council it was determined that the whole Warwick inheritance was to be divided, not just the lion's share in tail general that Clarence was occupying.

It was the best possible outcome for Anne. Duke Richard may have been her father's preferred choice for her during the 1460s. She shared the vicissitudes in Warwick's fortunes, into forfeiture and exile and then to next in the Lancastrian line of succession, and 'after his decease', as Rows put it, 'marvellously conveyed by all the corners and parts of the wheel of fortune'. Widowed, childless, ruined, dependent on her foes and with only the most unpromising prospects, yet was 'she exalted again' to be duchess of Gloucester and subsequently (as Rows was aware) 'higher than ever she was to the most high throne and honour'.[30] It was an amazing transformation. Certainly Anne had made the right choice for herself.

PARTITION OF THE WARWICK INHERITANCE

The principles of the partition were already agreed. Evidently Gloucester was to have everything in the North and Clarence the lands in the Midlands and the South – he was created earl of Warwick and Salisbury. By deduction, Gloucester was to have the marcher lordships in Wales. The division was convenient, since Gloucester already occupied the Neville castles in the North, where the king had allocated him military responsibilities, and Clarence those in the West Midlands. Historians have usually presumed that this was the dukes' preference, properties in Wales, the South, and elsewhere being little more than makeweights. Actually, however, the West Midlands had been more obviously home to the Duchess Isabel, the eldest sister who was entitled to have the first pick, whilst Anne's youth, after Warwick came into his father's Neville inheritance, may have been spent mainly in the North. The partition of the Warwick inheritance may therefore have conformed to the preference of the two ladies, who could indeed have had some input in the result. Surely Isabel did.

Next the estates had to be valued, the detailed division agreed, the legal niceties determined, and the actual transfer of properties carried out. When parliament next met (October 1472), only after Anne had pledged herself to Richard and the partition was agreed in principle, it was petitioned by Anne, Countess of Warwick for livery of her jointure and inheritance, without success. The only copy of her petition is in Gloucester's cartulary: presumably he had a copy taken when the issue was still in the balance.[31] But her plea came too late. The decisions had been made. Discussion of the petition and its progress were presumably halted and certainly came to nothing. Clarence, who was the loser, obstructed implementation of the partition of the inheritances by refusing to give up what he held and perhaps also with violence, comprehensibly since Gloucester was not yet legally married to his new duchess. Hence the stakes were raised. Early in June 1473, Gloucester's agent Sir James Tyrell removed the Countess Anne from sanctuary in Beaulieu Abbey to Gloucester's castle at Middleham. It may well be, as Rows was later to state, that she 'fled to him as her chief refuge', in which case she was to be sadly disappointed.[32] At the time it was reported that the king was to restore her inheritance, so that she could grant it to Gloucester. That King Edward was indeed complicit is suggested because the abbot of Beaulieu had to be released by him from her custody.[33] Gloucester already had a track record of coercing old ladies. Implicit in this action was the king's backing for the countess' restoration to her whole inheritance and its transfer to the duke and duchess of Gloucester, leaving Clarence with almost nothing. Perhaps this threat was sufficient. Perhaps it was the additional penalty of the resumption of Clarence's prized honour of Tutbury (Staffs.) in December 1473[34] – or maybe that was Edward's punishment of Clarence

for non-compliance – that brought Clarence to heel and enabled the implementation of the 1472 agreement. The whole
estate was valued, a partition was agreed – we possess the list of
Gloucester's share – and the legal formalities were concluded
in 1474 and 1475.[35]

There can be no doubt that both parties were greedy. Both
Clarence and Gloucester were acquisitive. Whether their duchesses were also we cannot tell. Isabel and Anne may have been
fully consenting parties: more probably, they were merely the
means that their husbands exploited as they acted nominally
on the ladies' behalf. Possibly, however, Anne played a larger
role, since Rows writes, with reference to the treatment of her
mother the countess, of Anne's 'election' (*electio*) or choice.[36]
Crowland was present in the royal council at which the two
dukes pushed their cases in person.

> So much disputation arose between the brothers and so many
> keen arguments were put forward on either side with the great-
> est acuteness in the presence of the king, sitting in judgement
> in the council-chamber, that all who stood around, even those
> learned in the law, marvelled at the profusion of the arguments
> which the princes produced for their own cases.[37]

It is hard to realise that the elder of the two dukes who debated
so confidently was aged only twenty-three and that Richard,
Duke of Gloucester was not yet twenty!

Clarence wished to hang on to the whole of the Beauchamp
(Warwick), Despenser and Montagu (Salisbury) inheritance in
right of his wife Isabel rather than divide it with his sister-
in-law Anne, the other co-heiress. Having pocketed the
Neville inheritance, to which Isabel had no hereditary claim,
Gloucester exploited his wife Anne to secure additionally her
half-share of the Beauchamp, Despenser and Montagu estates
as well. Both parties were agreed on the need to exclude the

male heir of the Neville estates – Warwick's nephew George, Duke of Bedford, son of his brother John, Marquis Montagu – and also, of course, their mother-in-law, the Countess Anne, rightful possessor of the Beauchamp and Despenser estates. If Clarence wanted to keep more than his duchess' strict entitlement, in line with plenty of precedents, Gloucester also aimed to end up with all the Neville lands and half the rest, together much more than half. It is to Edward's limited credit that the settlement he imposed treated them equally. Not too much praise should be heaped on him, however, for the whole quarrel, the aspiration of both dukes and duchesses, and especially the conclusion, affronted contemporary standards – property rights, rights of inheritance, filial respect, brotherly and sisterly etiquette, sexual and marital morality, chivalry and doubtless much else besides. Certainly Crowland, an informed and disinterested observer, was shocked: recognising that the inheritance properly belonged to the countess, whose rights were disregarded, and 'leaving these wilful men to exercise their will', he abandoned 'further inquiry into this hopeless business'.[38] Just as shocked was Rows, whose prime loyalty was to neither sister, nor their husbands, but the Countess Anne. 'Which good lady had in her days great tribulation for her lord's sake', he wrote. 'In her tribulations she was ever to the great pleasure of God full patient, to the great merit of her own soul and example for all others that were vexed with any adversity'.[39] If oblique, muted and less than explicit in the *Rows Roll* that he may have presented to Queen Anne, he does not spare her in the *History* that he wrote after her death.[40]

Invaluable though Clarence's services were in 1471, they would not have secured him such an enormous recompense – the greatest single act of patronage of any medieval English king – had not his Duchess Isabel been the real heiress. Similarly Edward IV would not have forced Clarence to disgorge so much for Gloucester – and probably, indeed, nothing – had

not the latter married the other heiress Anne. Probably neither
had the option of securing all they sought by a grant by their
brother the king. Once the whole Warwick inheritance was
reserved to them, however, it would have been much easier
– technically much less difficult legally – for them each to
have received their share by royal grant. All that was required
was for Warwick to be attainted as a traitor: no problem there,
as he undoubtedly was a traitor. He could be included in the
act of attainder that was passed against other traitors of the
Lancastrian Readeption. So could his brother John, Marquis
Montagu: that would have terminated the rights as next in
line of John's son George Neville, Duke of Bedford. But this
would have served only part of the purpose of Clarence and
Gloucester and their wives, partly because it would not have
given them everything – not, in particular, the lion's share
that properly belonged to the dowager-countess – and partly,
as Professor Lander long ago showed, because title by royal
grant was less secure.[41] Inheritance was forever. Royal grants
were subject to regular review and revision by acts of resumption. Had the Neville lands been forfeited and granted to the
dukes in their entirety, it would have been at the price that
at some later date, when the dukes themselves were out of
favour or deceased, the crown might take back from them or
their heirs what had been given. In 1473 Clarence had lost
his favourite lordship of Tutbury to such an act, Warwick had
suffered similarly in 1467, and both dukes had ample experience of Edward's changes of mind and consequent revisions
of his patronage.[42] Hence the dukes did not want Warwick
and Montagu attainted. Without these attainders, however, the
two royal dukes had no right to the Neville lands, since Isabel
and Anne had no rights over them. Moreover, some attainders
were necessary, since forfeiture was the basis for instance of
Gloucester's title to the lands of the De Veres, earls of Oxford.
Ironically the only way in which the royal dukes could have

their way was by authority of parliament, by special acts of parliament, which could be revoked by parliament in future just as easily as by acts of resumption. Ultimately they were.[43]

The circle of impossibility was duly squared. Parliament was induced to enable the two dukes to divide equally the whole inheritance, whatever the title and at once. First, in July 1474 Parliament accelerated Isabel and Anne's inheritance of the Montagu/Salisbury, Beauchamp and Despenser lands and the two earldoms by debarring the Countess Anne 'as if the said Countess were now naturally dead'.[44] Despite the blatant injustice to her, there was nobody powerful enough to put her case. The ladies she addressed apparently declined to intervene or did so ineffectively.[45] The Neville inheritance, which primarily interested the Gloucesters, had to wait for its act until the next parliamentary session in 1475. So did the act of attainder against the thirteen unfortunates selected for forfeiture out of all the rebels of 1469–71.

The Neville act was much more controversial, because it conferred by inheritance on the dukes lands to which neither they nor their duchesses had any rights and denied the inheritance to those who were entitled to it and who were, moreover, blameless and undeserving of such penalty. The next heir, George Neville, Duke of Bedford, had done nothing wrong himself, but would have lost out anyway had his uncle Warwick and father Montagu been attainted. No problem there, perhaps, except that through his mother he was a great heir of whom some account had to be taken. More seriously, however, he was not the last of the male line of the Nevilles covered by the entail created by Ralph, Earl of Westmorland (d.1425), because that earl had fathered other sons and indeed the youngest still has a male heir extant today in the marquis of Abergavenny. Next in line after George Neville was Richard Lord Latimer, born in 1469, who had powerful protectors in his guardian Thomas Bourchier, Cardinal-Archbishop of Canterbury and the cardinal's brother the earl of Essex, treasurer of England, both uncles of the king. It was their pressure surely that compelled even the royal dukes to compromise. Parliament was induced to accept the disqualification of George Neville, but not to extinguish the rights in reversion of the other Neville male heirs after his death. The Neville inheritance was therefore assured to the dukes for as long as George Neville had male heirs living. Gloucester's strategy thereafter was to buy out such reversionary rights before they arose. He failed.[46]

If the partition delivered the inheritance to the two couples immediately and made them the wealthiest magnates of their age, it satisfied neither of them. Both had wanted more and both still hoped for more. Certainly Clarence (together presumably with the Duchess Isabel) was aggrieved by what he had lost. Already the father of a legitimate daughter and by the 1475 act of a legitimate son, Clarence had heirs by Isabel's body and most likely hoped that if his rivals failed to secure a valid dispensation, the whole would revert to his own line on the deaths of Anne and Richard. The acts protected the reversionary rights of each line to the other's share by forbidding any alienations out of it. Certainly Gloucester (and perhaps the Duchess Anne) received less than he had wanted. They compiled a wish-list of what they would have liked to have. Several times the settlement was adjusted by further acts of Parliament and a wish list of at least nine items was served on King Edward in 1478. By then, Anne's sister Isabel was dead, probably the result of childbirth, and her brother-in-law Clarence was in prison, shortly to be attainted as a traitor and executed. Ahead of Clarence's conviction and even his trial, and most probably in return for his support in it, Richard was allowed to consolidate Anne's lordships in Wales, to adjust other boundaries, to degrade George Neville from the peerage and to wrest the earldom of Salisbury from Clarence for his own son. If nobody benefited more from Clarence's death than

Gloucester, adjustment to Anne's inheritance was a crucial part of it.[47]

Even so, the arrangement as a whole suffered from several flaws. Parliament agreed to debar George Neville, but not any subsequent male heirs. Gloucester had somehow to keep the boy alive and harmless and to buy out any contingent rights, which was to prove too difficult and which he failed to achieve. Duke Richard did secure the degradation of George Neville from his dukedom and indeed the peerage in 1478, and, following the death of his mother Isabel, Marchioness Montagu in 1476, obtained his wardship and marriage by 1480. He also did succeed in preventing the youth from marrying anyone dangerous. Unfortunately, however, George died without male heirs on 4 May 1483, at which point his rights passed to Richard Lord Latimer. All Gloucester's efforts had failed to wrest Latimer from his guardians and, as a minor, he was not capable of surrendering his heritage to the duke. On 4 May 1483, Anne and Richard's hold on the Neville lands that underpinned their northern hegemony was reduced to a life estate.[48] At that point Anne's home, heritage, and even the college they were jointly founding at Middleham ceased to be a part of their son's inheritance.

Secondly, the countess of Warwick declined to die. At least the Gloucesters provided for her, but that may have been because potentially she was too dangerous and could yet overthrow the 1474–5 settlement. She was confined in the North 'with the greatest strictness', according to Rows soon after 1483, at her daughter Anne's direction; a few years later it was Richard, Rows thought, who had 'locked her up for the duration of his life'.[49] She does not occur in any of our sources for the whole decade 1473–83. Was the Duchess Anne afraid that her mother, whose fiftieth birthday fell only in 1476, might remarry like many other noble dowagers to someone able to insist on livery of at least some of her inheritance and jointure? Actually the

countess, who survived until 1492, outlived both her daughters and both her sons-in-law and, following another dynastic
revolution, was able in 1487, with parliamentary support, to
disinherit the next generation of her grandchildren.[50] Again
the unfortunate lady had no choice.

Thirdly, and crucially for Anne Neville, it depended on the
legality of her marriage to Richard. It was never valid.

THAT DISPENSATION

Duke Richard had taken Anne into his custody by 16 February
1472 when, as we have seen, Clarence reluctantly conceded that
they could marry. At that point, therefore, Anne and Richard
were definitely not married. Apparently they were still unmarried on 18 March. They are first unambiguously recorded as
married on 6 June 1474.[51] Within this twenty-seven-month
timeframe the precise date of their marriage is unresolved.
No wedding is recorded. Since it used to be supposed that
their son Edward was born in 1473, some past historians
located the wedding in 1472. Pauli in 1858 plumped boldly
for 12 July 1472, the third anniversary of Isabel's marriage to
Clarence, but gave no reason and none has been uncovered
since. *The Complete Peerage* agreed.[52] The ceremony has often
been located in the spring of 1472 although, actually, canon law
forbade marriage during Lent. Since actually Edward's birth
was probably some years later,[53] such speculation is unfounded.
That the Warwick inheritance dispute still raged in November
1473 does not mean, as Peter Hammond wrongly supposed,
that Anne and Richard were still unmarried then and that the
marriage took place in 1474.[54] Where was Anne in the interim?
Did she remain in sanctuary throughout, which Crowland's
chronology did not exclude? Did she cohabit with the duke
or reside under his protection, scarcely less morally dubious?
Sheer convenience points to marriage as soon after the March

council as possible. Allowing for the dispensation of 22 April 1472 and its transmission from Rome, it is likely that, as Clarke has deduced, the wedding took place in the late spring or early summer of 1472.[55] Certainly it was concluded ahead of the comprehensive dispensation, since the act of June 1474, which settled Anne's inheritance, made provision for their divorce.[56] For divorce, read nullity. The act tells us that Anne and Richard had not yet secured a papal dispensation adequate to remove the impediments to marriage that was necessary for first cousins and siblings in law. It also foresees that if a dispensation was not granted, they might yet be put asunder. Richard protected himself against that eventuality.

Richard's brother Clarence and Anne's sister Isabel had required a papal dispensation for their marriage because they were closely related several times over. Clarence's mother Cecily, Duchess of York and Isabel's grandfather Richard, Earl of Salisbury were sister and brother. Both of them and Clarence's father Richard were descended from Edward III. They were related once in the second degree and twice in the fourth degree of consanguinity. There was moreover a spiritual tie, because the Duchess Cecily had been George's godmother. The necessary dispensation had required hard negotiation: it was not at all to be taken for granted and indeed Edward IV thought that he had stopped it.[57] Anne and Richard, also first cousins once removed, were also related in the second degree of consanguinity. Moreover, Richard was third cousin of Anne's first husband Edward of Lancaster, who had been Anne's third cousin: two further impediments in the fourth degree to add to those that Clarence and Isabel had to overcome. Numerous though these impediments were, none of them was proscribed by divine law – *Leviticus* – but only by the human laws, which popes routinely dispensed for people of their rank. Yet this was not all, because their siblings George and Isabel had also married. On this

account Anne and Richard were related in the first degree
of affinity. From 1469 to 1472 Anne and Richard must have
been accustomed to regard one another, albeit briefly and
intermittently, as brother and sister. Certainly *Leviticus* barred
marriage to a blood sister and to a wife's sister and such
unions were to be specifically forbidden by statute in 1540.[58]
Canon lawyers were not agreed whether cases covered by
Leviticus or similar to those in *Leviticus* could be dispensed
by the Pope. There could be no certainty what would result
from an application for a full dispensation that removed all
the impediments. Perhaps that was why Richard applied
initially for a dispensation that would enable him to marry
Anne, but which he must have known did not address all the
impediments. Surely here he was cynically manipulating the
rules? Moreover, these impediments were exacerbated by blatant cohabitation when aware that the previous dispensation
was insufficient. Perhaps the proximity of kinship and this
multiplicity of impediments meant that no such dispensation
could be forthcoming. Certainly another dispensation was
absolutely necessary to validate such a union. Apparently no
such dispensation was ever secured. Perhaps none was ever
sought.

The absence of an adequate dispensation is implied by the
1474 act that settled the countess of Warwick's lands on the two
dukes. This is a public document; however, it does not appear
to have become public knowledge. It may well be that it was
Clarence who, having established the details of the 1472 dispensation, secured the provision in the 1474 act that if no valid
marriage was contracted his own children – strictly Isabel's
children – would secure Anne's share of the inheritance on
Duke Richard's death. If so, Clarence was gambling, calculating, perhaps even expecting, that no dispensation would be
forthcoming. If not hitherto aware of the defects in his dispensation, Gloucester certainly knew about them afterwards.

Alternatively, it may have been the duke himself who here was ensuring his continued tenure of Anne's estates. Because officially the countess was dead, both dukes stood to gain from the clauses allowing them to keep the estates for life should their spouses predecease them: in Clarence's case the clause corresponded to the normal convention of courtesy of England because he had a child by Isabel, but in Gloucester's case no child was yet born to them. If he were to retain Anne's lands after her death, it would be at the expense of the Clarences or their heirs.

John Rows states that Richard was the product of 'true matrimony without discontinuance or any defiling in the law'.[59] Richard was thus distinguished, by implication, from Edward V, who had just been dethroned on the grounds that his parents were not properly married and whose father's legitimacy had also been impugned. Rows had no doubts that Anne and Richard were properly married, that Edward of Middleham was their 'son and heir', and 'inheritor to both royal possessions'[60] – that is, to both his parents' possessions. Anne and Richard were accepted as such. Maybe there had been a public wedding of which we know nothing conducted by a priest conned by the papal letter declaratory, unaware of or unconcerned by the extent of their relationship. The undispensed impediments were not publicly known, neither to Rows, nor even (as we shall see) to Crowland. Evidently, Anne and Richard lived together openly as man and wife. None of the critics of Richard III in his own time ever queried his marriage. Its invalidity is a modern discovery.

Yet without a second dispensation, the marriage was never valid. Duke Richard protected himself. The 1474 act provided that if they 'be hereafter divorced' – if the marriage was declared null as though it had never happened – he could nevertheless hang on to Anne's share of the Warwick inheritance for life. Whether he would have provided for and protected Anne, once she was no longer his consort, we cannot know. For Anne, it was a matter of trust. She would have been the principal loser, since it was her inheritance – not Richard's – that the duke was to retain for life. Anne knew Richard better than we do and whether he was worthy of such confidence. Richard had committed himself very little to her to leave the validity of their marriage – its permanence and her security – in doubt. Anne was fully aware of the impediments when she embarked on this contract: how could she be otherwise? The 1474 act indicates that any dispensation sought must have been for the couple already married to be allowed to remain in matrimony. Not to wait for a sufficient dispensation, like not to wait for a partner's divorce today, to jump the gun and to anticipate the legal formalities, is a type of decision with which we are familiar nowadays. Contemporary examples are not uncommon. The famous match that unified modern Spain in 1469 between Ferdinand of Aragon and Isabella of Castile involved second cousins: originally justified by a forged dispensation, it was not validated by a proper one until 1471. Isabella's rival Juana La Betraneja was married to her cousin King Alfonso of Portugal ahead of a dispensation that never arrived.[61] Anticipating dispensations was not unusual amongst royalty: not to seek a valid one at all, however, was wholly exceptional.

There are four alternative explanations of what happened next. The first option, that an adequate dispensation was indeed secured, can be discounted by evidence from 1485.[62] Moreover, Clarke failed to find a second dispensation for Anne and Richard in the penitentiary registers. The second option, that Anne and Richard were indeed divorced, obviously did not happen: Anne died as Richard's queen. To continue married after a further dispensation was refused, which was the third possibility, was forbidden as sinful by the Church, which was expected to take action to separate such couples after the verdict. Since Anne and Richard were not forcibly separated, it seems unlikely that their dispensation was declined. Yet surely a sufficient dispensation was never obtained, for in 1485, Crowland unwittingly reported, Richard thought a divorce easily attainable – thought the marriage easily declared invalid.[62] Not to seek an adequate dispensation at all, the fourth possibility and the one argued here, was surely very different.

Originally, no doubt, Anne and Richard meant to have their union ratified. Hence the initial petition that resulted in the 1472 dispensation. The couple had not then consulted their lawyers. Yet, afterwards, Anne and Richard perhaps, but far more probably Richard by himself, decided not to remedy the defects to a valid marriage and to continue living together as husband and wife without proceeding with the legal niceties. There is no evidence of the pangs of conscience that affected others who sought absolution from the Pope. Just possibly, a dispensation was sought but not pursued. If an application to the papacy had ever been made, a verdict – presumably unfavourable – must have been declared well before 1485 when Richard apparently considered setting Anne aside. Rather than risk divorce, Richard decided not to seek a dispensation that would probably have been denied. Their invalid union denied Anne the security to which she was surely entitled. Surely she was the victim here? If she was not Richard's spouse, Anne had no right to dower. Apparently she received no jointure. Normally she could have kept her own inheritance, but the 1474 act had assured it to Richard for life. Probably Anne did not know of that. The arrangement also denied legitimacy to their children. Surely Richard must have been concerned as he brazened it out, had Anne crowned as queen and their son invested as prince of Wales? Later, in Anne's last months, the illicit nature of their relationship and her dubious status caused her great anxiety. By then, at least, she knew her whole married life to be a lie. Yet it is hard to see how it could ever have turned out all right. Without a valid marriage, their offspring were bound to be illegitimate and unable to inherit, as any rival claimants – such as her sister's children – were certain to stress when the appropriate opportunity arose. Providing, that is, they knew: dispensations are seldom invoked in inheritance cases. As time passed and their marriage was accepted at face value, Anne and Richard may have hoped to get away with it. It was on this basis that Richard forged his political future.

CHAPTER FIVE

Her Husband's Wife
1475–83

WHAT ARE DUCHESSES FOR?

The Apostle Paul wrote that marriage was a means of carnal satisfaction without sin. Sex was certainly expected of their marriage by the duke and duchess and was duly delivered. Children were desired and indeed required. Wives were expected to have children, preferably sons. Though hardly essential to run the ducal household, for she had a host of officers and humbler servants to undertake such domestic tasks, and though often apart, the Duchess Anne was also her duke's companion, probably more equal in practice than in the formal record, and the source of his landed wealth and political power.

THE GLOUCESTERS' CHILDREN

The duke and duchess wanted children, above all a male heir. Together they achieved it. Young though she was, Anne cannot have been a virgin when she remarried. Her first union had to be consummated.[1] Whether she was sexually mature in 1470 we cannot tell. Her new husband, at twenty somewhat the older, was probably already sexually active.

In terms of offspring, it was not a very productive marriage. Anne and Richard had to wait to have children. Presumably they started sleeping together when they married, perhaps in 1472, maybe in 1473, certainly by 1474. By that time, Richard was twenty-two years of age and Anne was eighteen. Only one child is known to have been born to the marriage, a son, Edward. How joyful they must have been when he was born! No doubt he was named after his uncle Edward IV, who may have been his godfather, though inevitably absent from the christening. John Rows tells us that he was born at Middleham 'in the north country',[2] far away from Warwick, where Rows lived, or Tewkesbury. Hence neither Rows himself nor the Tewkesbury chronicler could reveal precisely when Edward of Middleham was born. It seems improbable that it was as early as 1473, as is usually supposed, since Rows, admittedly no expert where children were concerned, said the boy was about seven years old in 1483; Vergil, who did not see him, thought him nine.[3] If seven, he was born about 1476–7; if nine, perhaps as early as 1474. Surviving accounts for the lordship of Middleham do not even hint at any celebrations there in the financial year 1473–4.[4] The Tewkesbury chronicler says that Edward was born at Middleham in 1476 – an old-style year that continued until 25 March 1477, only shortly before the first explicit mention of him on 10 April 1477, when he was included with his parents in those to be prayed for in a chantry. Edward was the Gloucesters' 'first begotten son' on 1 July 1477.[5] No other child was mentioned in the licence, so at that point Edward was not merely their eldest son, but almost certainly their only child. As early as 1 July 1477 he was described as the Gloucesters' 'first begotten son the Earl of Salisbury' – properly Clarence's title – seven months before this firstborn (*primo-genitus*) son was formally created earl of Salisbury by Edward IV.[6] 'First begotten' is not necessarily indicative that there was also a last born or indeed any another offspring. Anne's father

Warwick had also been earl of Salisbury and so too had been Clarence in Isabel's right. It demonstrates the boy's significance to his parents, of which he was heir: his elevation to the peerage was especially gratifying to them. Although one sixteenth-century version of the Tewkesbury chronicle filled the blank left for the boy with the name George – a name perhaps pointing to Archbishop Neville, who died in 1476, or Clarence, who died in 1478, as godfather – it is much more likely that this was a simple error.[7] If born before Edward of Middleham, any such son had died by 1477; if afterwards, by 1483. Neither Rows nor the Tewkesbury chronicler mention any other child, but, living so far from the parents, they were unlikely to know of any miscarriages, stillbirths or children who had died in infancy.

Since there is no accurate record of Edward's birth, we know nothing of the rejoicing, the baptism, or the churching that followed – surely the highest points of his mother's short married life? That he was called Edward suggests forcibly that his godfather was the king, but that cannot be confirmed either. Presumably Anne was responsible for Edward's upbringing just as the Countess Anne had been for her own. As was customary at this time, the duchess did not suckle her son herself, but deputed that chore instead to a woman who had recently had her own baby. His wet-nurse was Isabel Burgh, the wife of Henry Burgh, who was rewarded with annuities by the duke.[8] Perhaps in succession, by 1480 Edward was in the care of Anne Idley, 'mistress of our [ducal] nursery'.[9] Mistress Idley was the widow of Peter Idley, an Oxfordshire squire and the educationalist who wrote *Instructions to his Son*. She may therefore have been known to have an interest in education.[10]

Our only evidence suggests that Anne was pregnant only once – or had only one live birth – during approximately twelve years of marriage. Probably she had to wait five years, until 1477, to produce a son. That was all. One son was

Anne Neville

enough, provided Edward of Middleham survived. Anne had performed the minimum to be expected of a wife, a duchess or a queen. But she never had another baby. Perhaps it was already likely by 1483, when she was only twenty-seven, that there would be no more children. History repeated itself: her mother's history. Yet Anne and Richard continued to try. Under 1485, Crowland reports that Richard then spurned his consort's bed.[11] The implication is that hitherto he had continued resorting to it and was known to have done so. Crowland was in a position to know. Lords and ladies, let alone kings and queens, did not normally share the same bed, nor the same chamber, nor even same household. Sharing the same bed was therefore a conscious decision made solely for the purposes of procreation – for sexual intercourse. It was also a public decision, obvious to the chamber staff of both households. The king could be observed commuting. Highly visible movement of the king from his apartments to those of the queen was required for intercourse to take place. Christmas 1484, like Christmas 1483, was celebrated at Westminster, where Crowland worked. Crowland knew the location of the apartments of both the king and the queen:[12] he or his colleagues were well-placed to monitor the king's sleeping (and therefore) marital sexual arrangements. We can therefore be confident that King Richard and Queen Anne continued trying to reproduce until 1485.

Edward of Middleham was an asset whether he was earl of Salisbury or prince of Wales. Had he survived, he was destined first to be duke of Gloucester and latterly King Edward VI, to continue the family line, and immeasurably to strengthen his parents' hold on and management of their estates. Whether he was seven years old in 1483 or older, it was not too early for his parents to be thinking of his marriage. Sir Thomas More reports agreement in principle for his marriage to a daughter of Henry, Duke of Buckingham (d. 1483), the wealthiest other magnate of the blood royal:[13] although within the prohibited degrees and no heiress, she was certainly eligible. As More tells it, moreover, it was a cement to the alliance that made Richard king. His account is unsubstantiated and the match anyway was soon outdated by Buckingham's rebellion. The boy's marriage became instead a factor in his father's diplomacy.

RICHARD'S BASTARDS

The relationship of Anne and Richard was certainly a sexual one. However, it was not exclusive, for Edward was not Richard's only child. He had at least two bastards and perhaps three. Whilst this is well known, Richard's modern supporters have argued that they were oats sown in the bachelor years before his marriage and are not evidence of infidelity to Anne.[14] That is a rather anachronistic line to take, applying modern morality (but not any longer, perhaps, contemporary morality) to a past period that had different standards. Women, married or unmarried, were expected to be chaste. For men, that was not so. There was a double standard. Numerous aristocrats had bastards, who were often publicly acknowledged: John of Gaunt's Beaufort by-blows, the bastards of Clarence and Fauconberg, are well known. There was not the stigma attached to it of later ages. Whilst one of Richard's bastards may predate his marriage, another probably did not. Anne, doubtless often separated from her husband, was not his sole source of sexual satisfaction.

Peter Hammond carefully examined the attribution of one Richard of Eastwell in Kent and concluded, almost certainly correctly, that Duke Richard was not his father.[15] Once king, however, Richard did acknowledge two bastards, a daughter Katherine Plantagenet and a son – 'the lord bastard' of his signet letter book – John of Pontefract, whom Richard knighted at York in 1483.[16]

On 28 February 1484 Richard negotiated Katherine's betrothal as second wife to the thirty-year-old widower William Herbert, Earl of Huntingdon. She had died by 1487. Katherine must indeed have been 'in her young age' as one pedigree puts it, since her father King Richard was only thirty. There were clauses in the contract requiring the bridegroom to settle jointure on her and her father to settle lands on them jointly. The wedding was to be concluded by Michaelmas (29 September), before which the earl was to make a settlement on them both jointly and Richard was to do likewise.[17] They were married before May, but not apparently by 3 April 1484, when Richard had indeed granted them revenues worth £152 a year.[18] Presumably lands could only be conveyed to Katherine after she had reached the female age of majority – fourteen. If that deduction is correct and Katherine was already fourteen in 1484, she was the product of a bachelor liaison dating from before Richard's wooing, betrothal or marriage to Anne. Most probably Katherine was born before Richard went into exile in 1470 – perhaps even some years earlier when Richard was in his mid-teens. Katherine is tangible evidence that Richard commenced his sex life early, though not unduly precociously. Tantalisingly, there is another Katherine, to whom the duke was paying an annuity of £5 from his East Anglian estates in 1476, but granted at least one financial year earlier.[19] She was Katherine Haute, presumably the Katherine wife of Jacques Haute, a kinsman of the queen, whose relationship with Richard could antedate her marriage. Such an annuity indicates services separate from any husband which, with the coincidence of forename, prompted Rosemary Horrox in 1989 and the present author, for lack of alternatives, to suggest that Katherine Haute may be the mistress by whom Richard had Katherine Plantagenet.[20] The name intrigues, since it implies a particularly close connection between Richard and the family of Edward's Wydeville queen during Edward IV's first reign.

The marriage indicates simultaneously Richard's awareness of his daughter, that he cared enough for her to provide for her, and her political utility to him as king.

The other known bastard, John of Pontefract, was presumably born at Pontefract, perhaps to a local girl. John's birth could also antedate Richard's exile in 1470. Assuming that he was born where he was conceived, he could have resulted from a liaison in 1465–8 when Richard was in the household of Warwick, who as chief steward of the duchy of Lancaster in the North and constable of Pontefract had the use of the great castle. Apart from Richard's youth, this appears unlikely, both because Warwick can never be shown to have been at Pontefract and because so early a birth would have made John a teenager mature enough in Richard's reign to have been used much more extensively than he was. Only after Prince Edward's demise does John crop up in records: as 'the Lord Bastard' escorted to and from Calais by Robert Brackenbury late in 1484. In March 1485, just a few days before Queen Anne's death, a payment was made for his clothing and he was appointed titular captain of Calais.[21] Perhaps Anne would have objected to such elevation earlier? From 1471 Duke Richard had also been chief steward of the northern duchy and constable of Pontefract and certainly visited it. He was there on 27 April 1473, moved there from Middleham in October, and was there between 1 March and 7 May 1474.[22] Possibly significantly, he was at Pontefract on 1 March 1474 when he granted his beloved gentlewoman Alice Burgh (*dilecte nobis Alesie Burgh generose sibi*) 'for certain special causes and considerations' an annuity for life from Middleham: a highly unusual event, especially as the sum, £20, was also substantial.[23] Alice was a lady most probably attendant on the Duchess Anne – a common source of mistresses for princes! Most likely she was a cadet of the Burghs of Knaresborough, a modest family of Yorkshire gentry. Was Alice Burgh, perhaps, Richard's mistress and the mother of John of Pontefract? The annuity was still due from Middleham in January 1485, when she was also drawing another 20 marks from Warwickshire,[24] evidence of further services that Richard evidently valued highly. Henry Burgh and his wife Isabel, surely kinswomen, were also feed (20 marks) from Middleham during Richard's reign. Isabel had been nurse to Prince Edward.[25] Was she the sister-in-law of Alice, perhaps selected because of Alice? There are too many occurrences of both forenames in grants and payments for Isabel and Alice to be identical. This is regrettable: how sad that the titillating possibility that Richard's mistress was wet-nurse to his legitimate son cannot apply. That John of Pontefract first appears in July 1483 at York is evidence perhaps that he was brought up in Yorkshire. However that may be, it appears much more likely that John was the product of a sexual liaison *after* Richard's marriage: evidence not necessarily that Richard was dissatisfied with his wife, sexually or otherwise, but that their relationship was not exclusive.

We know of Richard's bastards because he acknowledged them when he became king – more than that, he treated them with distinction, finding Katherine an earl for a husband and raising John to princely office. Whilst enticed by grants worth 1,000 marks a year (£666 13s 4d),[26] Huntingdon clearly did not feel disparaged by the bend sinister, but saw instead advantages, influence and favour at court in consequence. Richard also was not ashamed of his bastards. We cannot tell whether he was as blatant before his accession – could he have been so damnatory about his brother's peccadilloes had his own been known? – but if he was, one might expect it to be uncomfortable or even painful for his spouse. Here, however, our twenty-first-century reactions may mislead. Anne had of course to accept any by-blows who antedated their own relationship. We cannot know when she first learnt of their existence – at the latest when her husband the king brought

John and Katherine into public view. Anne's age observed a double standard, which permitted, condoned and perhaps even expected husbands to take sexual solace outside marriage, which wives were denied. Richard's brother Edward IV was a notorious practitioner.

If many magnates had bastards,[27] most of them were ungenerously treated. They were, after all, illegitimate. Anne's father Warwick had been exceptional in marrying his bastard daughter to the heir of a substantial gentry family, and in providing an attractive endowment.[28] That, surely, was the most that Katherine and John could have expected, had their father not become king. His accession was a boon that they did not live long enough to enjoy.

MARRIED LIFE

John Rows states that Richard and Anne were 'unhappily married', but these two words cannot be accepted as a definitive verdict on their married life. Not only is his comment over-brief, but he was ill placed to witness almost all of it and was writing in the later Latin version,[29] after Anne's final months that did deserve the title unhappy, her death, and possibly Richard's own fall. As consort of Richard, Duke of Gloucester, Anne should have accompanied him to public functions – ceremonial state occasions – and presided over his household. In reality she cannot be shown to have done any of these things. She was not mentioned in the heraldic accounts of the receptions of the Burgundian Lord Gruthuyse at Windsor and Westminster in 1472, at the creation of the queen's son as marquis of Dorset at Westminster in 1475, at the reburial of the king's father at Fotheringhay in 1476, at the marriage of the king's second son at Westminster in 1478, or at the funeral of Princess Mary at Windsor in 1482, all but the last attended by her husband. Heralds were not much interested in ladies, but surely she should have been there? Actually it is impossible to write a satisfactory account of Anne's married life.

Scarcely any relevant records survive between 1472 – or whenever matrimony commenced – and 1483. In some respects, this can be no great surprise. This was after all an era in which a married lady's property was regarded as her husband's and in which actions recorded as his may actually have been hers. That 'married women were often regarded as infants before the law' means 'that wives are often invisible in written records'.[30] By remarrying, Anne had surrendered the momentary autonomy that she had so briefly enjoyed as *femme sole*. We have already seen how little is known of the thirty-five-year marriage of her mother the Countess Anne. Moreover, a wife's sphere, even a wife who was a duchess, was domestic and not the stuff of public records, which do reveal some political actions of the duke. Not that even Richard occurs in such sources as frequently as many other magnates and princes did. Scarcely any private records survive of their affairs: a mere handful of accounts of receivers of estates in eastern England, one year's worth of accounts of one of their northern lordships, a cartulary of title deeds, a dozen or so miscellaneous deeds preserved by the recipients, and the impression of the ducal couple on other record-keeping bodies, such as the town council and Corpus Christi Guild at York, Durham cathedral priory, and bishops' registers. In total, it is not an impressive archive. Moreover, it relates almost entirely to Richard, scarcely at all to Anne.

Yet Anne's absence is hard to explain in purely archival terms. Amongst fifty references to the duke in the house books of the city of York, not a single one refers to her. Her intercession was not sought – perhaps it was not worth seeking? If so, that suggests that she did not count – that Anne lacked even the normal influence that fifteenth-century ladies had with their husbands. That is a big supposition to base on the absence of evidence.

But Richard was an egotist and no respecter of women: if Anne exercised no political influence on her husband it may not have been because she was especially ineffective.

Besides, Anne possessed no property of her own. Gloucester settled no jointure on her. Anne should have had some lands, of course. She was rightly heiress to half her father's Montagu/Salisbury lands. Actually, half her parents' whole estate had been secured in her right. It is evident, however, that Richard treated her lands as his own. He features at Middleham as 'lord' (*dominus*).[31] The Neville lands were the foundation of the duke's power in the North, which he extended in a highly personal way, exchanging properties that Anne had inherited when appropriate for others that complemented his other holdings better. Such transactions were in his name alone.[32] The chantries and colleges which they founded for both their souls were titled typically as the duke of Gloucester's, never the duchess's.[33] It was the duke's instructions that were obeyed both at Middleham and on the estates in eastern England, some of which – like Kirtling in Cambridgeshire – were properly Anne's.[34]

That does not mean either that Anne was ungenerously treated or unhappy. Richard need not have stinted on the house-keeping and indeed Anne seems to have attired herself in the most luxurious materials. Duke and duchess appear to have been together in London on 3–6 December 1476, when Gloucester issued a number of signet warrants for payment to the receiver of his East Anglian lands. Totalling £296, including some acquisitions from 1475, his purchases included tapestry (arras-work), velvet and other cloth, silks and furs, most of them purchased for his own use, but some for 'the most dear consort of the lord duke'. A tailor, John Lee, supplied her with cloth costing £10 18s 4d; a skinner, Thomas Cole, certain furs costing £19 7s 11d; and a mercer, John Knott, silk cloth and other things costing £20 12s 11d. The sum total, £50 9s

1d, was a considerable sum and indicates both bulk purchases
and luxuries.[35] Although the duke and duchess used the same
tradesmen and were paid from the same source, it is interesting
that their orders were separate – evidence perhaps that she (or
her purveyor) operated independently to meet her specific
needs and an indication that her allowance was not expected
to cover everything. That, of course, is to read a lot into very
little, regrettably almost all the direct evidence that we possess.
Although unrecorded, Anne probably accompanied Richard
on most of his visits to London, for parliamentary sessions and
on other occasions, at least once a year, but probably more
often. If often enough at court, Richard (and hence Anne) was
normally absent. Neither were courtiers.

For convenience, Anne's household surely was supported,
as others were, by estate revenues on which her officers could
draw. It is just that we do not know their identity or value.
Similarly, she must have had her own upper household of
chamberlain, chaplains and damsels in attendance on her,
and similarly all the other service departments found in any
other noble household. Anne certainly was not always in her
husband's household, for instance when he was campaigning
on the borders, invading France in 1475 and in Scotland in
1481–3, and doubtless at other times. She therefore required
her own establishment to cater for her needs when separated
from the duke. That in 1475–6 the duke's councillors conveyed
to the city of York a message from the duchess suggests, as one
would expect, that she deputised for him in his absence,[36] in
this instance probably when Gloucester was on campaign in
France.

Actually, we scarcely ever know for sure where the Duchess
Anne was. Often she must have been with her husband, and
his fragmentary itinerary is therefore a guide to her own. In
1483 the historian Mancini said that he lived mainly on the
Gloucester estates – for which, read his northern estates – and

certainly Richard is often reported in Yorkshire or in the West
March. He had major governmental and military responsibilities in the region and crops up regularly in the minutes of the
city council of York and in the correspondence of the Plumpton
family of Knaresborough. Most commonly Gloucester was at
Middleham, where their son was born. Never is the duke
recorded at Barnard Castle, although he certainly visited it and
commissioned works at the castle, and infrequently at Sheriff
Hutton or Penrith. Every year he spent some time in London.
There is no direct evidence after 1472 that the ducal couple
visited Warwick, Tewkesbury or Cardiff, all properties that had
earlier been regarded as Anne's home, although such visits are
implied by Gloucester's presence at Swansea in 1479.[37]

That Anne had her own staff, that she wanted to promote
them, and that she solicited and otherwise related to institu-
tions and other potential patrons independently of her husband,
as one would expect, is indicated by only one fragment of
evidence. Anne did seek for one of her clerks the vicarage of
Bossall, in the gift of Durham cathedral priory. Vicarages, which
vicars had to serve themselves, were not the most attractive or
prestigious of livings. We do not possess Anne's letter, but the
reply of Prior Richard Bell dated 19 March 1477, which hints
at an earlier supplication, perhaps one more general rather than
specific to Bossall, which may not then have been vacant. The
letter Bell was answering was borne to him by Anne's servant
Nicholas Hedlam. Again, it is not quite clear whether Hedlam
was the intended beneficiary, or whether Anne sought the right
to present whoever she chose. If the former, we may presume
that Hedlam himself told her of the vacancy, aspired to be vicar,
and solicited her intercession, in which case she took the initiative. However, she was too late – the living had been filled. 'For
the which matter', begged the prior, 'I will beseech your good
grace to take no displeasure, for I have a little overseen myself
in my simpleness for my lack of remembrance', presumably

of an earlier letter. This was more than an elegantly phrased excuse, for he promised amends. There were problems yet to be resolved relating to his choice. 'Nevertheless your good lady-ship shall be pleased either with it or with another as good', he writes, 'when it shall fall in our gift'. The duchess might have to wait, but the patronage of 'my full singular and gracious good lady' – and, by extension her husband – was something that Prior Bell was anxious not to lose.[38] Almost certainly it was on their recommendation that Bell was promoted bishop of Carlisle in 1478.[39]

ANNE'S PIETY

One final area offering some glimmerings of light is Anne's religion. Rows did not know Anne well enough to report on the quality of her religious faith and we know little more about it. Life in aristocratic households was constructed around Christian observance, with services timetabled every day and diet conditioned by the Christian calendar, its feasts, fasts and saints' days. The impressive college of priests, chaplains and choristers that was established in the chapel of Barnard Castle may indicate just how elaborate and just how choral were services in their household chapel.[40] Anne, like every other lady, gave offerings as appropriate. In 1477, moreover, the duchess and her husband joined the guild of Corpus Christi at York, albeit regrettably as 'the Duke of Gloucester and Lady *Elizabeth* his wife'. This was a fraternity or sisterhood that brought together all of northern high society and which moreover required its members, even peers, to process.[41] In 1476 it was Anne alone, this time without her husband, who was admitted to the sisterhood of Durham cathedral priory, whose monks thereby bound themselves to intercede for her good estate in life and her soul after death.[42] Dedicated to St Cuthbert, the premier northern saint, and indeed his shrine,

Durham cathedral housed the tombs of several of her Neville ancestors – there remains a splendid Neville screen – and was the mother church for the Warwick lordship of Barnard Castle. We do not possess the book of hours that she employed or any of her other books, except for Mechhild of Hackborn's *Book of Ghostly Grace*; even then the signature Anne Warwick, although associated with Richard's, may relate to her mother the Countess Anne. Much more can be inferred from his books about her husband Duke Richard, although even in his case a study of his religious life is not really feasible.[43]

The ducal couple were also notable benefactors of the Church, founders of religious establishments, and surely Anne played a role in this. She was certainly coupled with the duke; perhaps sometimes she was the first mover. The first in time was a chantry at the college of St Margaret and St Bernard at Cambridge, commonly called Queens' College, Cambridge, in 1477. Some of Richard's senior clerics were Cambridge graduates, but the duke of course was not. He had no earlier association with the college. Anne and Richard granted the college his advowson (right of presentation) of Fulmer in Cambridgeshire, forfeited by the De Vere earls of Oxford, in return for prayers for the souls of the earl and countess of Oxford and for the good estate of the king and queen, the duke and duchess of Gloucester, and their son Edward. Prayers were also reserved for those who fell at the duke's side at the battle of Barnet.[44] Thus far it sounds like an initiative of the duke and duchess in their own interests. That the patron was a queen – and that Anne herself patronised it also when she was queen – suggests that Anne's role may have been important. On the other hand, Anne was mentioned only once – as beneficiary – and there was clearly a political dimension to the benefaction. That the Gloucesters patronised the queen's foundation needs to be coupled with his donation in 1482 of two further advowsons of Olney (Bucks.) and Simonburn (Co.

Durham) to Edward IV's pet project at St George's Chapel, Windsor.[45] Moreover, such livings, which the colleges could appropriate, were worth much more to them than the duke and duchess, for whom the only cost was a loss of future appointments for their clerics. It is a complex episode, but it is one in which Anne may also have played a part.

That the duke and duchess, still in their early twenties, were thinking of their souls is shown by the two colleges that they were planning in February 1478. The first and largest within their castle at Barnard Castle was for a dean, twelve chaplains, ten clerks, six choristers and a clerk. The second, in Middleham parish church, was half that size: for a dean, six chaplains, four clerks, 6 choristers and the parish priest. Barnard Castle was endowed with lands to the value of 400 marks (£266 13s 4d) and Middleham to the tune of 200 marks (£133 6s 8d), which like Fulmer rectory was property late of the De Vere earls of Oxford.[46] Perhaps the services began at once, for the churches were already there, but the collegiate buildings had not proceeded very far by Richard's death. The endowments were retrieved by John, Earl of Oxford after 1485, rendering the foundations ultimately abortive. Apart from advancing the Gloucesters' souls and enhancing their household liturgy, these colleges may also have been intended as mausolea to replace those at Warwick and Tewkesbury allotted to Clarence although, it seems, Edward of Middleham may have been interred at Sheriff Hutton. Finally they augmented most prestigiously Anne's family seats and her Neville connection: it was her traditions that were celebrated here, surely with her approval if not primarily at her initiative. As always, however, we cannot really tell.

CHAPTER SIX

Her King's Consort
1483–5

BECOMING QUEEN

Anne, Duchess of Gloucester played no direct role in Duke Richard's usurpation of the crown. After a false alarm reported at York, Edward IV had died on 9 April 1483, and the coronation of his son and successor, the boy king Edward V, was scheduled for 4 May. The coronation was notified to King's Lynn (via Ludlow) on 16 April[1] and to Richard, Duke of Gloucester directly by the royal council, but surely somewhat earlier. The duke, perhaps accompanied by his duchess, may have held a memorial service for the old king and taken oaths of allegiance to the new one in York Minster before he proceeded southwards. On 30 April/1 May he met up with the king and his entourage, seized the young king (his first coup d'état), and on 4 May escorted the king into London, where he himself was appointed Lord Protector by the council. The coronation was postponed. The Duchess Anne had not accompanied him. Presumably she remained in the North: a surprising decision, since she surely wished to attend – and as the king's aunt was surely wanted at – the coronation on 4 May. Unless, of course, she foresaw – or, more probably, Richard knew – that the coronation would not happen and that events might materialise in which her participation was not desirable and her safety could not be guaranteed. Now Lord Protector, Gloucester was in complete control – and Queen Elizabeth, in sanctuary, completely sidelined – before the Duchess Anne arrived in London on 5 June,[2] in plenty of time for the new date set for King Edward V's coronation. Probably she and Richard resided at the Duchess Cecily's London house at Baynards Castle. Their son Edward, Earl of Salisbury was left in the North. The Duchess Anne was in London on 13 June, but not personally present at the council in the Tower, where Lord Hastings was arrested and executed (Richard's second coup), and also on 16 June, when Edward IV's younger son Richard, Duke of York was removed from sanctuary to join his brother Edward V in the Tower. Probably Anne did not attend Dr Ralph Shaa's notorious sermon at St Paul's Cross on 20 June, in which he argued that Edward IV's children were illegitimate because their parents had not been properly married and that Edward V should not therefore reign. Perhaps she was present at Baynards Castle on 25 June when her husband was offered and accepted the crown and Edward V ceased to be king. Whether she knew what was happening, shared in the planning and approved the result, actively or tacitly, we cannot know. The alarm and shock that Shakespeare portrays is fiction. Anne can never have been in company with Queen Elizabeth and Princess Elizabeth, who were immured in sanctuary. Yet it was Anne's northerners who overawed London at the crucial time, who were to crush those who rebelled against Richard, and to whom Richard turned to rule the recalcitrant South. When the duke became King Richard III on 26 June, Anne Neville did become his queen. They were crowned together on 6 July and Anne shared most of his reign. She did not live to witness the collapse of their regime.

For a king to be already married at his accession was highly unusual: Edward I was the last instance, although Henry IV had been a widower and the Black Prince, though married, had predeceased his father. Moreover, English kings normally selected foreign princesses as their queens. Anne was only the third since the Norman Conquest to be of English birth. English noblemen naturally picked from amongst their peers. Royal princes, who were not expected to become kings, followed the example of the nobility, wedding heiresses who could bring them great estates and hence great power. Thus John Lackland was married first to the Gloucester heiress Isabella, whom he set aside for a foreign princess, and Henry Bolingbroke wed the Bohun co-heiress Mary, who died before he acceded and was replaced by a foreign queen. Richard, Duke of Gloucester, as we have seen, married Anne Neville, an even greater heiress. Leaving aside John's brief and chronologically distant consort, there had been no English queen for two centuries except Edward IV's consort Elizabeth Grey (née Wydeville).

To marry clandestinely, on impulse and for love, affronted contemporary values. For a reigning king to act thus was scandalous. Edward's choice moreover was deplored for many reasons: Elizabeth, as an Englishwoman, was his subject; she was a lady of genteel origins rather than royal or even noble blood; she was a widow who had been married before and not the virgin that was traditionally expected; and she brought with her an extensive family of her own – a pack of sons, brothers, sisters and cousins – and hence political complications that conventionally lonely foreign princesses did not. Of course it was Edward who compounded all this by his over-generosity to them all, to the great displeasure especially of Anne's father Warwick, and it was his enemy, Warwick again, who attributed the king's infatuation to Wydeville sorcery.[3] Anne and Richard, of course, were already married before she became queen: it would have been scandalous for him to set her aside as King John had done to his consort. Anne, moreover, was of both noble and royal blood, well able to trace her descent repeatedly

– albeit remotely – from King Edward III. Yet she too was already an English subject, had a former husband – admittedly a royal prince – and was no virgin (but also no mother) when she married Richard. A virgin was desired, and indeed Anne's repeated depiction with blonde hair loosed portrays her as virgins and queens were normally painted.[4] Actually, the tradition that queens were virgins and not widows was (like many traditions) of recent creation, breached most recently by Henry IV's queen and rejected by no less than the Black Prince. Had Richard III been unmarried in 1483, he would probably have looked abroad for his queen. Although there was no choice, one can imagine that Anne was not regarded everywhere as ideal queen-material. She had been brought up of course with such ambitions in mind and had a decade of experience as a royal duchess behind her. Moreover, she had done her duty by bearing Richard a son and heir. If any criticisms were thought or murmured, however, they have not been passed down to us and were submerged by the strident opposition and condemnations of King Richard.

Coronations did not make kings or queens. Consecration and anointing did, however, confer a sacral quality and divine approval on them and hence did strengthen and confirm their positions. Evidently Richard wanted that reinforcement as soon as possible, setting the date for the coronation for 6 July, only ten days after his accession. Those in London for Edward V's abortive coronation and parliament or in Richard's northern army remained in attendance. Whilst much that was prepared for Edward V's coronation remained usable, for example the decorations for Westminster Abbey, this clearly was not true of the robes of either the adult king, adult queen, nor the queen's ladies in waiting. Moreover, this was the first double coronation since 1308 and the first occasion that the special provisions for a double coronation set down in the Royal Book (*Liber Regalis*) were brought into operation.[5] Evidently the tailors, silkwomen and other artisans had to work flat out. It was a tall order, yet the great wardrobe, abbey and other offices appear to have coped, and no hitches are recorded. Primarily, of course, it was the king's coronation: he took precedence throughout over his consort, whose ceremonial was in a lesser key.

The great wardrobe received its orders on 27 June, but our first evidence of Anne's direct involvement comes on Thursday 3 July, when king and queen apparently exchanged gifts. Richard gave Anne four yards of purple cloth of gold – both imperial and royal – and twenty more yards of the same wrought with garters, plus seven yards of purple velvet. Anne responded with twenty yards of purple velvet adorned with garters and roses.[6] Next day, Friday 4 July, they moved to the royal apartments in the Tower, where the coronation ceremonial traditionally began. On Saturday 5 July, the vigil of the coronation began with Richard's dubbing of forty-nine knights of the bath, who then served dinner – fish – to the monarchs, who solemnly proceeded through the City to Westminster in the afternoon. After the king and his entourage there followed those of Queen Anne. The way was headed by two of Anne's gentlemen ushers, William Joseph and John Vavasour, as representatives of her two duchies of Aquitaine and Normandy. Next came the queen's chamberlain and the queen herself traditionally attired. As befitted the more usual virgin, she wore her fair hair loose over her shoulders, and a gold circlet adorned with pearls and precious stones. She wore white cloth of gold, with a cloak and train furred with ermine and trimmed with lace, gold thread and tassels. Given the July date, one can only hope that the weather was mild! She did not ride, but was seated on a litter borne by two palfreys, led by Richard Lord Grey of Powis, attended by Thomas Hopton, gentleman of her chair, and flanked by twelve knights. Borne by palfreys trapped in white damask, the litter itself was of white damask and white cloth of gold garnished with ribbon, fringed with gold and bells, and topped by an imperial canopy of gilded staves with bells. Next came her five henchmen, her riding horse led by the yeoman of her horse William Danyell, four carriages containing twelve great ladies, and seven ladies of the queen's chamber. Pausing only at St Paul's Cross to receive 500 marks in gift from the City, she proceeded to Westminster Hall for a light snack (void) of wine and spices. Supper was taken in the great chamber of Westminster Palace.

Sunday 6 July, coronation day, saw the procession assemble at 7a.m. in Westminster Hall. Cardinal Bourchier, Abbot Eastney, the coronation regalia, knights of the bath, nobility, mayor of London and other dignitaries preceded the king into Westminster Abbey. Queen Anne followed. Anne was clad in a smock of lawn, a kirtle laced with seventy annulets beneath a royal surcoat and a mantle, and a train of crimson velvet secured by heavy silk and gold laces. Again she was bare headed, her hair loose over her shoulders and kept in place with a bejewelled circlet of gold. She was preceded by her chamberlain, attended by Margaret, Countess of Richmond, who perhaps bore her train, flanked by Bishops Goldwell and Courtenay, and followed by two duchesses, her ladies decked in crimson robes, her knights and her esquires. Within the abbey church they stopped at a stage specially erected under the crossing and covered in red worsted where each had a throne. King Richard's was St Edward's Chair, Queen Anne's was to the left and somewhat lower. First of all at the high altar King Richard was anointed with the holy oil, vested, crowned and enthroned, Anne sitting on a stool to one side. Escorted to the altar by the two bishops, Anne prostrated herself on cushions, and then knelt. Her circlet was replaced by a crown, she too was anointed on temple and breast with holy oil, a ring was placed on the fourth finger of her right hand and a crown on her head, and she was invested with her sceptre in her right hand and a rod featuring a dove of peace in her left. Next followed high mass. They advanced to St Edward's shrine, near where the monarchs breakfasted and changed their robes. Anne now wore a kirtle, a sleeveless surcoat and a mantle with a train, furred with miniver and ermine, together using fifty-six yards of material. Returning to their thrones, they proceeded to Westminster Hall, and to their chambers. The next stage, at 4p.m., saw king and queen back in Westminster Hall for the coronation banquet, seated at the marble table of king's bench and attended by two countesses. Surely it was the most impressive and the most debilitating day of Anne's short life. One and probably both of her weddings had been quiet affairs. Certainly Rows, the artist of the Salisbury Roll and *Beauchamp Pageant*, thought so, as each chose to depict Anne in her coronation robes.[7] The jousts and other jollifications that followed are not recorded.

Once crowned, Richard set off on progress through the Thames Valley, the West and North Midlands, to York, the centre of his former hegemony. He was concerned to show himself to his subjects and to win their acceptance and adherence, and to reveal himself as a right-minded and gracious king. He professed for example his commitment to justice and renounced the fiscal extortion associated with his late brother. King Richard spread his bounty lavishly, patronising not merely individuals, but also towns and other communities that received new charters. An impressive escort of bishops and noblemen accompanied him. On Saturday 19 July the king and queen proceeded from Greenwich to Windsor, where they surely viewed Edward IV's splendid half-built chapel of St George and visited his tomb within his two-storey chantry. Anne remained at Windsor Castle for perhaps as long as a fortnight, whilst Richard proceeded on 21 July to Oxford, Woodstock, Tewkesbury (4 August), Gloucester, Worcester and Warwick. Anne was spared thereby the tedious Latin speeches with which Oxford University regaled her husband. He arrived at Warwick on Friday 8 August, where she joined him, with other ladies of noble rank; so did her nephew, her sister Isabel's son Edward, Earl of Warwick, to whom town and castle properly belonged.[8]

Unless she went there independently, Anne did not go to Tewkesbury Abbey, where her first husband had been buried. The mausoleum of her Despenser ancestors and of her grandmother the Countess Isabel, the abbey's patronage had been allocated to Clarence at the partition of the Warwick inheritance. When the Duchess Isabel died in 1476, Clarence had had her interred at Tewkesbury and had erected for them both a splendid new monument, now lost, in which he himself was interred following his execution.[9] When in Tewkesbury, King Richard worshipped in the abbey, prayed and surely also made offerings at his brother's tomb. Clarence's forfeiture meant that the abbey had not been repaid the 310 marks (£206 13s 4d) that they had spent on the tomb, which King Richard now reimbursed.[10] Although Richard was to move the body of the Lancastrian Henry VI to a more honoured location at St George's Chapel, Windsor, he evidently felt no need to mark with a fitting monument the tomb of Henry's son and Queen Anne's first husband Prince Edward, whom supposedly he had slain. We cannot know whether he prayed or offered at Prince Edward's tomb. Strangely, the abbey's historian did not extend the chronicle that ended in 1477 to include this royal visit of the founder's kin. He ends with the arms of the two royal dukes, not those of Gloucester as king.[11]

Queen Anne's absence from much of Richard's fatiguing progress is perhaps surprising, since the most was made of her connections with her home country in the new monarch's love-in with his subjects. If not at Warwick as frequently as might have been expected in her youth, it was nevertheless one of her principal homes and perhaps one that she had last visited in 1470 during the Lincolnshire Rebellion. Since then Clarence had had consecrated her grandfather's

Beauchamp Chapel at Warwick College, where there also lay buried her cousins Henry Neville and Oliver Dudley slain at Edgecote in 1469, and further progress had been made on the still unfinished great tower of Warwick Castle that represented the highest fashion in contemporary architecture.[12] Richard committed himself to further expenditure. The king and queen stayed for a whole week. Presumably they stayed in the castle, worshipped and made offerings at St Mary's church, and visited Guyscliff, where the aged Rows continued to officiate. Almost certainly it was on this occasion that Rows presented the queen with the English version of his *Roll of the Earls of Warwick* and that the queen, perhaps in consequence, commissioned the splendid illustrated biography of her grandfather Earl Richard Beauchamp now known as the *Beauchamp Pageant*. King Richard earned Rows' approval 'as special good lord to the town and lordship of Warwick' by conceding, without fee or fine, undocumented privileges supposedly awarded by William the Conqueror and which Clarence as earl of Warwick had sought to no avail.[13]

In its progression of illustrations and accompanying text for each lord of Warwick and his consort, Rows' *Rolls* resembles the *Salisbury Roll* of Anne's Montagu and Neville ancestors, but Rows conceived them on a much grander scale, both in the sheer number of tableaux and the much more elaborate commentary. He also focused more single-mindedly on the direct line in preference to collateral kin. If Rows' achievement stimulated a new version of the *Salisbury Roll* culminating in Anne and Richard in their coronation robes, there was no historian like Rows to enhance its commentary.[14] Rows' *Rolls* incorporated a lifetime of devoted antiquarian research. Two versions were made, one English and another Latin. Preparing the sixty drawings of past lords, real and fantastic, earls and countesses, their coats of arms and emblems of any one version would have taken even an accomplished artist many months to execute: much longer time than Rows possessed between Anne's accession and her visit to Warwick if that was indeed when it was presented to her. Fortunately her accession required modification only of the last few entries: rather than erasing and rewriting, which did not befall the surviving *Roll*, it is possible that updated versions for Anne and Richard and their son Edward of Middleham were substituted. They are still located after the accounts of Isabel, appropriately as the younger sister, but in the final pedigree Anne is placed first, in the position of seniority,[15] which has been interpreted as Rows' flattery. That Rows' *Rolls* as history are imperfect – there is a good deal of factual inaccuracy and the family legends are recounted as though they actual happened – probably did not matter: almost certainly Anne was as credulous about the family myths as was Rows himself. The *Rolls* made the most of Anne's ancestral renown. A unique survival from this era, different and superior to other contemporary genealogies, it was a splendid gift that surely gave her much pleasure. Surely it was a further pride to her as much as for Rows that she had brought the crown that her father had sought to the house of Beauchamp and Warwick.

Of course it was difficult for Rows to present recent history entirely positively and indeed he dodged as far as possible the disasters for the earldom of Warwick of 1397, 1471 and 1478. The treasons and come-uppance of Anne's father Warwick in 1471 and the attainder and execution of her brother-in-law Clarence in 1478 were euphemistically treated: 'forward fortune', in Warwick's case, 'him deceived at his end' and in Clarence's case 'maligned for against him and laid all apart'.[16] Yet Rows did not merely massage the past into the most acceptable form. An octogenarian and vulnerable to the disapproval of his patrons, it was understandable and pardonable if he was timeserving, as he is usually charged, and he did tailor his message to suit the politics of his day. How could he have presented a roll to the current queen, also his ancestral patroness, that deplored her dispossession of her mother, the rightful lady of Warwick? Certainly he did amend the Latin *Roll* in this way after Richard's fall, evidently for his own satisfaction and at no Tudor prompting. His *History of the Kings of Britain* was decidedly hostile and incorporated much Tudor propaganda against the king.[17] But even the English version is not wholly uncritical. Rows, we must recall, was committed to the lords of Warwick, amongst whom Anne and Richard were not to be counted. He reported on all Earl Richard Beauchamp's children, including the three elder daughters who did not succeed, but he did not pursue their lines down to his own day. He knew the Countess Anne– she was born after he came to Guyscliff, she had inherited Warwick and made it her own – and also the Duchess Isabel, for whom it was the principal seat in 1471–6. Rows records the dates and places of birth of each of the Duchess Isabel's children,[18] but he knew Anne much less well. She had resided principally in Calais and the North before leaving her parental home at fourteen, never to return. He possessed no such precise information on Anne's own son, whom he had probably never seen. Rows was committed to the Countess Anne – the kingmaker featured in his *Rolls* merely as her consort – and considered that she was still his rightful lady. 'By true inheritance countess of Warwick', Rows, English *Roll* reports her sufferings because of the kingmaker's death and her patience through all her tribulations. In the Latin *Roll*, which he had kept for himself, he notes that she was deprived of her heritage and kept straitly by decision of Anne Neville. Later in his *History,* Rows tells more explicitly how it was Duke Richard who had responded to her appeal by locking her up for life.[19] Careful reading of the English *Roll* is necessary to appreciate Rows' ambivalence – more careful reading, probably, than Anne gave it and than most modern historians seem to have undertaken – and the Latin *Roll* never came to Anne's notice. What one would like to know and cannot know is how far Rows' later strictures against King Richard dated back to 1483 or whether they were merely added in consequences of his failure, in response to Tudor propaganda, and because Rows came to believe that Richard had indeed poisoned Queen Anne.[20]

From Warwick the royal party proceeded on 15 August via Coventry, Leicester and Nottingham to Pontefract (28th), where they overnighted once again at the great castle and elevated the little town into a borough.[21] After that they stayed for three weeks from 29 August at York, probably in the archbishop's palace. York, of course, was the principal city of the North, the region that Richard had made his own as duke, centre of Anne's Neville connection, and whence they drew most of their support. It was moreover a city that both had visited regularly and knew well, over whose affairs Richard had established his ascendancy, and where he appears to have been popular. Even more than Warwick, York was where the new regime was at its strongest, where existing loyalties must be maintained, and whose display of loyalty might serve to reinforce the fidelity of any doubting southerners. Thirteen thousand of Richard's white boar badges were commissioned. The king's secretary John Kendal was sent in advance to lay on the celebrations and much treasure was laid out on magnificent feasts and entertainments.[22]

It was at this point that the royal couple were joined by their only son Prince Edward, Earl of Salisbury. He had remained in the North when they went south and had missed both the usurpation and their coronation. Since he was their heir, the assurance of a future to their dynasty, one wonders why. Now, however, they had come to him and the family group was complete. Moreover, he could now take pride of place: the highpoint of the forthcoming festivities was to be a splendid public ceremony at which he took centre stage – his formal creation and investiture as Prince of Wales. Not only were such investitures highly infrequent, but they occurred almost always in Westminster during parliamentary sessions: York was a unique venue. The great wardrobe supplied appropriately splendid clothes and horse-gear and the burghers of York laid on their best entertainment. Combined with King Richard's own crown-wearing, this visit was designed to signal to northerners and Anne Neville's traditional retainers the succession of a northern house and indeed of the Neville line to the English crown at last. To southerners, it demonstrated both Richard's power and popularity in the North.

King Richard, Queen Anne and Prince Edward, five bishops, three earls, six other peers and many gentry set off from Pontefract on 29 August. They were met outside the city walls by the mayor, aldermen and councillors and processed past three pageants to York Minster – it was the feast of the beheading of St John the Baptist. A splendid service featured the *Te Deum* before the royal couple proceeded to the adjacent palace of the archbishop. King and queen attended two banquets and a performance of the Creed play. The visit culminated on 8 September, the feast of the Nativity of the Blessed Virgin, when the royal party processed from the palace to the Minster for mass. Richard munificently presented twelve silver gilt figures of the apostles to York Minster. The Minster's relics were displayed on the high altar. Immediately afterwards Prince Edward was knighted, created prince of Wales and invested with the insignia of the golden wand and wreath. His nephew Edward, Earl of Warwick and the king's bastard John of Pontefract were also knighted. Following dinner, another banquet, the king, queen and prince sat crowned for four hours. So splendid was the occasion that Crowland called it a second coronation. Amongst a very large and sumptuous order to the great wardrobe were suits of armour, five heralds' doublets, five banners of the Trinity, SS George, Cuthbert and

Edward, and of the king's arms, and 13,000 cushions embroidered with boars – that number again, somewhat greater than the population of York itself. King Richard also founded a chantry college for a hundred extra priests at the Minster. A foundation so unprecedented in size required large buildings, which were indeed commenced, and large endowments that were never transferred. Professor Dobson has suggested that at this stage Richard may even have been contemplating York Minster as his burial place.[23] (If Barnard Castle was still an option, Middleham was no longer part of Anne and Richard's hereditary estate, and neither college was really worthy of a sovereign.) Additionally Richard reduced the city's fee farm and scattered benefits lavishly amongst other northern churches, communities and individuals. York had seen nothing like it since the enthronement of Archbishop Neville, which both Anne and Richard had attended, eighteen years before.

Proceeding southwards to Pontefract on 21 September, they stayed for three weeks, before moving on to Lincoln on 11 October, where the royal party were greeted by news of Buckingham's rebellion. Richard took on the task of suppression himself, whilst Anne, presumably, proceeded to London independently. However, the honeymoon period was over. Although the rebels were soon routed, there was never to be another time when Richard's right to rule was unquestioned.

THE QUALITY OF QUEENSHIP

Warwick had hoped to make his daughters royal and at different points had schemed for each to become a queen. That had been Anne's destiny during her brief first marriage. It was an expectation and aspiration that she surely abandoned when she married Duke Richard. No better than third in the male line to the throne, rather further away if Edward IV's daughters were admitted, he was a youngest son and never scheduled for the crown. That he became king was unexpected and surely unplanned. Anne was carried with him to throne and crown. Given the weight attached at the usurpation to legitimacy and to the invalidation of Edward IV's marriage, it was important that there was no question about the validity of the union of King Richard and Queen Anne: unlike that of Edward IV, Rows rather forcefully hinted.[24] They lived their lie. If Richard had not been scheduled to be king, neither was Anne to be queen. After Edward of Lancaster's death, she must have abandoned any such pretensions. As a mature Englishwoman, she brought to the throne much baggage – traditions, biases and connections – which were very much Richard's as well. He used them to make himself king and found himself obliged to rely quite heavily on them once this was accomplished. However, Anne's heritage was either to be submerged in Richard's own royal line of succession or to follow a different course once their line faltered: its preservation, as we shall see, was no longer his concern.

Was Anne a good queen? Ricardians today wish to establish whether Richard was a good king. Because his reign was so brief, it is an impossible question to answer, besides being anachronistic. Richard's age did not judge their rulers by the standards – such as reforms and legislative activity – that we do today. What are kings for? When assessing Anne as queen, moreover, we need to consider what queens were for. They had neither the power nor the responsibility of their husbands as rulers. To be queen, in Anne's case, was not fundamentally different from being the wife, mother and duchess that she had been before. That is why late medieval theorists found it unnecessary to say anything more about queens.[25] As queen, her rank was simply higher, her establishment, income and following all larger.

Her prime function, of course, was as breeding stock. It was her duty to supply the necessary son and heir, and this Anne had already fulfilled. This, however, was the barest requisite. It was desirable to have not just an heir, but also a spare, as Prince Harry is today. To ensure the succession and facilitate diplomatic alliances, a whole litter of princes and princesses was the ideal. Unfortunately Prince Edward was all she had delivered and all, moreover, that she could produce. That was to prove a fatal flaw that came to outweigh every other use and service.

A queen was also expected to preside over her husband's court, to appear at, participate with the king in, and to lead major ceremonies, all of which (as we have seen) Anne appears to have performed satisfactorily. To Faunger she was 'the social companion of the king in the ritual performance of the regal rites'. Laynesmith waxes lyrical here:

> A woman was required in this context not just as an ornament to the king's court but to complement the king's masculine qualities with perceived feminine virtues of mercy and peace-making... The ideal queen thus consummated her husband's kingship by beauty, chastity and noble character that were an inspiration to good deeds, by mercy and emotion which complemented his judgement and logic, by an inclination to peace that tempered his courage, and by the flesh of the most human that complemented his spirit approaching the divine.[26]

One hopes that Anne was up to this role, but once again, regrettably, we cannot know.

We cannot even tell how often she was with the king. They were on progress together from Warwick to Lincoln in 1483, for both Christmases at Westminster and in 1484 at Nottingham. Cohabitation is also implied by Richard's repeated visits to Greenwich, his adolescent home but probably the queen's residence. Yet Anne may have shared little of his restless itinerary through England's provinces, dictated as it was by political and military considerations to which she had little to contribute.

A bachelor court like that of Edward IV, which had however been morally disreputable, was conceivable. That King Edward in the 1480s and King Richard were married did not guarantee respectability. It was kings, not their queens, who set the tone. If there was a role as patroness of the arts and literature, there are indications that Anne fulfilled it. Perhaps Anne as queen was expected to intercede with the king, to induce his exercise of his prerogative of mercy. We cannot tell. Certainly it was desirable that she should not represent any particular interest or become involved in court factions, whether actively or passively, as her predecessor Elizabeth Wydeville had done. It was one of the dangers of a queen who was English that she brought with her to office kinsfolk and dependants who expected patronage and influence on affairs. Anne, at least, was not like that, both because she had few kin of her own – and because those she possessed, like the Beauchamp and Despenser heirs, were not her supporters – and because those she might have advanced, her Neville retainers, were of the utmost value to her husband and more generously rewarded by him than she could have achieved. It is hard, indeed, to show that she exercised any influence on Richard's patronage or clemency. However Sir William Knyvet thought it worth paying her to escape the penalties of treason.[27]

Anne's Warwick inheritance and the Neville connection derived from it had been crucial in creating Richard's hegemony in the North as Duke of Gloucester, assisted him in securing the throne and was to be an important source of reliable manpower as king. We have already seen the propaganda value of Anne's Beauchamp and Salisbury antecedents and perhaps also how much they still meant to the queen. To Richard, however, they were superseded by his accession. What he wanted to pass on to his son was the crown, not merely his estates as duke, and the Warwick inheritance had ceased to be material. One clear indication of this is that he felt free to dispose of it as he wished and, in the interests of winning friends, to acknowledge claims that he had hitherto resisted. Whether Anne shared his changed perceptions must be doubted.

Take, for instance, Richard's changed attitude to the Neville inheritance, which, as we have seen, was the core of his estates, power-base and plans for the future in the north of England. Under the 1475 act, he had held this for as long as there were male heirs of the Marquis Montagu living. Before his accession, Richard had been striving to protect his tenure of these properties by minimising the dangers posed by George Neville, by degrading him and securing his wardship himself, and to acquire the reversionary rights of the next heir Richard Lord Latimer, by seeking his wardship also. Once of age, he needed the boys to release their rights to him or, at the very least, to marry them off to safe and powerless ladies. He secured custody of George but had yet to marry him off, so that his line continued, and had failed to wrest control of Richard from his uncle Cardinal Bourchier. Duke Richard's plans were thwarted, however, when George died on 4 May 1483, still unmarried and childless. Gloucester's title was reduced to that of a life-tenant: he could keep the Neville inheritance for life, but could not pass it on his son.[28] His dominance of the North was limited to his own lifetime. Once king, he did secure custody of Latimer, but no longer was he interested in extending his estate in the Neville lands beyond his own days and in barring Latimer from his Neville inheritance. Almost at once, instead, Richard sold Latimer's marriage to Humphrey Stafford of Grafton, who married him to his daughter Anne. Stafford certainly expected Latimer to succeed in due course not merely to his modest barony, but to Middleham, Sheriff Hutton, Penrith and potentially Gloucester's dominance in the

North and the West March. A great future had been purchased for Anne Stafford and her heirs.[29]

Another part of the great Warwick inheritance had been inherited from the Despensers. The lordship of Glamorgan in the marches of South Wales had been allotted to Anne and most of the rest, including Tewkesbury and Hanley, to Isabel and hence her son Edward, Earl of Warwick. The underlying title derived from the Countess Anne was debatable, however: she should have divided the lands with the son of her half-sister George Neville, Lord Abergavenny, whose title had been recognised to no avail both in 1449 and in 1470.[30] The two royal dukes of Clarence and Gloucester had firmly rebutted his claims. Now, however, Richard acknowledged them and granted livery of at least some of the lands to Lord Abergavenny.[31] It was a signal favour to him deserving of the most committed service. If applied to the whole inheritance, it could have transformed Abergavenny from a middle-ranking noble in Kent and Sussex to one of the greatest Welsh marcher lords of his day. Whilst it cannot be demonstrated that Richard's award was implemented and that many Despenser lands actually changed hands – indeed T.B. Pugh demonstrated that Richard kept his grip on Glamorgan[32] – the grant indicates that Richard no longer cared particularly about keeping the estate intact or honouring the act of 1474. He was giving away his nephew Warwick's lands as well as Anne's own; moreover, once Prince Edward had died, it would all be at Warwick's long-term expense.

Another sign that such issues scarcely concerned him any more is that on 1 July 1484 the countess of Warwick was allocated £80 a year to support herself. Most probably this indicates that she was released from custody and allowed to set up house herself. The revenues arose not from her own inheritance, but from the estate in Yorkshire of Richard's former chamberlain in the minority of his son at the hands

of the custodians Sir Thomas and Lady Jane Wortley.[33] Perhaps
Richard no longer feared any threat that she posed to his
tenure of her estates. Now in her sixties, she did not remarry.
Richard also allowed a Beauchamp rival, Edward Grey Lord
Lisle, whom he himself raised to viscount, to secure Chaddesley
Corbett in Worcestershire, a part of the Beauchamp trust that
first the kingmaker and then Clarence had treated as their
own.[34] Richard granted away parts of Anne's inheritance, the
London house of le Erber, which he gave to the new college of heralds as their headquarters.[35] There was also a further
grant to Queens' College, Cambridge, this time of lands in
the East Midlands of Beauchamp and Despenser origin. The
king was already committed to endowing Queens' College by
16 March 1484, when it was licensed to acquire property in
mortmain to the value of 700 marks (£466 13s 4d) a year, of
which the king granted 'at the request of my dearest consort'
lands valued at £329 3s 8d a year, in capital value worth over
£6,000. Including lands of Anne's inheritance in East Anglia,
they constituted both a major endowment for the college and
a substantial alienation of the family estate, a breach once again
of the 1474 act, and ultimately a loss to Isabel Neville's son and
Anne's nephew Edward, Earl of Warwick. Richard was giving
away his wife's inheritance. The souls of both king and queen
were to be prayed for, of course. The original warrant appears
in Richard's signet letter book and was therefore authenticated
by him. However, the college's petition was addressed to him,
initialled by him, and recalled how 'of late it pleased your said
highness of your grace especial to grant'. The grant of course
was to Queens' College, not King's: the apostrophe in the title
Queens' reminds us that it was Anne who was patroness alongside Elizabeth Wydeville and Margaret of Anjou rather than
King Richard. It may therefore be that this lavish benefaction
should really be credited to the intercession of 'the most serene
Queen Anne' rather than King Richard himself.[36]

The principal source for the study of a fifteenth-century queen ought to be the records of her estates and her household. For late medieval queens lived even more separate lives from their consorts than ladies did from their lords. Many royal palaces like Westminster had separate apartments for the king and queen. Queens had their own estates – in particular, the ancient queen's lands across southern England – and their own residences. In 1467–8 these had been worth approximately £4,500; those of Queen Margaret of Anjou had been even more extensive. The principal charge on these revenues was the queen's household, an elaborate establishment that mirrored that of the king, with carvers, knights and gentlemen above stairs, serving departments below, smaller only than that of the king, but larger than that of the greatest other subject in the realm. That was what ought to have happened to Queen Anne. Most probably it did, but there is no conclusive evidence of it.

We know more of royal patronage during Richard III's brief reign than of either Edward IV before him or Henry VII afterwards because we possess the king's signet letter book, but strangely Anne herself is almost completely absent. Both Margaret of Anjou and Elizabeth Wydeville feature frequently in the patent rolls as recipients of a whole series of grants of the particular estates that comprised their dower. For Anne, there are neither any such grants nor any record of signet warrants to the estate officials implementing such decisions. Whereas her son Prince Edward was formally created Prince of Wales by charter dated 24 August 1483,[37] there are no grants or parliamentary ratifications conveying to him his principality of Wales, duchy of Cornwall and county of Chester like those for Edward IV's heir in 1471–2. In neither case need this mean that the queen and prince went unendowed: it is unlikely, but we cannot be sure. Richard III may have argued that Edward IV, as a bastard, was never king and therefore he himself was.

He certainly asserted that Edward IV had never been married to Elizabeth Wydeville and therefore she had never been queen and her son never prince nor King Edward V. The ex-queen and ex-king therefore did not need to be dispossessed of that to which they had no title. In similar vein, as queen to the king and eldest son to the king, it could be asserted that Anne and Edward automatically succeeded to the queens' lands and to the appanage of the princes of Wales. There was no need therefore for any formal grants. Whilst possibly correct, this is still very odd. Medieval officers wanted assurance and authorisation for their actions – by what warrant did you act? – and the issue of legal title, if not to the lands themselves then to appurtenant rights of way etc., were surely bound to arise. Not only were no grants enrolled, but none of these properties feature in the lists in Richard's signet letter book, nor were the estate officers included in his lists. That a grant was made after Anne's death from Higham Ferrers (Northants.) suggests that it had just become available.[38] Probably, therefore, Queen Anne succeeded to the whole dower formerly held by Queen Elizabeth. Unfortunately, however, there are no estate accounts or other archives indicating Anne's tenure or what she did with these lands in the National Archives. We really cannot tell. On the evidence cited above of Richard's alienations, it seems unlikely that Anne secured control of her own inheritance.

However large her dower was, it seems certain that Anne controlled a substantial estate to fund her expenditure as queen. The largest charge should have been her household. That Anne was not always with the king, resided in other royal palaces, and travelled independently, for example to Warwick and from Lincoln in 1483, indicates that she possessed an autonomous household like any other queen. Almost certainly it mirrored that of her predecessor: King Richard was careful to maintain the standards of display expected of a king. However, we know almost nothing about it.

A mere handful of members of her household are known by name. Walter Graunt, a yeoman usher of her chamber in 1484, and John Snowden, a yeoman of her chamber in 1485, attracted royal grants and appear in Richard's own records. Robert Roo transferred from her son's household, where he was gentleman of the pantry. We know also of a chamberlain and two chamberers, a carver, gentlemen and yeomen of her horse, chair, and great chamber, and five henchmen, mostly nameless.[39] Laynesmith has attempted to fill the gaps. 'The majority of those who appear to have been in Anne Neville's household were members of northern gentry families, and were probably her attendants as duchess of Gloucester also'. Anne's cousin Elizabeth Parr, her illegitimate half-sister Margaret Huddleston, and another cousin Elizabeth Lady FitzHugh 'were almost certainly among her personal attendants', she speculates.[40] Here she may be extrapolating from records of the queen's coronation, which report more of Anne's attendants than any other source, including seven married ladies from northern aristocratic families: Elizabeth Bapthorpe, Anne's bastard half-sister Margaret Huddleston, Elizabeth Mauleverer, Grace Pullan, Joyce Percy, Katherine Scrope, Alice Skelton and Anne Tempest.[41] At that point, evidently, Anne Neville had not taken on Elizabeth Wydeville's staff and most probably was continuing her own as duchess. Whether this northern bias persisted in her much larger household as queen is doubtful: her spouse at accession sought to be inclusive and was forced to 'northernise' his regime only after the rebellious southerners opted out. Laynesmith, however, may well be right. There is nothing unreasonable about what she writes, but at present we cannot know. Queen Anne certainly required such genteel tirewomen.

Anne shared with Richard suffrages for the good of her soul. It used to be argued that Richard was a most lavish founder of chantries. Certainly, as we have seen, the couple did establish a chantry at Cambridge, collegiate chantries at Barnard Castle, Middleham and most splendidly at York, all of which prayed assiduously for Anne's soul. Also, however, she was prayed for at All Hallows the Less in London, St Leonard's Chapel in Wolverley (Worcs.), St Mary Rykill in York and Wilberfoss nunnery (Yorks.), Carlisle cathedral priory, and the College of Heralds, at Old Sleaford and Brown's Hospital in Stamford (Lincs.), St Helen Abingdon (Berks.), at Wem and Ludlow in Shropshire, Bishops Stortford in Hertfordshire and Ashbourne in Derbyshire, where other founders set up chantries licensed by the king on condition he and his consort were prayed for.[42] Whilst evidence of the accumulation of merit for her in purgatory, one benefit of being a queen, they do not actually imply any pious actions by Anne herself.

CHAPTER SEVEN

Past Her
Sell-By Date

QUEEN ANNE'S FINAL SORROWS

Queen Anne had little opportunity to enjoy being queen. Her reign was exceptionally short. She may have been in ill-health at her succession. By January 1485 she was certainly a sick woman who, despite her relative youth, was past childbearing. The son, whom she loved, had died. Her husband played fast and loose with her inheritance, which no longer mattered to him. He appears also to have identified a younger princess as replacement and waited in eager anticipation for her death, which soon followed. At least Anne was spared the destruction of her husband and all he stood for. Whereas Richard is remembered as the most wicked of kings and uncles, Anne was another victim that he used, exhausted, and inevitably discarded. In this instance Shakespeare was right.

We have already seen how Edward of Middleham's investiture as prince of Wales was made the centrepiece of Richard's visit to York in 1483. The prince was left in the North as figurehead of Richard's regional rule – the king's hegemony was to be continued in his absence and Anne's Neville connection maintained through the household and council of their son. In February 1484, whilst parliament was in session at Westminster, 'almost all the lords spiritual and temporal and the leading knights and gentlemen of the king's household', assembled by royal command in a downstairs room on the corridor leading to Anne's own apartments, were induced to swear a new oath of allegiance to the prince, 'on whom' – Crowland wisely observes 'all hope of the royal succession rested'.[1] Prince Edward fell ill, however, and died on 9 April 1484, one year to the day since the demise of Edward IV. It was a staggering blow, certainly politically, but also personally, to his parents, who were then together at Nottingham. Separation from their son did not indicate that they did not care for him. 'You might have seen', reported Crowland, who evidently had seen, 'the father and mother … almost out of their minds for a long time when faced with the sudden grief'.[2] It is the clearest testimony that we possess (and the only one) that Anne and Richard enjoyed a genuinely companionate marriage, that they felt towards their son both the love that we expect today (and which is sometimes denied of past parents by modern historians), and that they were really distraught at their son's death. Immediately afterwards Richard proceeded via York (1 May) to Middleham (5–6 May), Durham (15th), Scarborough (22nd) and back to York (27th), an itinerary most probably shared by Queen Anne. Both may have attended their son's funeral, perhaps at Sheriff Hutton.

Prince Edward's death was a personal grief, but it was much more than that. It left his parents childless, and this was in particular worrying for King Richard. We may readily believe that he 'began to complain unto many noble men of his wife's unfruitfulness, for that she brought him forth no children, and that chiefly did he lament with Thomas Rotherham, Archbishop of York', who supposedly repeated the story with his own riders. Rotherham is an unexpected confidant, since he was the chancellor who allegedly surrendered the great

seal to Edward IV's widow and whom Gloucester therefore superseded. Since the archbishop died in 1500, several
years before our source the historian Polydore Vergil came to
England, this anecdote reached Vergil at best at second-hand
from Rotherham's audience.[3] Politically the prince's death was
especially important because it left Richard bereft of an heir.
He desperately needed one. The future of his dynasty required
that retainers and subjects had the security that more than his
own life stood between the regime, their careers and fortunes,
and oblivion. That security was a male heir. Richard's own
future demanded that commitment. Without it, he could not
hope to continue: 'Or else my kingdom stands on brittle glass',
Shakespeare made the king say.[4] First Richard seems to have
turned to his nephew Edward, Earl of Warwick, son of his
brother Clarence, but he soon changed his mind. This may
have been because he realised that Warwick's hereditary claim
was better than his own. The fact that Warwick was only nine
years old and hence merely a figurehead may have been more
significant. Instead Richard designated another nephew, John
de la Pole, Earl of Lincoln, son of his sister Elizabeth, Duchess
of Suffolk, who at least was of age. A de la Pole pedigree of
the time does identify Lincoln as Richard's heir.[5] Richard
also foregrounded his bastard John of Pontefract:[6] if he ever
considered making him his heir, he surely decided – as his
great-nephew Henry VIII was to do with his bastard Henry,
Duke of Richmond – that this would be counter-productive.
Probably John was also too young to be really useful.

Such measures, however, were merely stop gaps until
Richard could produce another legitimate son of his own.[7]
He was still in the prime of life. Apparently he was still sleeping with Queen Anne.[8] Reading between the lines, indeed, he
may have made a final effort to impregnate his queen. Anne,
however, was in ill health: she began, says Crowland, to 'sicken
most vehemently'.[9] Perhaps she had tuberculosis. Her chances

of conceiving may already have been recognised to be slim. She was breeding stock that had ceased to breed. Given that she was aged only twenty-eight, Richard might have had to wait many years and perhaps all his life to remarry and try again for a legitimate heir. His great-nephew Henry VIII was famously to dispense with four superfluous consorts by other than natural means, two by execution. Henry set a precedent where hitherto there was none. Such predecessors as Richard I, Richard II and Henry IV were less inventive and had to stick with barren queens.

Queen Anne died on 16 March 1485. She was promptly on cue. So convenient was her death that there was understandable speculation that King Richard had helped her on her way. The historian John Rows was not alone in reporting that Richard had poisoned her. The rumour was current on 30 March, only a fortnight after, when Richard denied it. The allegation occurs also in the *Great Chronicle of London* and Vergil's *English History*.[10] Vergil reports, at several removes, that Rotherham mused that Queen Anne would not live much longer 'and foreshadowed the same to divers of his friends':[11] presumably he expected Richard to help her on her way. The story duly passed into Tudor myth and was broadcast to later generations by Shakespeare. Taken together, Richard's denial, repetitions by later chroniclers, and the prophetic speculations of the archbishop are grounds to believe the story. But none of our sources can have had access to reliable medical information – if the diagnoses of poisoning of fifteenth-century doctors is to be credited – and no better data is likely to emerge now. Besides, there was no need to kill her. Queen Anne had been ailing for some months before she died. It was on the doctors' advice that Richard abstained from sexual intercourse.[12] A natural death is indicated. There is no reason to doubt the grief that Richard asserted, that he was as sorry & in heart as heavy as man might be',[13] albeit sorrow not untinged with relief. Yet there are good grounds for crediting Shakespeare's story, that Richard had in mind a consort as Anne's successor. If Anne had passed her sell-by date, nevertheless King Richard required a consort to bear him an heir and to fulfil all the other functions required of queens. His first choice apparently was his own niece, Elizabeth of York, the daughter of his brother Edward IV, who had been bastardised by the precontract story and whom he is supposed to have designated even before Queen Anne was dead. This allegation requires more careful consideration than it has ever received to date.

THE ELIZABETH OF YORK STORY

The best contemporary evidence for these aspersions is that on 30 March 1485 King Richard held a news conference in the great hall of St John's Priory at Clerkenwell, at which he made a statement to the mayor, aldermen, councillors, and livery companies of London, whom he had summoned to hear it.

Whereas a long saying and much simple communication among the people by evil disposed persons contrived and sown to very great displeasure of the king, showing how that the queen as by consent and will of the king was poisoned for and to the intent that he might marry and have to wife Lady Elizabeth, eldest daughter of his brother, late king of England deceased, whom God pardon etcetera. For the which and other the king... showed his grief and displeasure aforesaid and said it never came in his thought or mind to marry in such manner wise nor willing or glad of the death of his queen, but as sorry and in heart as heavy as man might be, with much more in the premises spoken. For the which he admonished and charged every person to cease of such untrue talking on peril of his indignation.[14]

As our source is a record made at the time and as it was the king himself who reported these aspersions against him, we cannot doubt that the allegations of poisoning, of remarriage, and of his selection of Princess Elizabeth were in circulation in the spring of 1485 immediately following Anne's death, nor that Richard vehemently and publicly denied them. He cannot have wished to give currency to such damaging rumours. It was because they were already in circulation that a denial was needed and that he could afford to be explicit. A king's word should normally have been conclusive and the story quelled.

Unfortunately, Richard's public statement failed to do the trick. The poisoning reappears both as fact in Rows' *History* and at least as a possibility to Polydore Vergil and the London chronicler *c.*1512, who all accept his rumoured remarriage.[15] Moreover, we know that Richard made this public declaration because his councillors insisted that he did so, as Crowland reports in his chronicle.[16] Note that the record of the Clerkenwell declaration confirms much of Crowland's narrative. Crowland also reveals, at first hand, that in spite of Richard's repeated denials, he himself believed that Richard did indeed intend to marry Elizabeth of York, and that he, Crowland, personally disbelieved that part of the king's denial. At second hand, Crowland states that other royal councillors and especially the key figures of Sir Richard Ratcliffe and William Catesby shared his own views. To Crowland's mind, they knew.[17] He did not mention the poisoning charge and presumably did not credit it. Although he can hardly have been unaware of the story, which was current at the time and mentioned by the king himself, Crowland presumably disbelieved it. He knew murder to be unnecessary, since he also knew that Anne had been ailing for several months and that her death was apparently expected several weeks in advance. What Crowland did relay was damaging enough.

Even in the fifteenth century, convention demanded a decent interval for mourning between the death of one wife and the wedding of another. The planning of a second marriage before the ending of the first was not approved. Many forthcoming widowers must have foreseen such an eventuality, especially when there were young children to care for and households to run. Post-Reformation parish registers frequently reveal rapid remarriages. Kings, furthermore, were always a special case. Reasons of state undoubtedly demanded on occasions both a precipitation and a calculation in matrimony to be eschewed by ordinary mortals. Once single, Richard was free to marry again. It was not so much his intention to marry that aroused criticism – that was to be expected and was actually his public duty – but his supposed choice of bride. Because of the supposed precontract between her father Edward IV and another lady, Princess Elizabeth had been bastardised just as much as her younger brothers the Princes in the Tower, who had disappeared, who were believed to be dead, and whom Elizabeth surely thought had suffered at Richard's hands. Of all the noble young ladies who could bear him sons, it was her claim to the crown, Elizabeth must have realised, that singled her out. Elizabeth of York was also closely associated with her mother Elizabeth Wydeville, who was no longer categorised as a queen at all, her uncle Anthony, Earl Rivers and half-brother Lord Richard Grey, both of whom Richard had had executed, on whose behalf, so Crowland reports, Richard's supporters feared her vengeance.[18] If Shakespeare was seeking a paradox, a marriage between those whom past events should have made incompatible opposites, surely it should have been Elizabeth of York and Richard III in 1485 rather than Anne Neville and Richard, Duke of Gloucester. Furthermore, Elizabeth was Richard's niece: a blood tie so close to the king that Crowland (and, on his evidence, many others) considered any such joining into one flesh to be incest.[19] So did the Reformation

Parliament, which legislated against such matches. It was for this latter reason, not mere decorum, that Richard had publicly to deny any such plan.

From Richard's angle, Elizabeth's disqualification was a pity. A match with her had obvious political advantages. She could only strengthen Richard's title. For any Yorkists sceptical of the bastardy of Edward IV and his children, Elizabeth was their preferred claimant. At the very least, such a match would disarm their opposition to Richard. At the best, Richard could enlist their support. Besides, the king's rival Henry Tudor had pledged himself at Christmas 1483 to marry Elizabeth in order to secure the support of Yorkist fugitives from Buckingham's Rebellion and their adherents within England for his candidacy as king. Tudor even secured a papal dispensation for his marriage to Elizabeth on 27 March 1484, albeit an insufficient one and obtained without her consent.[20] If Richard did marry Elizabeth, Tudor could not do so himself: where was he to find so advantageous a replacement? Such a union was surely the necessary incentive for recalcitrant Yorkists to swallow their hostility, to relinquish their plans to dethrone the king, and to seek instead his forgiveness and the restoration of their forfeited properties, which Richard was prepared to concede. Elizabeth, moreover, had other advantages. Now eighteen, she was nubile, physically healthy, and no doubt attractive. Apparently she so resembled her aunt the queen physically in height, build, colouring etc. that they could wear the same clothes.[21] Queen Anne, after all, was less than ten years her senior. Perhaps Elizabeth reminded Richard of what had first attracted him to Anne Neville. Elizabeth could be expected to provide the desired heir speedily. Her Wydeville kin were as prolific as the Nevilles: Elizabeth was the eldest of ten children. Elizabeth, in short, could quickly supply the defects in title and expectations that Richard in 1485 so obviously lacked. She was more than an adequate substitute for Queen Anne: to a beleaguered and desperate usurper, she was ideal.

Three contemporary sources report that Richard was considering his match with Elizabeth ahead of Anne's death: the Clerkenwell declaration, Crowland's chronicle, and the report of a letter in her own hand from Elizabeth herself to John Howard, Duke of Norfolk.

The original of Elizabeth's letter is lost. Perhaps it never existed and was forged by our source, the pro-Ricardian Jacobean historian Sir George Buck. Yet Buck himself reported its existence (and provided a paraphrase) in 1619 'among precious jewels and rare monuments' in the 'rich and magnificent cabinet' of Thomas Howard, Earl of Arundel, heir of the recipient, to whom it had descended.[22] Arundel was interested in his family's history and was a noted connoisseur and collector. It was in his cabinet that the scholarly earl displayed all his particular treasures. A royal letter (autograph?) of a princess and a future queen to an ancestor was just such a treasure. Buck wrote for publication: surely he expected his reference to be pursued? Moreover, it seems to have been overlooked that Buck not only acknowledged the earl's permission to consult the letter, but also dedicated his book to him. Had it ever been published, Arundel would have received a presentation copy, which – as a scholar himself – he could be expected to read. Obviously the earl knew whether such a prized letter was actually in his cabinet. By seventeenth-century standards, this was as good a provenance and as precise a citation to a publicly accessible location where the original was to be found as could be imagined at the time. For all these reasons forgery is unlikely. Partly because the original, four centuries further on, is now lost and partly because Buck's manuscript history was damaged by fire in 1731, modern historians anxious to rebut the story as discreditable to Richard have questioned exactly how the original text read.[23] Buck rendered into the third person what must originally have been in the first person, but the version published in 1647 by Buck's nephew certainly confirms the meaning that his uncle had intended if not his actual words.[24] After an appropriately respectful introduction,

> First she thanked him for his many courtesies and friendly offices and then she prayed him as before to be a mediator for her in the cause of the marriage to the king, who as she wrote, was her only joy and maker in this world, and that she was his in heart and in thoughts, in body, and in all. And then she intimated that the better half of February was past, and that she feared the queen would never die.[25]

If genuine, Elizabeth's letter indicates that the marriage was indeed projected and that Elizabeth herself had consented to it – indeed, in highly enthusiastic terms! She fancied her uncle as well as wanting a crown. This was in February 1485, more than a fortnight before Queen Anne died. If not quite explicit about Richard's intentions, it indicates that there was opposition to the match. It was to win over Norfolk and to secure his support in persuading Richard to proceed that Elizabeth's letter purports to have been written.[26] This conforms to Crowland's statement that there were those who knew about it despite Richard's denials that such a project was afoot.[27] Since Buck had also read Crowland's account, however, consistency between it and any letter that he might have forged is to be expected and the two sources cannot safely be considered to substantiate one another. Furthermore, Crowland, it could be argued, may not only have been wrong to disbelieve the solemn denials of a king he disliked, but he may also have read the rumours of the proposed marriage that were current in the spring of 1485 back to Christmas 1484. He may have found it difficult to separate what happened before Queen Anne's death from what ensued afterwards. Hindsight is a wonderful thing. Later developments can make better sense of what happened earlier.

On 1 March 1484 Richard had made a deal with Elizabeth Wydeville that enabled Edward IV's erstwhile queen and her daughters to emerge from sanctuary and to live under his protection, evidently at court.[28] The deal was definitely not struck with the marriage between King Richard and Princess Elizabeth in mind, as Vergil says,[29] for Prince Edward was still living and the oaths of allegiance to him had just been administered. The prince still took priority. The contract survives. It contains nothing about such aspirations,[30] for which it is at least nine months too early. As the eldest and most adult daughter, Elizabeth of York was present at Richard's court at Westminster Palace for the Christmas celebrations of 1484. She attracted much attention. In Crowland's case, it was highly disapproving. Elizabeth's conduct that Christmas was amongst the 'things unbefitting' and 'evil examples' with which 'the minds of the faithless' should not sullied. 'There are many other things besides, which are not written in this book and of which it is grievous to speak', wrote Crowland.

Nevertheless it should not be left unsaid that during this Christmas feast too much attention was paid to singing and dancing and to vain exchanges of clothing between Queen Anne and Lady Elizabeth, eldest daughter of the dead king, who were alike in complexion and figure. The people spoke against this and the magnates and prelates were greatly astonished; and it was said by many that the king was applying his mind in every way to contracting a marriage with Elizabeth either after the death of the queen, or by means of a divorce for which he believed he had sufficient grounds. He saw no other way of confirming his crown and dispelling the hopes of his rival.[31]

People were acutely conscious of differences in status. The 1483 sumptuary law set monarchs apart from royalty and royalty from mere nobility. Whether a princess or a bastard, Elizabeth was not Queen Anne's equal in rank. For them to wear similar outfits – and even exchange them – struck the wrong note immediately and excited the suspicions that Crowland relates. We would be wrong to underrate the importance of what he reports. We may, however, reasonably wonder whether Crowland was attaching undue significance to these celebrations in the light of later rumours and whether he perhaps also read public disapproval back a few weeks in time, although this chronicler was usually scrupulous in guarding against such dangers. One circumstance, however, demonstrates that this is not a correct interpretation, and that at this point Crowland's recollections were strictly contemporary.

When dispensing with his consorts, Richard III's great-nephew Henry VIII resorted to divorce on two occasions. Divorce did not involve sundering a valid knot as it does today. Adultery, cruelty or mere incompatibility were not yet grounds for divorce, still less the brief period of separation that enables so many millions of valid marriages contracted 'till death us do part' today to be terminated prematurely and routinely. There were two categories of divorce in this period. The first, the divorce *a mensa et thoro*, was not a divorce at all by our standards but a legal separation, which neither terminated the marriage nor permitted either party to marry whilst the other was still living. The second type that applies here, the *divortium a vinculo*, did release both parties from the marriage, but was possible only because the marriage had never really occurred, because forbidden or because never consummated, and was thus null from the outset. Henry VIII could divorce Katherine of Aragon because she was his dead brother's wife: they were therefore, at canon law, tantamount to brother and sister and thus related within the degrees within which marriage was forbidden. So closely were they related, moreover, so Henry alleged, that the Pope could not dispense the impediments away. Under 1485, Crowland also reports that Richard was contemplating 'a divorce for which he believed he had sufficient grounds'.[32] Crowland did not state what these grounds were, almost certainly because he did not know – indeed, had no idea and had not thought further about it. On his own admittance, he was not a doctor of theology; if a canon lawyer, he had not practised for many years. Had he known what Richard's grounds were, as we shall see, he would surely have made much of it both here and earlier in his chronicle.[33] A divorce, of course, presupposes a living wife. This report must therefore antedate Anne's death and when it was first expected, which Elizabeth's letter locates some time before late February. Crowland demonstrates that Richard's intent to remarry preceded Anne's death. Divorce could serve no purpose thereafter. It seems that Richard first considered divorce, but then Anne's ill health and death rendered it unnecessary. At the latest that was in the last days of February 1485. Any idea of divorce must therefore be earlier.

Divorce between the king and queen was feasible because the marriage between the duke and duchess of Gloucester – brother- and sister-in-law – had never been properly validated by a papal dispensation. In this event, the act of 1474 resettling the Warwick inheritance had anticipated a divorce – that their marriage might be declared null. Because the 1472 dispensation had not covered the key issues, the 1474 parliament 'ordained that if the said Richard Duke of Gloucester and Anne, be hereafter divorced and after lawfully married' – that if the Church applied the letter of the law to nullify their union and subsequently allowed them to remarry – that then the parliamentary settlement of the Warwick inheritance would be 'as good and valid' as if there had been no divorce and as if Anne and Richard had been married throughout.

However, if they were divorced and not allowed to remarry, and if Richard did his utmost to remain married and did not marry anyone else during Anne's life – only possible with a divorce *a vinculo* – then he could retain her lands during her life and for his life after her death.[34] In 1474, of course, it had been so important to Richard to retain Anne's lands that he was prepared to forego any other marriage. Companionship and sex was available without. Up until 1484, of course, it had been in the interests of Anne and Richard to affirm the validity of their union and to conceal this crucial flaw. That they were married was just another lie that they successfully concealed. Nobody questioned the royal marriage at the time, Laynesmith reminds us.[35] Richard had wanted Anne's estates by inheritance, both to secure his title and to transmit it to his own descendants. Anne had no incentive to undermine her own position. Once monarchs, neither King Richard nor Queen Anne wanted to cast doubt on the legitimacy of their son Prince Edward, the hope of their dynasty, nor indeed the moral probity which they denied in Edward IV. Even though children remained legitimate if born to unions within the prohibited degrees in which the partners were ignorant of affinity, this did not apply if they were aware of the impediments at the time of Edward's conception, as Richard and most probably Anne emphatically were.[36]

Now that Prince Edward was dead, however, and Anne appeared incapable of supplying a replacement, the situation was radically changed. With access to the resources of the crown, possession of Anne's estates was no longer essential for her husband. King Richard now had good reason to seek release from his marriage. All that was necessary was to reveal the absence of a dispensation and the Church would decree that the original marriage was null and that it had indeed never been valid. No doubt Richard could purport to discover the impediment just as he had with his brother's precontract. The king could then marry again. That was why, around Christmas 1484 and in the New Year of 1485, Richard may have considered himself eligible for a divorce. That he did indeed think thus is indicated by Crowland's report with its reference to his case for a divorce – a case that Crowland did not understand. To report what he did not understand is the surest evidence of veracity: Crowland had no ulterior motive. Had he understood, the truth would certainly have shocked him. To live openly as man and wife when related in the second, fourth, fourth, and fourth degrees of consanguinity, knowingly without a valid dispensation, was prohibited, incestuous and sinful, though matters might have been righted in arrears by a dispensation if appropriately penitent. To do so openly with one's brother- or sister-in-law, a relationship in the first degree of affinity, was yet more grave and perhaps beyond what could be dispensed. To combine all five impediments was obviously worse. It had not occurred to Crowland that the original match between Anne and Richard might not be dispensable, nor that the impediments had not been dispensed. Had Crowland appreciated that no dispensation had been obtained, not only must he have understood why Richard thought a divorce to be feasible, but this stern critic would surely have referred to it both at this point and in the passages relating to Richard's first marriage, about which Crowland's narrative was anyway sharply disapproving.[37]

We may be sure of this because of Crowland's horror at Richard's proposal to marry his niece incestuously. Evidently he was ignorant that Richard's first marriage was also incestuous. Uncle and niece constituted another blood relationship that was normally regarded as incestuous in the fifteenth century and is still so considered today. Princess Elizabeth herself was also, of course, closely related to Anne and to Richard through other lines also. The number of impediments is impressive. Crowland was horrified. He was certainly not unusual in his reaction. Just as horrified, he indicates, were the nobility, the

bishops and even the general public.[38] Richard's 'unlawful
desire', so the two historians Polydore Vergil and Edward Hall
declared, 'provoked the ire of God and the sword of vengeance
against him, whereby his final ruin and fatal fall shortly after
ensued'... [39] It was public opinion that Richard sought to still
in his declaration at Clerkenwell.

That Richard knew the value of sexual morality and
immorality for propaganda purposes emerges in his successive denunciations of Edward IV's precontract and bastardy,
the sexual adventures of the Wydevilles and Greys, and Henry
Tudor's bastardy on both sides. Opposition to his proposed
second marriage worried Richard. Perhaps it caused him to
waver, as Elizabeth's letter implies, if not to drop the project,
which he appears extremely reluctant to abandon. It was opposition that provoked his qualms, not the message itself that what
he projected was incestuous and damnable. That evidently did
not trouble the king. After all, he had done it before. A man who
could marry his sister [in-law] in defiance of convention and
indeed religious law – an incestuous union by the standard of
the time – was unlikely to be deterred by another such union,
in this case marriage to his niece. Of incest Richard was a serial
practitioner. To coin a phrase, he was a 'serial incestor'. Maybe
another marriage was to be celebrated and consummated ahead
of the arrival of (or request for) a dispensation. Could he afford
to wait on negotiations at the papal curia that were bound to be
protracted if they were to achieve their objective? The instant,
automatic negative that was to be expected would be difficult
to overcome. Too much depended politically on the match to
enable him to wait on prior papal approval.

Besides, the Lady Elizabeth was willing enough. Presumably
her mother was too. How imperfect once again appear the
moral standards of the house of York! Did its members
regard the prohibited degrees and papal dispensations as mere
technicalities that could be squared rather than the moral issues

and dictates of God that Crowland and public opinion so respected? Richard could do it and therefore he would do it.

Certainly the king did appreciate that the projected match was bound to arouse hostility. Hence it was politic to keep it secret and to deny any such plans in public, but not at once to abandon it. If Crowland is to be believed, he floated his project with key advisers – perhaps including the Duke of Norfolk, recipient of Princess Elizabeth's supposed letter. They were averse. After Anne's death, his councillors invoked a special session of council – maybe even a great council – for this issue alone. It met in late March, between 17th and 30th, and it sounds as though opposition was unanimous. Richard denied having any such match in mind or ever having intended it, which, apparently, was not regarded by those who knew him best as evidence that he would be deflected from his purpose. 'Some at that council', states Crowland, 'knew well enough that the contrary was true'. When the king denied it, therefore, Sir Richard Ratcliffe and the esquire William Catesby, key advisers and agents, retorted

> That if he did not deny any such purpose… the northerners, in whom he placed the greatest trust, would all rise against him, charging him with causing the death of the queen, the daughter and one of the heirs of the earl of Warwick and through whom he had obtained his first honour, in order to complete his incestuous association with his near kinswoman, to the offence of God.

They also produced more than a dozen doctors of theology who stated that the Pope could not dispense so close a degree of consanguinity.[40]

Perhaps the doctors were right, although the opinion of canon lawyers was more relevant on such a topic than those of theologians, and canonists are likely to have been divided.

Although *Leviticus* chapter 18 verses 12–13 banned the marriage of a man to his aunt, it did not explicitly proscribe the marriage of a man to his niece, although the nature and proximity of the relationship was the same. Taking the literal meaning rather than the spirit of God's law, what Richard proposed was not explicitly forbidden. Perhaps, therefore, the marriage of the king and the princess was not in breach of divine law, which was absolute, but human law, which could be dispensed. Precedents could be found both for such marriages being allowed and disallowed.[41] All dispensations to set aside canon law required serious grounds, popes usually placing the desires of kings into that category. The curia found it hard to rebuff kings and princes. In practice royalty secured dispensations covering the greatest impediments, which mere nobility and gentry could not, whilst ordinary mortals could not obtain them at all. Hence, perhaps, clerics and gentry deplored a union that Richard and Elizabeth of York thought acceptable. Their senses of Christian morality differed.

The *Great Chronicle* suggests that 'a licence purchased' would permit this union[42] – a dispensation by another name – and Professor Kelly considers that such a dispensation was not altogether impossible.[43] Kelly reviewed what a range of canonical authorities had to say and examined several case studies, all of which Richard's advisers may have known. One aunt-nephew marriage in direct contravention of Levitical decrees was when Henry IV's son Thomas, Duke of Clarence was allowed to remain married to his aunt *by marriage*, Margaret, widow of John, Earl of Somerset (d. 1410). Despite this precedent, Cardinal Torquemada and some other notable canonists considered that popes could not dispense for marriages between uncles and nieces. Perhaps that represented the balance of canonical opinion, but from the next decade a whole series of matches involving royalty and contradicting the Levitical decrees were indeed dispensed. Thus Pope Alexander VI allowed King

Ferrante of Naples to marry his Aunt Joanna and a series of marriages to siblings-in-law involving offspring of Ferdinand and Isabella were permitted.[44] That was in the future and cannot have been known to Richard, who also could not have waited on lengthy deliberations at the curia. Moreover, Kelly considered the case in isolation, without considering all the other degrees in which Richard and Elizabeth were related. What of his first wife, aunt to his proposed second wife, and her cousin several times over? Even if her marriage was invalidated, the carnal relationship remained, and of course Richard had not secured (or even sought) the necessary dispensation.

In this instance, legal arguments took second place to political ones. Accordingly, as his councillors insisted, Richard declared publicly at St John's Hall Clerkenwell that he had never intended any such thing. 'Many people', including Crowland, did not believe him.[45] But his project to marry Elizabeth was dropped – as far as we know.

Of course the marriage did not happen. Because Anne died, divorce was unnecessary. So was murder. The poisoning of his queen nevertheless became a highly effective piece of Tudor propaganda against Richard, which was silenced neither by his denial or by improbability. So was Richard's incest with his niece.[46] The London chroniclers knew the whole story. About 1512, the *Great Chronicle* states:

But after Easter much whispering among the people that the king had put the children of King Edward to death, and also that he had poisoned the queen his wife, and intended with a licence purchased to have married the elder daughter of King Edward. Which rumours and sayings with other things have caused him to fall in much hatred of his subjects as well as men of [good be]haviour as of others. But how so[ever] the queen were dealt with, were it by his means or the visitation of God, she died shortly after... which was a woman of gra-

cious fame, upon whose soul & all Christian [soul]s, Jesus have
mercy. Amen.[47]

Whether the charges were true or false, including those relating to the queen's death, Anne was exonerated, but public
opinion blamed her husband, so the chronicler testifies.[48] Yet
how much more effective would such propaganda have been
had it related to the fact of an incestuous marriage rather
than merely an incestuous intent, and had it been revealed
that Richard's twelve-year-long first marriage had also been
illicit, incestuous, sinful and surely damnable. He was a serial
incestor. Because Anne died, it never became expedient for
Richard to reveal his first marriage as invalid. Richard was
induced to repudiate Elizabeth of York. Approaches were made
to appropriate princesses of Spain and Portugal. King Richard
perished at Bosworth, still single, on 22 August 1485. Whether
he would have revived his matrimonial project had he been
victorious we cannot tell. That he contemplated the match
– and did so whilst Anne was still living – we cannot doubt
any more. Strangely his apparently willing partner appears to
have escaped unsullied: within the year, Elizabeth of York had
married his successor and was crowned and was on course to
be ancestress of the Tudor, Stuart and all subsequent dynasties.
It is remarkable that in 1485 such a potentially anti-Tudor story
was written of the fiancée of the current Tudor king.[49]

LAST DAYS

Following the distressing death of her son, therefore, and perhaps the king's last desperate attempt to father another, Anne's
last days were clouded indeed. 'Unhappy' (*infelix*), as Rows said,
may her marriage have become.[50] The king spurned her bed:[51]
he considered repudiating her as his spouse and potentially as
his queen. The death of her son had removed the cement to

their relationship: shared sorrow did not keep them together, but threatened a decisive parting of the ways. Whether or not illegitimacy really disqualified a king who had been publicly recognised and acclaimed, as historians have questioned, the slur certainly sufficed to strip Edward V of his crown and kingdom, and would have done so also in Anne's case. Richard wished to marry another lady, henceforth his queen, and could do so, because Anne had never been married to him. Crowned and anointed or not, she could not have continued as queen – a proper ecclesiastical court could not have adjudicated her marriage valid – and would certainly have lost her dower as queen to her supplanter, and perhaps also, one wonders, the Warwick inheritance that the 1474–5 acts had assured to Richard himself for life. There was not as yet the comfortable single life after marriage of Katherine of Aragon and Anne of Cleves as divorced queens to serve as a precedent. What was to become of Anne? Although no divorce in the modern sense was necessary, Anne was no longer useful to her husband King Richard and was, in modern parlance, past her sell-by date. Vergil has another unattractive story how Richard had her death rumoured whilst she was still living, which came to her ears and which she raised with him and which he denied in reassuring terms.[52] Since there is no confirmation of this – which, indeed, is incompatible with Crowland's circumstantial analysis – it can be rejected, yet talk of divorce or remarriage could still have been rather a nasty psychological tactic designed to hasten her end (and more likely, surely, to loosen her wits than to kill her) as Hanham suggests?[53] Sorrow, rather than poisoning, was Vergil's preferred cause of death.[54] Queen Anne was aware, of course, of the grounds for divorce. Did she perceive in Elizabeth her potential successor? Were her last days clouded by the apprehension that she would be set aside, disgraced, and/or suffer from qualms of conscience arising from her illicit marriage, for which the death of her son was punishment? Did she see all her misfortunes as punishment for her sin and fear for her soul? We cannot tell: she has not left us her will. That in itself is surprising, since her death was anticipated by others if not herself: surely Anne wished to compose herself and to settle her earthly accounts before she died? Whilst married women, even queens, possessed no property of their own, it was by no means unusual – and surely normal in her circumstances – for her husband to allow her some testamentary dispositions. Moreover, she was unwell, languishing, and died, unattended and indeed unregretted by her husband. If heavy at heart over her death, nevertheless it served Richard's purpose and appeared to offer him a way forward. If Richard's treatment of Anne was ruthless and cruel, his assessment purely material and utilitarian, we must recognise also that his action was the desperation of a rat in a trap as Shakespeare indeed so clearly perceived and need not preclude a genuine affection for her.

Anne died on 16 March 1485 at Westminster, 'on the day when the great eclipse of the sun took place':[55] an omen that Crowland cannot have been alone in recognising. She was buried not at any of her family mausolea – not at Bisham with her father Earl Richard Neville, not at Warwick with her grandfather Earl Richard Beauchamp, not at Tewkesbury with her grandmother or her sister Isabel, Duchess of Clarence, not at her colleges of Barnard Castle, Middleham or York, where she and Richard may formerly have intended to be interred, but with previous monarchs at Westminster Abbey. No heraldic account survives for her funeral, unlike those for other members of the house of York, yet Crowland tells us that she was buried 'with honours no less than befitted the burial of a queen'.[56] Presumably King Richard was present. She was interred in the presbytery in front of the high altar, reported Rows, but the *Great Chronicler*, after all a Londoner, locates her 'by the south door that leads into St Edward's Chapel'.[57]

No monument was ever erected over her tomb. Perhaps none was intended. Far more probably, however, her husband's reign ended before any such project could be undertaken. Her sepulchre, however, was nobler than those of either husband, Edward of Lancaster at Tewkesbury Abbey or Richard III in his unmarked grave at Leicester.

Besides a monument to Anne, Laynesmith speculates that Richard intended 'perhaps even a double one to share her privileged position in the sanctuary' of Westminster Abbey.[58] Of course the couple's earlier plans for colleges implied their interment together. Once Richard was thinking of a second queen, perhaps even of repudiating Anne both as his spouse and queen, this was surely far from his thoughts. He had other things on his mind. Both his queen at Westminster and his son at Sheriff Hutton were allowed to rest where they fell. Longer term planning was left to the longer term – which never arrived. But if Richard had indeed remarried, Anne and Edward were less likely to feature in any re-interments or grandiose monuments.

Ratcliffe and Catesby touched a vital nerve when they drew attention to Anne's Warwick inheritance and especially the Warwick connection of which they were a part.[59] However egotistical he was and however much his own man, Richard had founded his power on Anne's inheritance. Even though the Neville lands had been in tail male, Anne was regarded as Warwick's, Salisbury's and Westmoreland's heiress. Much more than a miscellany of properties or indeed an assembly of employees incentivised by pay and spoils of office, Anne brought Richard a devoted following united by family tradition focused on herself that caused them to hazard their lives on her behalf and that endured beyond the grave.[60] However little control he allowed her of her own affairs as duchess and queen, they remained hers. The Neville retainers were the core of the northern army that had watched over Richard's usurpation and that had enabled him to rule the insurgent South. Richard could not count on adherents of the house of York or the Yorkist establishment of his brother Edward, many of whom indeed had become his foes, nor had he much opportunity to build up much committed support from his own subjects. If Anne's death enabled Richard to look for another consort capable of extending his support, it also threatened to deprive him of his original power base. Deploying his son and residual heirs in the North may have reinforced traditional ties. Whether Anne's death actually did weaken his connection is unclear. Richard had legal tenure for life. Certainly Ratcliffe and Catesby did not fail him: both were at Bosworth, Ratcliffe falling in battle and Catesby being executed thereafter. The division of his army that Northumberland failed to engage in battle most probably included Anne Neville's northern retainers. Whether they were lukewarm to their erstwhile lord – absent inadvertently or by design – we cannot tell. King Henry, however, was anxious to ensure that the connection never operated effectively again. At first in the North, then everywhere, he destroyed it. The Warwick inheritance and Neville connection hardly outlived Anne Neville.

CHAPTER EIGHT

Epilogue

By any standards, Anne crammed a great deal into her twenty-eight years. She had a full life. She enjoyed status and high rank – the highest which any woman could attain. She experienced high society and lots of parties, two husbands, fashionable and expensive clothes, plenty of sex, child-bearing, and lots of admiration and deference. Anne was a housewife who ran a big establishment with lots of servants, had several homes and entertained on the most lavish scale. Even in our modern era of careers for women, we are familiar with advancement by marriage, the trophy wives, husbands who marry for money, and proud mothers who resort to a lot of childcare. Anne exemplified all these types in their fifteenth-century form: it was, moreover, what she was meant to do – the female ideal – and what she was trained for. It was surely not just the aspiration of her father to make her into the queen that she became.

Anne's life was not all positive, of course. There was plenty of bereavement. Much of it was unpredictable, as wholesale slaughter eliminated most of her uncles and great-uncles and exaggerated the complement of widows within her extensive family. One should stress the violent deaths of Anne's father, grandfather, first husband and brothers-in-law, but perhaps none of them was particularly close to her. The death of her sister (presumably in childbirth), her stillborn nephew and the

death of her son touched her more closely, but such premature deaths, for reasons that could have been averted today,
were commonplace, to be expected, natural and indeed facts
of life. Perhaps her extensive experience of mortality was not
as traumatic as we ourselves might expect. It is not at all the
same today, when infant mortality is minimal, violent death
(even on the roads) is relatively uncommon, few people are
struck down in their prime, the old are really old, and death is
no longer a familiar occurrence to the young. We should not
suppose, therefore, that each death of a loved one made the
impact that it does nowadays nor, indeed, collectively.

More difficult for us to accept, perhaps, is marriage without
love. The arranged marriage is something that we find difficult to understand, and hence we encourage and rejoice in
those daughters of Asian immigrants who repudiate spouses
designated for them and marry for love. We find it hard to
understand that such arranged marriages could be companionate and satisfying, so that mothers seek them out for their
offspring, and that Anne's twelve-year marriage to Richard as
duke and king could have fallen into that category. Much has
been made of the tragedy of her end, when she was no longer
wanted and was threatened by divorce. Divorce as a way to
dispense with an unwanted spouse is less drastic, of course, than
murder by poisoning, which now looks highly unlikely. If we
are right to regard divorce as tragic, it is an everyday tragedy
in our modern age, the breakdown of marriage that literally
millions of people currently endure, and from which they
recover. Nowadays there are plenty of divorcees of twenty-
eight with their whole lives ahead of them. We take divorce far
less seriously than did people in the past. Of course it carries
less stigma than a generation ago, when the queen declined to
receive divorced people. Even whilst we recognise that divorce
is not the end of the world and that it can be a new beginning, perhaps for Anne too, we should not underestimate the

blow to her *amour propre*, as she was potentially degraded, and the shame to be incurred not so much from the divorce but from her decade of illicit unmarried fornication. Marriage was what she was bred for – marriage her whole destiny – and that, potentially, was what she was about to lose. What all this meant to Anne, therefore, depended on her sense of values and on those of her age by which she was judged, and which we, at five centuries removed and in a very different era, find hard to comprehend and, still more, to appreciate and apply. Perhaps Anne was lucky that death intervened and saved her the horrors that she surely saw ahead.

Anne was a central figure in great events, yet she appears a powerless one. Perhaps she was. In part, this is the reality of the inferiority of women, even duchesses, princesses and queens, which Anne was born into, lived with and surely accepted. In part perhaps it was because Anne's father Warwick and husband Richard III were particularly powerful, Richard indeed as autocratic and egotistical as any husband. He seems to have denied his duchess many of the trappings of autonomy that other noblemen extended to their consorts. Yet partly this is a problem of the sources. If we possessed for Anne the household and estate accounts of Margaret of Anjou and Elizabeth Wydeville, the privy purse expenses of Elizabeth of York, the letters of Margaret or her own register of correspondence, Anne might be found doing much more than we can actually reveal, and being far more in control of and managing her own affairs. Certainly Anne went along with Warwick's choice of partner, shacked up with Duke Richard and operated as his wife and queen as he wished, went along with his accession, and remained with him through all the unsavoury scandals of his reign. Had she a choice? Was this the helplessness, the passivity that Shakespeare depicts, or did she believe in it? Surely she must have believed in her father's insurrections in 1469–71, just as he, public opinion and many generations of historians have believed as well? It was Anne herself, as we have seen, who leapt into the arms, bed and ducal coronet of Richard, Duke of Gloucester. If there is a case for the precontract, which some at least believed, even possibly her husband, may not Anne have believed it too? Why should she not wish her husband to be king and herself to be queen? Because Richard failed, because in retrospect he has been seen to be a bad thing, because Tudor subjects like Shakespeare found it impossible to suppose that anybody really accepted his arguments or supported him, it does not mean that he did not possess supporters who believed in him and in his cause, and wanted him king. We know he did. And it is entirely conceivable, indeed probable, that Anne was among them. We possess not a jot of evidence to the contrary. She was crowned with him, was his queen, and acted out the role until her end.

At the end of this book, as at the beginning, Anne remains an enigma. How could it be otherwise? The sources speak to us – but not at length or in depth. In their absence, nobody speaks. The gaps, actually enormous gulfs, are insurmountable. There is just too much we cannot know. This book has not added significantly to the hard facts about Anne's life and about her age. What it has shown is what these events mean or may mean – the implications, the options, and wherever possible the choices that were made and Anne's role within them. If Anne was the model daughter, wife and queen, as she appears, who fulfilled the dictates of her menfolk, yet she was also highly exceptional both in her choice of second husband and the lie that they lived for most of their adult life. If she made it possible for Richard to be king, her death may have deprived him of the means to survive. Did she matter to him more in death than life? What is certain is that Anne herself counted, that she was more than merely a symbol, stereotype or sidekick, and that in 1471–2 she herself chose the course that brought her, until her final illness, the most successful of marital careers.

Genealogical Tables

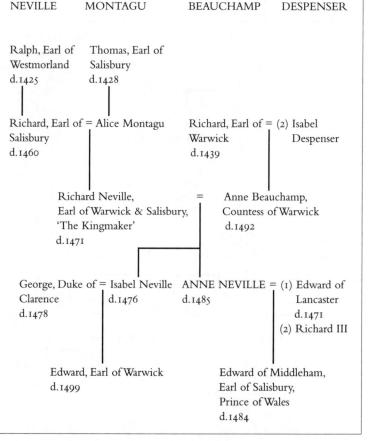

NEVILLE	MONTAGU	BEAUCHAMP	DESPENSER

Ralph, Earl of Westmorland d.1425

Thomas, Earl of Salisbury d.1428

Richard, Earl of Salisbury d.1460 = Alice Montagu

Richard, Earl of Warwick d.1439 = (2) Isabel Despenser

Richard Neville, Earl of Warwick & Salisbury, 'The Kingmaker' d.1471 = Anne Beauchamp, Countess of Warwick d.1492

George, Duke of Clarence d.1478 = Isabel Neville d.1476

ANNE NEVILLE d.1485 = (1) Edward of Lancaster d.1471 (2) Richard III

Edward, Earl of Warwick d.1499

Edward of Middleham, Earl of Salisbury, Prince of Wales d.1484

Anne Neville's Pedigree

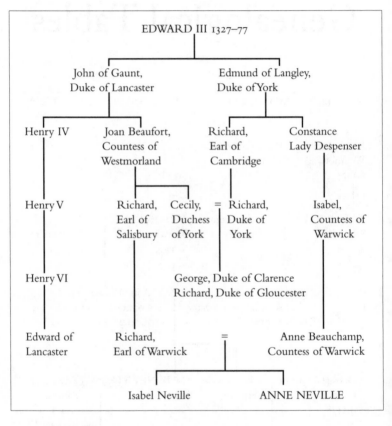

Anne Neville and the Prohibited Degrees

Abbreviations

CCR	*Calendar of the Close Rolls*
CFR	*Calendar of the Fine Rolls*
Clarke	Clarke, P.D., 'English Royal Marriages and the Papal Penitentiary in the Fifteenth Century', *English Historical Review* cxx (2005)
CPR	*Calendar of the Patent Rolls*
Crowland	*The Crowland Abbey Chronicles 1459-86,* ed. Pronay, N. and Cox, J.C. (Gloucester, 1986)
Hammond & Sutton	*Richard III: The Road to Bosworth Field,* ed. Hammond, P.W., and Sutton, A.F. (1985)
GEC	*The Complete Peerage of England etc,* ed. Gibbs, H.V. and others (13 vols. London, 1910–59)
Hanham	Hanham, A., *Richard III and his earlier historians* (Cambridge, 1975)
Harl.433	*British Library Harleian Manuscript 433,* ed. Hammond, P.W., and Horrox, R.E. (4 vols. Upminster, 1979–83)
Hicks, *Clarence*	Hicks, M.A., *False, Fleeting, Perjur'd Clarence: George Duke of Clarence 1449–1478* (Gloucester, 1980)
Hicks, *Richard III*	Hicks, M.A., *Richard III* (Stroud, 2000)
Hicks, *Rivals*	Hicks, M.A., *Richard III and his Rivals: Magnates and Their Motives during the Wars of the Roses* (1991)
Hicks, *Warwick*	Hicks, M.A., *Warwick the Kingmaker* (Oxford, 1998)
Laynesmith	Laynesmith, J.L., *The Last Medieval Queens* (Oxford, 2004)
Oxford DNB	*Oxford Dictionary of National Biography* (64 vols, Oxford, 2004)
RP	*Rotuli Parliamentorum* (6 vols. Record Commission, 1832), v and vi.

Ross, *Richard III*   Ross, C.D., *Richard III* (2nd edn. 1999)

Rows Rolls   *The Rows Rolls,* ed. Courthope, W.H. (1859)

TNA   The National Archives

Waurin   Waurin, J., *Recueil des Croniques et Anchiennes Istories de la Grant Bretaigne*, ed. Hardy, W. and E.L.C.P. (5 vols. Rolls Series, 1891)

Worcester   'Annales Rerum Anglicarum', *Letters and Papers illustrative of the Wars of the English in France*, ed. J. Stevenson (Rolls Series, 1864), ii (2).

Notes

1 WHY STUDY ANNE NEVILLE?

1   W. Shakespeare, *Richard III*, ed. E.A.J. Honigman, New Penguin Shakespeare (1995), Act 1 scene 2 ll.227–8.
2   *Ibid.* Act 2 scene 1 ll.1-239.
3   *Ibid.* Act 1 scene 4 ll. 1-62.
4   *Ibid.* Act 4 scene 2 ll. 59-431.
5   *Hall's Chronicle*, ed. H. Ellis (1809), 301.
6   *RP* v.478; vi.193–5.
7   Laynesmith, 20.
8   Hicks, *Richard III,* 169–82.
9   *Rows Rolls,* no.62; *The Beauchamp Pageant,* ed. A. Sinclair (Richard III and Yorkist History Trust, 2003), pl. lv; A. Payne, 'The Salisbury Roll of Arms, c.1463', *England in the Fifteenth Century*, ed. D. Williams (Woodbridge, 1987), pl. viii; BL MS Egerton 3510 f.104.
10 *Crowland,* 174–5.
11 Laynesmith, 52 & n.
12 See below p.212
13 *Crowland,* 121–2, 132–3, 174–5; *Rows Rolls,* no.62.
14 E.g. P.J.P. Goldberg, 'Women', *Fifteenth-Century Attitudes: Perceptions of Society in Late Medieval England*, ed. R.E. Horrox (Cambridge, 1994), 112–31; *Medieval London Widows 1300–1500*, ed. C.M. Barron and A.F. Sutton (1994); P.R. Coss, *The Lady in Medieval England 1000–1500* (Stroud, 1998); *Young Medieval Women*, ed. K.J. Lewis, N.J. Menuge, and K.M. Phillips, (Stroud, 1999); J.C. Ward, *English Noblewomen in the Later Middle Ages* (Harlow, 1992); F. Swabey, *Medieval Gentlewoman. Life in a Woman's Household in the Later Middle Ages* (Stroud, 1999); Laynesmith.
15 Goldberg, 'Women', 112.

16 *Oxford Dictionary of National Biography*, 64 vols (2004), ii.180–1.

17 Lewis, Menuge and Phillips, xi.

18 Barron and Sutton, *Medieval London Widows* ; Lewis, Menuge and Phillips; Ward, *English Noblewomen*; Laynesmith *passim*.

19 E.g. H. Maurer, *Margaret of Anjou. Queenship and Power in Late Medieval England* (Woodbridge, 2003); D. Baldwin, *Elizabeth Woodville: Mother of the Princes in the Tower* (Stroud, 2002); A.Okerlund, *Elizabeth Wydeville: The Slandered Queen* (Stroud, 2005); Laynesmith *passim*.

20 R.H. Helmholz, *Marriage Litigation in Medieval England* (Cambridge, 1974), 77–87; C. McCarthy, *Marriage in Medieval England. Law, Literature and Practice* (Woodbridge, 2004), 35, 140–1; H.A. Kelly, 'Canonical Implications of Richard III's Plan to Marry his Niece', *Traditio* xxiii (1967), 270–311.

2 WHO WAS ANNE NEVILLE?

1   Unless otherwise stated, this section is based on *GEC passim*; *Warwick*, 7–28.

2   *Warwick,* 7, 16.

3   J.R. Lander, *Crown and Nobility 1450–1509* (1976), 95–6.

4   J.M.W. Bean, *The Estates of the Percy Family 1416–1537* (1958), 83.

5   *Rows Rolls*, no.50; *Beauchamp Pageant*, passim.

6   *Rows Rolls*, no.56.

7   *Warwick*, 26–8.

8   *Ibid*. 37–48.

9   C. Wood, 'The Nature and Extent of the Royal Family 1399–1509' (BA dissertation, King Alfred's College, 2002).

10 *Rows Rolls*, no.62.

11 *Rows Rolls; Beauchamp Pageant*; A. Payne, 'The Salisbury Roll of Arms, *c*.1463', *England in the Fifteenth Century*, ed. D. Williams (Woodbridge, 1987). Coincidence of date, rather than anything explicit, links each to Anne as queen.

12 Richard: 2 daughters; Thomas: childless; John: 5 daughters, *GEC* ix.93n; xii.ii.393.

13 Lander, *Crown & Nobility*, 97.

14 *An English Chronicle 1377–1461*, ed. W.Marx (Woodbridge, 2003), 73.

15 *Rows Rolls*, nos 50, 57.

16 Hicks, *Rivals*, 342.

17 Bodleian Library MS Top.Glouc.d.2.

18 *Warwick*, 9–10.

19 *Ibid*. 17–18.

20 Thus Anne was depicted with Neville arms in a church window at Skipton (Yorks.), BL MS Egerton 3510 f. 104.

21 Hicks, *Rivals*, 324.

22 *Rows Rolls*, no.58.

23 *Calendar of Papal Letters 1447–55,* 151.

24 *Rows Rolls*, no.62.

25 *Ibid.* no.59.

26 The fullest account of the rule of the Nevilles is now *Warwick*, ch.8.

27 *The Brut or the Chronicles of England*, ed. F.W.D. Brie (Early English Text Society cxxxvi, 1908), 524; *Chronicles of London*, ed. C.L. Kingsford (Oxford, 1905), 167.

28 *Brut*, 529; Kingsford, *London Chronicles*, 170; 'John Benet's Chronicle 1400–62', ed. G.L. and M.A. Harriss (Camden Miscellany xxiv 1972), 225; *Worcester*, 772.

29 Waurin, v. 305, 307–8.

30 *Ibid.* 310; *Warwick*, 185.

31 *Warwick,* 200.

32 *Rows Rolls*, nos 57, 58.

33 *Ibid.* no.56.

34 *The Great Chronicle of London*, ed. A.H. Thomas and I.D. Thornley (1938), 207.

35 M.A. Hicks, *Edward V: The Prince in the Tower* (Stroud, 2003), 35–6.

36 *Issues of the Exchequer*, ed. F. Devon (1837), 490.

37 *Young Medieval Women*, ed. K.J. Lewis, N.J. Menuge & K.M. Phillips (Stroud, 1999), esp. 1, 4, 7; N. Orme, *From Childhood to Chivalry* (1984), 27–31.

38 *Rows Rolls*, no.62.

39 Warwick County Record Office MS 26/4 f.69.

40 J. Leland, *De Rebus Britannicis Collectanea*, ed. T. Hearne (6 vols. Oxford, 1770), vi. 3–4.

41 *Great Chronicle,* 234.

42 *Warwick,* 233.

43 *CPR 1461–7,* 270.

44 *Warwick,* 234.

45 Hicks, *Rivals,* 324.

46 *Ibid.* 347. Lady Latimer's son Henry Neville and son-in-law Oliver Dudley were interred in the Beauchamp Chapel.

47 Devon, *Issues,* 490.

48 Hicks, *Rivals*, 292.

49 Waurin, *Recueil*, v.458-9.

50 *Worcester*, 785.

51 *Ibid.* 786.

52 *Ibid.* 788

53 *Clarence,* 42.

3 HER FATHER'S DAUGHTER 1469–71

1   TNA PSO 1/64/61.

2   *The Great Chronicle of London*, ed. A.H. Thomas and I.D. Thornley (1938), 206.

3   *Rows Rolls*, no. 59.

4   *Crowland*, 132–3.

5   *Collection of Ordinances and Regulations for the Government of the Royal Household* (Society of Antiquaries, 1790), 89–105.

6   *Rows Rolls*, no. 59.

7   *Collection of Ordinances*, 98.

8   *Clarence,* 45.

9   *Worcester*, 788.

10 *Clarence*, 44.

11 Bodleian Library, MS Dugdale 15 p. 75. Strangely this dispensation is not discussed by Clarke.

12 *Registrum Thome Bourgchier Cantuariensis Archiepiscopi 1454–86*, ed. F.R.H. Du Boulay (2 vols. Canterbury and York Soc. liv, 1957), 35–6.

13 *Collection of Ordinances*, 98; see also *Chronicle of John Stone*, ed. W.G. Searle, Cambridge Antiquarian Society octavo ser. 34 (1902), 109–11.

14 *Collection of Ordinances*, 98.

15 M.A. Hicks, *Edward V: The Prince in the Tower* (Stroud, 2003), 52–3; J. Calmette and G. Périnelle, *Louis XI et L'Angleterre 1461–83* (Paris, 1930), 306–7.

16 *Warwick*, 286–7.

17 *Crowland,* 116–17.

18 *Clarence*, 55–61.

19 Waurin, v. 586.

20 *Clarence*, 69.

21 *Ibid.*

22 *Warwick*, 280–1.

23 *Ibid.* 286, 300.

24 P. de Commines, *Mémoires*, ed. J. Calmette and G. Durville (3 vols., Paris 1923–5), i. 194.

25 *Warwick*, 287.

26 Commines, i. 194.

27 P.M. Kendall, *Louis XI* (1971), 229.

28 Hicks, *Warwick*, 289.

29 *CSPM* i. 139.

30 *Ibid.* 138.

31 *Ibid.* 117.

32 *Ibid.* 140.

33 Laynesmith, 167.

34 *Warwick*, 289–99.

35 *Crowland*, 123.

36 *The Politics of the Fifteenth Century: John Vale's Book*, ed. M.L. Kekewich, C. Richmond, A.F. Sutton, L. Visser-Fuchs, and J.L. Watts (Richard III and Yorkist Trust, Stroud, 1995), 217.

37 *Ibid.*; C.D. Ross, *Edward IV* (1974), 147; Calmette and Périnelle, 118.

38 *CSPM* i.140–1. Louis had decided to apply for a dispensation no later than 24 July, when payment of expenses was authorised; the decision could have been earlier, Clarke, 1021; Calmette and Périnelle, 118.

39 *CSPM* i.117.

40 Ross, *Edward IV*, 147.

41 *CSPM* i. 142.

42 *Ibid. Pace* Clarke, 1027, this explicit statement demonstrates that it was Warwick who postponed the marriage.

43 *John Vale's Bk*. 218.

44 *Ibid.*

45 *Clarence*, 82; Calmette and Périnelle, 118 n.1; Clarke, 1021 & n. For what follows, see P. Erlanger, *Margaret of Anjou, Queen of England* (1970), 221.

46 Clarke, 1021n.

47 Calmette and Périnelle, 133.

48 *Ibid.* 133, 319.

49 *Ibid.* 133.

50 *John Vale's Bk.* 222–5.

51 *Historie of the Arrivall of Edward IV*, ed. J. Bruce (Camden Society i, 1838), 10.

52 *Clarence*, 93.

53 J. Fortescue, *The Governance of England,* ed. C. Plummer (1885), 348–53.

54 *CPR 1467–77,* 252.

55 *Clarence*, 93.

56 *Ibid.*, 96–7.

57 *Ibid.*, 104

58 *Arrivall*, 10.

59 *Ibid.* 22.

60 *Ibid.*

61 J. Gairdner, *History of the Life and Times of Richard III* (Cambridge, 1898), 22n.

62 *Arrivall*, 23.

63 *Ibid.*

64 *Ibid.*

65 *Ibid.*, 11; *Clarence*, 105–6. The *Arrivall* was apparently wrong in attributing recruitment in the South-West to Warwick, *Arrivall*, 23.

66 *Ibid.*, 23.

67 *Ibid.*, 23–8.

68 *Ibid.*, 31.

69 *English Historical Documents*, iv, *1327–1485*, ed. A.R. Myers (1969), 315.

70 *Ibid.*, 314–15.

71 A.F. Sutton and L.Visser-Fuchs, *Richard III's Books* (Stroud, 1997), plate ix, from Besançon MS 1168.

72 *Arrivall*, 31.

73 C.L. Kingsford, *English Historical Literature in the Fifteenth Century* (London, 1913), 37.

74 *Ibid.*

75 *Ibid.*

76 N.J. Rogers, 'The Cult of Prince Edward at Tewkesbury', *Transactions of the Bristol and Gloucestershire Archaeological Society* 101 (1984), 187–9.

4 BETWEEN PRINCES 1471–5

1 *RP* vi. 9-11.

2 J.T. Rosenthal, 'Other Victims: Peeresses as War Widows 1450–1509', *History* lxxii (1987), 213–30.

3 *CPR 1477–85*, 254.

4 Laynesmith, 44; P.W. Hammond, *Edward of Middleham, Prince of Wales* (Cliftonville, 1973), 27-8.

5 *Warwick*, 29; *CPR 1429-36*, 598.

6 Hicks, *Edward V*, 31–5, 43–5.

7 *Ibid.* 31–5, 43–5.

8 BL MS Julius BXII ff.314-v; J.Gairdner, *History of the Life and Times of Richard III* (Cambridge, 1898), 22.

9 Hicks, *Rivals*, 327.

10 Gairdner, *Richard III*, 22n.

11 *CSPM* i. 177.

12 *Crowland*, 132–3.

13 *GEC* xii.i. 442–3.

14 E.g. Thomas, Duke of Gloucester, husband of Eleanor Bohun, wanted to prevent the marriage of her sister Mary.

15 Hicks, *Rivals*, 309.

16 *Crowland,* 132–3.

17 *Ibid.*

18 *Paston Letters and Papers of the Fifteenth Century*, ed. N. Davis (2 vols. Oxford, 1971–6), i. 447.

19 *Arrivall*, 39; 'Richard of Gloucester visits Norwich, August 1471', *Ricardian* 95(1986), 333.

20 TNA DL 29/648/10485.

21 *CPR 1467–77*, 297.

22 I. Wigram, 'Clarence and Richard', *Ricardian* 76 (1982), 17.

23 *Paston L & P* i. 447.

24 J.C. Ward, *English Noblewomen in the Later Middle Ages* (Harlow, 1992), 28.

25 *Illustrations of Ancient State and Chivalry*, ed. W.H. Black (Roxburghe Club, 1840), 30; see also the process regarding Henry VII and Elizabeth of York, related in the fourth degree of consanguinity, *CPL* xiv. 14–27.

26 E.g. J.J.N. Palmer, 'England, France, the Papacy and the Flemish Succession, 1361-9', *Journal of Medieval History* ii (1976), 339–64.

27 Clarke, 1021 & n., who wrongly supposes the dispensation to be sufficient.

28 *Paston L & P* i. 447.

29 *Crowland*, 132–3. *Pace* Clarke, 1023, 'the only solution was' *not* 'for Edward to persuade Clarence to compromise', still less on terms that satisfied none of the principal parties.

30 *Rows Rolls*, no.62.

31 BL MS Julius B XII f.314v partly printed in Gairdner, *Richard III*, 22.

32 *Clarence*, 117; Hanham, 121.

33 Gairdner, *Richard III*, 22.

34 *Clarence*, 122–3; *Crowland,* 142–3.

35 *RP* vi. 100–1, 124–5; TNA DL 26/29.

36 *Rows Rolls,* no.56 note (Latin version).

37 *Crowland*, 132–3.

38 *Ibid.*

39 *Rows Rolls*, no.56.

40 *Ibid.* no.57, note (Latin version); Hanham, 121.

41 J.R. Lander, *Crown and Nobility 1450–1509* (1976), 139n.

42 *Ibid.*

43 *RP* vi. 391–2.

44 *RP* v. 100–1.

45 Gairdner, *Richard III*, 22.

46 *RP* v. 124–5; Hicks, *Rivals*, 273–6, 295–6.

47 *Clarence,* 150–1.

48 Hicks, *Rivals*, 276.

49 *Rows Rolls*, no.56, note (Latin version); Hanham, 121.

50 *RP* vi. 391–2.

51 *CPR 1467–77*, 455.

52 *County History of Glamorgan*, iii, *The Middle Ages*, ed. T.B. Pugh (Cardiff, 1971), 613; *GEC* v.741.

53 See below p.152.

54 Hammond, *Edward of Middleham*, 11.

55 Clarke, 1023.

56 *RP* vi. 101. Strangely, Clarke, 1023, does not query this.

57 See above p.66.

58 H.A. Kelly, 'Canonical Implications of Richard III's Plan to Marry his Niece', *Traditio* xxiii (1967), esp. 269, 290–1, 306.

59 *Rows Rolls,* no.63.

60 *Ibid.* 64.

61 W.H. Prescott, *History of the Reigns of Ferdinand and Isabella,* 2 vols (3rd edn. 1851), i. 164–5, 195, 208–9, 214; F. Fernandez-Armesto, *Ferdinand and Isabella,* London (1975), 44; H. Kamen, *Spain 1469–1714: A Society in Conflict* (2nd edn 1991), 1.

62 *Crowland,* 174–5; see below chapter 7.

5 HER HUSBAND'S WIFE 1475–83

1   See above pp.88–9.

2   *Rows Rolls,* no.64.

3   Hanham, 122; *Three Books of Polydore Vergil's English History,* ed. H. Ellis, Camden Society xxix (1844), 190; G. Smith, 'One Prince or Two?' *Ricardian* 149 (1999), 467–8.

4   TNA DL 29/648/10485 m.6d.

5   W.G. Searle, *History of the Queens' College of St Margaret and St Bernard in the University of Cambridge 1446–1560,* Cambridge Antiquarian Society 9 (1867), 90; *CPR 1476–85,* 34. The use of the Salisbury title certainly indicates the Gloucester's dissatisfaction with the 1474–5 settlement. Does it also indicate that Clarence's forfeiture was intended, that Gloucester was already committed to it, and that the title was the first fruit of his support seven months before his brother Clarence's destruction?

6   *CPR 1476–85,* 34.

7   M.A. Hicks, 'One Prince or Two? The Family of Richard III', *Ricardian* 122 (1993), 467–8.

8   *CPR 1476–85,* 512.

9   *Stonor Letters and Papers of the Fifteenth Century,* ed. C.L. Kingsford, Camden 3rd series xxx (1919), ii. 81.

10 A.F. Sutton, 'Anne and Peter Idley', *Ricardian* 74 (1981), 402–3.

11 *Crowland,* 174–5.

12 *Ibid.* 170–1.

13 T. More, *History of King Richard III,* ed. R.S. Sylvester (New Haven, Conn., 1963), 44.

14 P. Hammond, 'The Illegitimate Children of Richard III', *Richard III: Crown and People,* ed. J.Petre (Gloucester, 1985), 18.

15 *Ibid.* 19–23.

16 *Ibid.* 20–23.

17 C.A. Halsted, *Richard III as Duke of Gloucester and King of England,* 2 vols. (1844), ii. 569–70.

18 *CPR 1476-85*, 538; *Harl.MS 433*, i.271; ii.211.

19 TNA DL 29/637/10360A mm.2–2d.

20 R.E. Horrox, *Richard III: A Study of Service* (Cambridge, 1989), 81.

21 *Harl MS 433* i.191; ii.185–6.

22 TNA DL 29/648/10485 m.6d.

23 *Ibid.*

24 *Harl MS 433* i.191; ii.185–6.

25 *CPR 1476-85*, 512; *Harl MS 433* i.197.

26 Halsted, *Richard III,* ii.570.

27 E.g. the bastards of Clarence, Exeter and Fauconberg.

28 *Warwick*, 234, 237. This was the Margaret Huddleston who was among Anne Neville's ladies at her coronation, *The Coronation of Richard III. The Extant Documents*, ed. P.W. Hammond and A.F. Sutton (Gloucester, 1983), 168, 170, 360,

29 *Rows Rolls*, no.62 note (Latin version).

30 P.J.P. Goldberg, 'Women', *Fifteenth-Century Attitudes: Perceptions of Society in Late Medieval England*, ed. R.E. Horrox (Cambridge, 1994), 115

31 TNA DL 29/648/10485.

32 *CPR 1476–85*, 67, 254.

33 *Ibid.*

34 TNA DL 29/637/10360A mm.2–2d; R.E. Horrox and A.F. Sutton, 'Some Expenses of Richard Duke of Gloucester, 1475–7', *Ricardian* 83 (1983), 267.

35 TNA DL 29/637/10360A mm.2–2d; Horrox & Sutton, 267.

36 *York City Chamberlain Account Rolls 1396–1500*, ed. R.B. Dobson, Surtees Society xcii (1980), 152. For what follows, see D. Mancini, *Usurpation of Richard III*, ed. C.A.J. Armstrong (Oxford, 1969), 70–1.

37 *County History of Glamorgan*, iii, *The Middle Ages*, ed. T.B. Pugh (Cardiff, 1971), 201.

38 *Historiae Dunelmensis Scriptores Tres*, ed. J. Raine, Surtees Society (1839), ccclviii–ix.

39 R.B. Dobson, *Church and Society in the Late Medieval North of England* (1996), 153–5.

40 *CPR 1476–85,* 67.

41 *Register of the Guild of Corpus Christi in the City of York*, ed. R.H. Skaife, Surtees Society 57 (1871), 101n.

42 *Historia Dunelmensis*, ccclvii–viii.

43 A.F. Sutton and L.Visser-Fuchs, *The Hours of Richard III,* Richard III and Yorkist History Trust (Gloucester, 1990); J. Hughes, *The Religious Life of Richard III* (Stroud, 1997) .

44 Searle, *Queens' College*, 88–92; C.D. Ross, 'Some Servants and Lovers of Richard III in his Youth', *Crown and People*, 146–8; *CPR 1476-85*, 34.

45 *CPR 1476–85*, 67, 255, 260.

46 *Ibid.* 67.

6 HER KING'S CONSORT 1483-5

1   Historic Manuscripts Commission, 11th Report III: *MSS of the Borough of King's Lynn* (1887), 170.

2   *Stonor Letters and Papers of the Fifteenth Century*, ed. C.L. Kingsford, Camden 3rd ser. xxx, 1919, 162.

3   *CPR 1467–77*, 190.

4   Laynesmith, 52.

5   *The Coronation of Richard III. The Extant Documents*, ed. A.F. Sutton and P.W. Hammond (Gloucester, 1983), 1.

6   *Ibid.* esp. 27, 78. Unless otherwise stated, the next two paragraphs are based on *Coronation, passim*.

7   *Rows Rolls*, no.63; A. Payne, 'The Salisbury Roll *c*.1463', *England in the Fifteenth Century*, ed. D. Williams (Woodbridge, 1987), pl.8; *The Beauchamp Pageant*, ed. A. Sinclair, Richard III and Yorkist History Trust (Stroud, 2003), plate lv.

8   Hanham, 122.

9   W. Dugdale, *Monasticon Anglicanum* (1846), ii.64; *Clarence*, 128, 142. For the next sentence, see A.F. Sutton, 'The Death of Queen Anne Neville', *Richard III: Crown and People,* ed. J. Petre (Gloucester, 1985), 16–17.

10 *Harl MS 433* ii.7.

11 Bodleian MS Top.Glouc d.2 f.38.

12 *Clarence*, 195–6; *Rows Rolls*, no.59.

13 *Beauchamp Pageant;* Hanham,122.

14 Payne, 'Salisbury Roll',

15 *Rows Rolls*, espec. 62 & pedigree.

16 *Ibid.* nos 48, 57, 59.

17 *Rows Rolls, passim*; Hanham, 120–3.

18 *Rows Rolls*, nos 58, 60, 61.

19 *Ibid.* no.56 & note (Latin version); Hanham, 121.

20 Hanham, 121.

21 Hicks, *Richard III,* 144–7.

22 *Ibid.* 146–8. For what follows, see A. Compton-Reeves, 'King Richard III at York in Late Summer 1483', *Ricardian* 159 (2002), 542–53.

23 R.B. Dobson, 'Richard III and the Church of York', *Kings and Nobles in the Later Middle Ages*, ed. R.A. Griffiths and J.W. Sherborne (Gloucester, 1986), 147.

24 *Rows Roll*, no.63.

25 Laynesmith, 4.

26 *Ibid.* 5, 51, 54.

27 *Coronation*, 364.

28 Hicks*, Rivals*, 276.

29 M.A. Hicks, 'Richard Lord Latimer, Richard III and the Warwick

Inheritance', *Ricardian* 154 (2001), 314–19.

30   *Warwick*, 42, 297.

31   *Harl MS 433* ii.108.

32   *County History of Glamorgan,* iii, *The Middle Ages,* ed. T.B. Pugh (Cardiff, 1971), 201.

33   *Harl MS 433* i.171, 192; iii.155.

34   Hicks, *Rivals*, 347.

35   *Harl MS 433* iii.155.

36   *Ibid.* i.171, 192, 263; Laynesmith, 256; *CPR 1476–85*, 423; TNA C 81/1530/33; *History of the Queens' College of St Margaret and Bernard at the University of Cambridge 1446–1560*, ed. W. Searle, Cambridge Antiquarian Society 9 (1867), 95–101.

37   P.W. Hammond, *Edward of Middleham, Prince of Wales* (Cliftonville, 1973), 29–30.

38   *Coronation*, 84.

39   *Ibid.* 33–4, 84; R.E. Horrox, *Richard III: A Study of Service* (Cambridge, 1989), 105n; *CPR 1476–85*, 417, 496; Laynesmith, 105n.

40   Laynesmith, 228–9.

41   *Coronation*, 84.

42   *CPR 1476–85*, 372, 375, 377, 385, 386, 464, 473, 498, 505, 510, 511; *Harl MS 433*, i. 251.

7 PAST HER SELL-BY DATE

1   *Crowland*, 170–1.

2   *Ibid.*

3   *Three Books of Polydore Vergil's English History*, ed. H. Ellis, Camden Soc. xxix (1844), 211.

4   W. Shakespeare, *Richard III*, ed. E.A.J. Honigman, New Penguin Shakspeare (1995), Act IV scene 2 l.59.

5   P. Morgan, '"Those were the days": A Yorkist Pedigree Roll', *Estrangement, Enterprise, and Education in Fifteenth Century England*, ed. S. Michalove and A. Compton Reeves (Stroud, 1998), 114–16.

6   Harl. 433 i.271.

7   He had several bastards, see above, chapter 6.

8   *Crowland*, 174–5.

9   *Ibid.* 174.

10   P.W. Hammond and A.F. Sutton, *Richard III: The Road to Bosworth Field* (1985), 199; see below note 15.

11   Vergil, 226.

12   As demonstrated by H.A. Kelly, 'Crowland Observations', *Ricardian* (1990), correcting the mistranslation of Crowland, 174–5.

13   Hammond & Sutton, 199.

14 *Ibid.*

15 *Great Chronicle of London*, ed. A.H. Thomas & I.D. Thornley (1938), 234; *Chronicles of London*, ed. C.L. Kingsford (Oxford, 1905); Vergil, 211; Hanham, 121.

16 *Crowland*, 174–7.

17 *Ibid.* 174–7.

18 *Ibid.* 176–7.

19 *Ibid.* 174–5; H.A. Kelly, 'Canonical Implications of Richard III's Plan to Marry his Niece', *Traditio* xxiii (1967), 270.

20 Clarke, 1024-5.

21 *Crowland*, 174–5.

22 G. Buck, *History of King Richard III (1619)*, ed. A.N. Kincaid (Gloucester, 1979), 3–5, 191.

23 L. Visser-Fuchs, 'Where did Elizabeth of York turn for consolation?' *Ricardian* 122 (1993), 473.

24 Hanham, 19n.

25 Buck, *Richard III*, 191.

26 *Ibid.*

27 *Crowland*, 174–5.

28 Hammond & Sutton, 165–6.

29 Vergil, 210–11.

30 Hammond & Sutton, 165–6.

31 *Crowland*, 174–5.

32 *Ibid.* Strangely, Clarke, 1025n., makes no comment here.

33 Dr John Gunthorpe, one candidate to be Crowland, certainly would have known, since it was he who produced the dispensation that allowed Prince Richard to wed Anne Mowbray in 1477, *Illustrations of Ancient State and Chivalry*, ed. W.H. Black (Roxburghe Club, 1840), 30.

34 RP vi.100–1.

35 Laynesmith, 80.

36 R.H. Helmholz, 'The Sons of Edward IV. A Canonical Assessment of the Claim that were Illegitimate', *Richard III: Loyalty, Lordship and Law*, ed. P.W. Hammond (Gloucester, 1986), 95.

37 *Crowland*, 132–3.

38 *Ibid.* 174-7.

39 Kelly, 'Canonical Implications', 269.

40 *Crowland*, 174–7.

41 E.g. Kelly, 'Canonical Implications', 286.

42 *Great Chronicle*, 234.

43 Hanham, 53.

44 Kelly, 'Canonical Implications', 269–311, esp. 286, 305, 307.

45 *Crowland*, 176–7.

46 Hicks, *Richard III*, 181.

47 *Great Chronicle*, 234.
48 *Ibid.*
49 *Crowland*, 176–7.
50 *Rows Rolls*, no.63 note (Latin version).
51 *Crowland*, 174–5; Vergil, 211.
52 Vergil, 211.
53 Hanham, 52.
54 Vergil, 211.
55 *Crowland*, 174–5.
56 *Ibid.*
57 *Great Chronicle*, 234; *Rows Rolls*, no.62 note (Latin version).
58 Laynesmith, 122.
59 *Crowland*, 174–5.
60 Hicks, *Rivals*, 332–3.

Select Bibliography

PRIMARY SOURCES: MANUSCRIPTS

London, British Library [BL]
Cotton MSS
Egerton MSS
Harleian MSS

London, The National Archives [TNA]
C 81	Chancery, Warrants for the Great Seal
DL 26	Duchy of Lancaster, Ancient Deeds
DL 29	Duchy of Lancaster, Ministers Accounts
E 159	Exchequer, King's Remembrancer, Memoranda Rolls
E 404	Exchequer, Treasury of Receipt, Warrants for Issue
PSO 1	Privy Seal Office, Warrants for the Privy Seal
SC 6	Special Collections, Ministers' Accounts, General Series

Oxford, Bodleian Library
MS Dugdale 15
MS Top Glouc d.2

PRIMARY SOURCES: PRINTED BOOKS

The Beauchamp Pageant, ed. Sinclair, A. (Richard III and Yorkist History Trust, Donnington, 2003)
Bruce, J., ed., *Historie of the Arrivall of Edward IV*, Camden Society i (1838)
Buck, G., *The History of King Richard III,* ed. Kincaid, A.N. (Gloucester, 1979)
Calendar of the Close Rolls 1452–94

Calendar of Papal Registers: Papal Letters 144–84

Calendar of the Patent Rolls 1452–94

Calendar of State Papers Milanese i.

Commines, P., *Mémoires*, ed. Calmette, J., and Durville, G., 3 vols. Societé de l'histoire de France 23-5 (Paris 1923–5)

Courthope, W.H., ed., *The Rows Rolls* (1859)

Crawford, A., ed., *Letters of the Queens of England 1100–1547* (Stroud, 1994)

Davis, N., ed., *Paston Letters and Papers of the Fifteenth Century*, 2 vols. (Oxford, 1971-6)

Ellis, H, ed., *Three Books of Polydore Vergil's English History*, Camden Society xxix (1844)

Hammond, P.W., and Horrox, R.E., eds, *British Library Harleian Manuscript 433* (4 vols. Upminster, 1979–83)

Hammond, P.W., and Sutton, A.F., ed., *Richard III: The Road to Bosworth Field* (1985)

Kekewich, M.L., Richmond, C., Sutton, A.F., Visser-Fuchs, L., and Watts, J.L., eds., *Politics in the Fifteenth Century: John Vale's Book* (Richard III and Yorkist History Trust, 1996)

Kingsford, C.L., ed, *Chronicles of London* (1905).

—, *Stonor Letters and Papers of the Fifteenth Century*, 2 vols, Camden 3rd series xxix, xxx (1919)

Mancini, D., *The Usurpation of Richard III,* ed. C.A. J. Armstrong (2nd edn. Oxford, 1969)

Leland, J., *De Rebus Britannicis Collectanea*, ed. T. Hearne (6 vols. Oxford, 1770)

Marx, W., ed., *An English Chronicle 1377-1461* (Woodbridge, 2004),

More, T., *History of King Richard III*, ed R.S. Sylvester, Yale Edition of the Complete Works (New Haven, Conn., 1963)

Pronay, N. and Cox., J.C., eds., *The Crowland Abbey Chronicles 1459–86* (Gloucester, 1986)

Rotuli Parliamentorum (6 vols. Record Commission, 1832), v and vi.

Shakespeare, W., *Richard III*, ed. Honigman, E.J., New Penguin Shakespeare (1995).

Stevenson, J.S., ed., 'Annales Rerum Anglicarum', *Letters and Papers illustrative of the Wars of the English in France* (4 vols., Rolls Series, 1864)

Sutton, A.F., and Hammond, P.W., eds., *The Coronation of Richard III: The Extant Documents* (Gloucester, 1983)

Sutton, A.F., and Visser-Fuchs, L., eds, *The Reburial of Richard Duke of Y ork, 21–30 July 1476*, Richard III Society (1996)

Sutton, A.F., Visser-Fuchs, L., and Griffiths, R.A., eds., *The Royal Funerals of the House of York at Windsor*, Richard III Society (2005)

Thomas, A.H., and Thornley, I.D., eds., *The Great Chronicle of London* (1938)

Waurin, J., *Recueil des Croniques et Anchiennes Istories de la Grant Bretaigne*, ed. Hardy, W. and E.L.C.P. , 5 vols. (Rolls Series, 1891)

SECONDARY SOURCES

Baldwin, D., *Elizabeth Woodville: Mother of the Princes in the Tower* (Stroud, 2002)

Barron, C.M., 'The Education and Training of Girls in Fifteenth-century London', *Courts, Counties, and the Capital in the Later Middle Ages*, ed. Dunn, D.E.S. (Stroud, 1996)

Bean, J.M.W, *The Estates of the Percy Family 1416–1537* (1958), 23

Calmette, J. and Périnelle, G., *Louis XI et L.Angleterre 1461–83* (Paris, 1930)

Clarke, P.D., 'English Royal Marriages and the Papal Penitentiary in the Fifteenth Century', *English Historical Review* cxx (2005)

Cokayne, G.E., *The Complete Peerage of England etc*, ed. H.V. Gibbs and others (13 vols., 1910–59)

Edwards, R., *The Itinerary of King Richard III 1483–1485* (Richard III Society, 1983)

Erlanger, P., *Margaret of Anjou, Queen of England* (1970)

Gairdner, J., *History of the Life and Times of Richard III* (Cambridge, 1898)

Goldberg, P.J.P., 'Women', *Fifteenth-Century Attitudes: Perceptions of Society in Late Medieval England*, ed. Horrox, R.E. (Cambridge, 1994)

Hammond, P.W. *Edward of Middleham, Prince of Wales*, Gloucester Group Publications (Cliftonville, 1973)

—, 'Edward of Middleham', *Ricardian* 146 (1999)

—, 'The Illegitimate Children of Richard III', *Richard III: Crown and People*, ed. J. Petre (Gloucester, 1985)

—, 'John of Gloucester', *Ricardian* 72 (1981)

—, ed., *Richard III: Loyalty, Lordship and Law* (Gloucester, 1986)

Halsted, C.A., *Richard III as Duke of Gloucester and King of England*, 2 vols. (1844)

Hanham, A., *Richard III and his earlier Historians* (Cambridge, 1975)

Helmholz, R., *Marriage Litigation in Medieval England* (Cambridge, 1974)

Hicks, M.A., *Edward IV* (2004)

—, *Edward V: The Prince in the Tower* (Stroud, 2003)

—, *English Political Culture in the Fifteenth Century* (2002)

—, *False, Fleeting, Perjur'd Clarence: George Duke of Clarence 1449-1478* (Gloucester, 1980)

—, 'One Prince or Two? The Family of Richard III', *The Ricardian* 122 (1993)

—, *Richard III* (Stroud, 2000)

—, *Richard III and his Rivals: Magnates and Their Motives during the Wars of the Roses* (1991)

—, *Richard III as Duke of Gloucester: A Study in Character*, Borthwick Paper 70 (1986)

—, 'Richard Lord Latimer, Richard III and the Warwick Inheritance', *The*

Ricardian 154 (2001)

—, *Warwick the Kingmaker* (Oxford, 1998)

Horrox, R.E., *Richard III: A Study of Service* (Cambridge, 1989)

—, 'Some Expenses of Richard Duke of Gloucester 1475–7', *Ricardian* 83 (1983)

Kelly, H.A., 'Canonical Implications of Richard III's Plan to Marry his Niece', *Traditio* xxiii (1967)

Kingsford, C.L., *English Historical Literature in the Fifteenth Century* (1913)

Lander, J.R., *Crown and Nobility 1450–1509* (1976)

Laynesmith, J.L., *The Last Medieval Queens* (Oxford, 2004)

Lewis, K.J., Menuge, N.J., and Phillips, K.M., eds., *Young Medieval Women* (Stroud, 1999)

McCarthy, C. *Marriage in Medieval England. Law, Literature and Practice* (Woodbridge, 2004)

Myers, A.R., *Crown, Household and Parliament in Fifteenth Century England*, ed. Clough, C.H. (1985)

Okerlund, A., *Elizabeth Wydeville: The Slandered Queen* (Stroud, 2005)

Orme, N., *From Childhood to Chivalry: The Education of the English Kings and Aristocracy 1066–1530* (1984)

Oxford Dictionary of National Biography, 64 vols. (Oxford, 2004)

Payne, A., 'The Salisbury Roll of Arms c.1463', *England in the Fifteenth Century*, ed. Williams, D. (Woodbridge, 1987)

Petre, J., ed, *Richard III: Crown and People* (Gloucester, 1985)

Pollard, A.J., *Late Medieval England 1399–1509* (2000)

—, *Richard III and the Princes in the Tower* (Stroud, 1991)

—, *The Worlds of Richard III* (Stroud, 2001)

Reeves, A.Compton, 'King Richard III at York in Late Summer 1483', *Ricardian* 159 (2002)

Ross, C.D., *Edward IV* (2nd edn., 1997)

—, *Richard III* (2nd edn. 1999)

Saul, N., *The Three Richards: Richard I, Richard II, and Richard III* (2005)

Sutton, A.F., 'Anne and Peter Idley', *Ricardian* 74 (1981)

—, 'The Death of Queen Anne Neville', *Richard III: Crown and People* , ed. Petre, J. (Gloucester, 1985)

—, 'The Hautes of Kent', *Ricardian* 77 (1982);

—, 'Richard of Gloucester visits Norwich, August 1471', *Ricardian* 95 (1986)

Sutton, A.F., and Visser-Fuchs, L., *Richard III's Books* (Stroud, 1997)

Ward, J.C., *English Noblewomen in the Later Middle Ages* (Harlow, 1992)

List of Illustrations

Geoffrey Wheeler.

13 King Henry VI, the politically ineffective but pious father-in-law whom Anne never knew, depicted *c.*1500 as a saint on the screen at Ludham in Norfolk. Courtesy of Jonathan Reeve. JR PC1.

14 A fanciful Victorian depiction of the death of Anne's father Warwick on the battlefield of Barnet on Easter Sunday 1471. Courtesy of Jonathan Reeve. JR858b61p601 14501500.

15 Edward of Lancaster as Prince of Wales, from the *Rows Roll* in the College of Arms. Courtesy of Geoffrey Wheeler.

16 A modern plaque in the chancel floor at Tewkesbury Abbey commemorating the death of Prince Edward, 'the last hope of thy race'. Courtesy of Geoffrey Wheeler.

17 Tewkesbury Abbey. Courtesy of Geoffrey Wheeler.

18 Crowland Abbey, Lincolnshire, where the best chronicler of the Yorkists wrote in 1485. Courtesy of Geoffrey Wheeler.

19 John Rows, the aged chantry priest of Guyscliff, Warwick, author of the *Rows Rolls* of the earls of Warwick and partisan of the Countess Anne, as depicted by himself. Courtesy of Geoffrey Wheeler.

20 John Rows' portrayal of Anne's sister Isabel, Duchess of Clarence and her husband George, Duke of Clarence. Author's Collection.

21 The family of Anne Neville from the *Beauchamp Pageant*. Tempus Archive.

22 Middleham Castle, Yorkshire, the best known of Anne's ancestral seats, where she and Duke Richard resided in 1472–83 and where their son Edward was born. Courtesy of Geoffrey Wheeler.

23 Barnard Castle towers over the Tees. Courtesy of Geoffrey Wheeler.

24 Surrounded by courtiers, King Edward IV receives the book proffered by the author, his brother-in-law, Earl Rivers. Courtesy of Jonathan Reeve. JR861b4p582 14501500.

25 Sir John Millais' sympathetic portrayal of the Princes in the Tower, whose legitimacy Richard III had to discredit to make himself king and Anne queen. Courtesy of Jonathan Reeve. JR859b61p620 14501500.

26 Anne and Richard III as king and queen. Author's Collection.

27 King Richard and Queen Anne from the Salisbury Roll. By kind permission of His Grace The Duke of Buccleuch & Queensberry, KT.

28 Queen Anne Neville, redrawn from a lost stained glass window at Skipton church, Yorkshire. Courtesy of Geoffrey Wheeler.

29 Anne Neville as Queen of England, crowned and at prayer. From a modern memorial window at Middleham Church given by the Richard III Society in 1934. Courtesy of Geoffrey Wheeler.

30 King Richard and Anne Neville in stained glass by William Burges at Cardiff Castle. Courtesy of Geoffrey Wheeler.

Index

TEMPUS – REVEALING HISTORY

Britannia's Empire
A Short History of the British Empire
BILL NASSON

'Crisp, economical and witty' *TLS*
'An excellent introduction the subject' *THES*

£12.99   0 7524 3808 5

Madmen
A Social History of Madhouses,
Mad-Doctors & Lunatics
ROY PORTER
'Fascinating'
The Observer

£12.99   0 7524 3730 5

Born to be Gay
A History of Homosexuality
WILLIAM NAPHY

'Fascinating' *The Financial Times*
'Excellent' *Gay Times*

£9.99   0 7524 3694 5

William II
Rufus, the Red King
EMMA MASON
'A thoroughly new reappraisal of a much
maligned king. The dramatic story of his life is
told with great pace and insight'
John Gillingham

£25   0 7524 3528 0

To Kill Rasputin
The Life and Death of Grigori Rasputin
ANDREW COOK

'Andrew Cook is a brilliant investigative historian'
Andrew Roberts
'Astonishing' *The Daily Mail*

£9.99   0 7524 3906 5

The Unwritten Order
Hitler's Role in the Final Solution
PETER LONGERICH

'Compelling' *Richard Evans*
'The finest account to date of the many twists
and turns in Adolf Hitler's anti-semitic obsession'
Richard Overy

£12.99   0 7524 3328 8

Private 12768
Memoir of a Tommy
JOHN JACKSON
FOREWORD BY HEW STRACHAN

'A refreshing new perspective' *The Sunday Times*
'At last we have John Jackson's intensely personal
and heartfelt little book to remind us there was a
view of the Great War other than Wilfred Owen's'
The Daily Mail

£9.99   0 7524 3531 0

The Vikings
MAGNUS MAGNUSSON

'Serious, engaging history'
BBC History Magazine

£9.99   0 7524 2699 0

If you are interested in purchasing other books published by Tempus, or in case you have difficulty finding any
Tempus books in your local bookshop, you can also place orders directly through our website

www.tempus-publishing.com

TEMPUS – REVEALING HISTORY

D-Day The First 72 Hours
WILLIAM F. BUCKINGHAM

'A compelling narrative' *The Observer*

A *BBC History Magazine* Book of the Year 2004

£9.99   0 7524 2842 x

The London Monster
Terror on the Streets in 1790
JAN BONDESON

'Gripping' *The Guardian*

'Excellent... monster-mania brought a reign of terror to the ill-lit streets of the capital'
The Independent

£9.99   0 7524 3327 x

London
A Historical Companion
KENNETH PANTON

'A readable and reliable work of reference that deserves a place on every Londoner's bookshelf'
Stephen Inwood

£20   0 7524 3434 9

M: MI5's First Spymaster
ANDREW COOK

'Serious spook history' *Andrew Roberts*

'Groundbreaking' *The Sunday Telegraph*

'Brilliantly researched' *Dame Stella Rimington*

£20   0 7524 2896 9

Agincourt A New History
ANNE CURRY

'A highly distinguished and convincing account'
Christopher Hibbert

'A *tour de force*' *Alison Weir*

'*The* book on the battle' *Richard Holmes*

A *BBC History Magazine* Book of the Year 2005

£25   0 7524 2828 4

Battle of the Atlantic
MARC MILNER

'The most comprehensive short survey of the U-boat battles' *Sir John Keegan*

'Some events are fortunate in their historian, none more so than the Battle of the Atlantic. Marc Milner is *the* historian of the Atlantic campaign... a compelling narrative' *Andrew Lambert*

£12.99   0 7524 3332 6

The English Resistance
The Underground War Against the Normans
PETER REX

'An invaluable rehabilitation of an ignored resistance movement' *The Sunday Times*

'Peter Rex's scholarship is remarkable'
The Sunday Express

£12.99   0 7524 3733 x

Elizabeth Wydeville: The Slandered Queen
ARLENE OKERLUND

'A penetrating, thorough and wholly convincing vindication of this unlucky queen'
Sarah Gristwood

'A gripping tale of lust, loss and tragedy'
Alison Weir

A *BBC History Magazine* Book of the Year 2005

£18.99   0 7524 3384 9

If you are interested in purchasing other books published by Tempus, or in case you have difficulty finding any Tempus books in your local bookshop, you can also place orders directly through our website

www.tempus-publishing.com

TEMPUS – REVEALING HISTORY

Quacks Fakers and Charlatans in Medicine
ROY PORTER

'A delightful book' *The Daily Telegraph*
'Hugely entertaining' *BBC History Magazine*

£12.99   0 7524 2590 0

The Tudors
RICHARD REX

'Up-to-date, readable and reliable. The best introduction to England's most important dynasty' *David Starkey*

'Vivid, entertaining... quite simply the best short introduction' *Eamon Duffy*

'Told with enviable narrative skill... a delight for any reader' *THES*

£9.99   0 7524 3333 4

The Kings & Queens of England
MARK ORMROD

'Of the numerous books on the kings and queens of England, this is the best' *Alison Weir*

£9.99   0 7524 2598 6

The Covent Garden Ladies
Pimp General Jack & the Extraordinary Story of Harris's List
HALLIE RUBENHOLD

'Sex toys, porn... forget Ann Summers, Miss Love was at it 250 years ago' *The Times*

'Compelling' *The Independent on Sunday*

'Marvellous' *Leonie Frieda*

'Filthy' *The Guardian*

£9.99   0 7524 3739 9

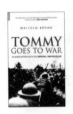

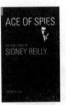

Okinawa 1945
GEORGE FEIFER

'A great book... Feifer's account of the three sides and their experiences far surpasses most books about war' *Stephen Ambrose*

£17.99   0 7524 3324 5

Tommy Goes To War
MALCOLM BROWN

'A remarkably vivid and frank account of the British soldier in the trenches' *Max Arthur*

'The fury, fear, mud, blood, boredom and bravery that made up life on the Western Front are vividly presented and illustrated' *The Sunday Telegraph*

£12.99   0 7524 2980 4

Ace of Spies The True Story of Sidney Reilly
ANDREW COOK

'The most definitive biography of the spying ace yet written... both a compelling narrative and a myth-shattering *tour de force*' *Simon Sebag Montefiore*

'The absolute last word on the subject' *Nigel West*

'Makes poor 007 look like a bit of a wuss' *The Mail on Sunday*

£12.99   0 7524 2959 0

Sex Crimes
From Renaissance to Enlightenment
W.M. NAPHY

'Wonderfully scandalous' *Diarmaid MacCulloch*

£10.99   0 7524 2977 9

If you are interested in purchasing other books published by Tempus, or in case you have difficulty finding any Tempus books in your local bookshop, you can also place orders directly through our website

www.tempus-publishing.com